McDougal Littell Science

Earth's Waters

water
cycle

ocean

HABITAT

hydrosphere

EARTH SCIENCE

A ▶ Earth's Surface
B ▶ The Changing Earth
C ▶ Earth's Waters
D ▶ Earth's Atmosphere
E ▶ Space Science

PHYSICAL SCIENCE

A ▶ Matter and Energy
B ▶ Chemical Interactions
C ▶ Motion and Forces
D ▶ Waves, Sound, and Light
E ▶ Electricity and Magnetism

LIFE SCIENCE

A ▶ Cells and Heredity
B ▶ Life Over Time
C ▶ Diversity of Living Things
D ▶ Ecology
E ▶ Human Biology

Acknowledgments: Excerpts and adaptations from *National Science Education Standards* by the National Academy of Sciences. Copyright © 1996 by the National Academy of Sciences. Reprinted with permission from the National Academies Press, Washington, D.C.

Excerpts and adaptations from *Benchmarks for Science Literacy: Project 2061.* Copyright © 1993 by the American Association for the Advancement of Science. Reprinted with permission.

ISBN-13: 978-0-618-84242-1

ISBN-10: 0-618-84242-X   2 3 4 5 VJM 10 09 08 07

Internet Web Site: http://www.mcdougallittell.com

Science Consultants

Chief Science Consultant

James Trefil, Ph.D. is the Clarence J. Robinson Professor of Physics at George Mason University. He is the author or co-author of more than 25 books, including *Science Matters* and *The Nature of Science.* Dr. Trefil is a member of the American Association for the Advancement of Science's Committee on the Public Understanding of Science and Technology. He is also a fellow of the World Economic Forum and a frequent contributor to *Smithsonian* magazine.

Rita Ann Calvo, Ph.D. is Senior Lecturer in Molecular Biology and Genetics at Cornell University, where for 12 years she also directed the Cornell Institute for Biology Teachers. Dr. Calvo is the 1999 recipient of the College and University Teaching Award from the National Association of Biology Teachers.

Kenneth Cutler, M.S. is the Education Coordinator for the Julius L. Chambers Biomedical Biotechnology Research Institute at North Carolina Central University. A former middle school and high school science teacher, he received a 1999 Presidential Award for Excellence in Science Teaching.

Instructional Design Consultants

Douglas Carnine, Ph.D. is Professor of Education and Director of the National Center for Improving the Tools of Educators at the University of Oregon. He is the author of seven books and over 100 other scholarly publications, primarily in the areas of instructional design and effective instructional strategies and tools for diverse learners. Dr. Carnine also serves as a member of the National Institute for Literacy Advisory Board.

Linda Carnine, Ph.D. consults with school districts on curriculum development and effective instruction for students struggling academically. A former teacher and school administrator, Dr. Carnine also co-authored a popular remedial reading program.

Donald Steely, Ph.D. serves as principal investigator at the Oregon Center for Applied Science (ORCAS) on federal grants for science and language arts programs. His background also includes teaching and authoring of print and multimedia programs in science, mathematics, history, and spelling.

Sam Miller, Ph.D. is a middle school science teacher and the Teacher Development Liaison for the Eugene, Oregon, Public Schools. He is the author of curricula for teaching science, mathematics, computer skills, and language arts.

Vicky Vachon, Ph.D. consults with school districts throughout the United States and Canada on improving overall academic achievement with a focus on literacy. She is also co-author of a widely used program for remedial readers.

Content Reviewers

John Beaver, Ph.D.
Ecology
Professor, Director of Science Education Center
College of Education and Human Services
Western Illinois University
Macomb, IL

Donald J. DeCoste, Ph.D.
Matter and Energy, Chemical Interactions
Chemistry Instructor
University of Illinois
Urbana-Champaign, IL

Dorothy Ann Fallows, Ph.D., MSc
Diversity of Living Things, Microbiology
Partners in Health
Boston, MA

Michael Foote, Ph.D.
The Changing Earth, Life Over Time
Associate Professor
Department of the Geophysical Sciences
The University of Chicago
Chicago, IL

Lucy Fortson, Ph.D.
Space Science
Director of Astronomy
Adler Planetarium and Astronomy Museum
Chicago, IL

Elizabeth Godrick, Ph.D.
Human Biology
Professor, CAS Biology
Boston University
Boston, MA

Isabelle Sacramento Grilo, M.S.
The Changing Earth
Lecturer, Department of the Geological Sciences
San Diego State University
San Diego, CA

David Harbster, MSc
Diversity of Living Things
Professor of Biology
Paradise Valley Community College
Phoenix, AZ

Richard D. Norris, Ph.D.
Earth's Waters
Professor of Paleobiology
Scripps Institution of Oceanography
University of California, San Diego
La Jolla, CA

Donald B. Peck, M.S.
*Motion and Forces; Waves, Sound, and Light;
 Electricity and Magnetism*
Director of the Center for Science Education (retired)
Fairleigh Dickinson University
Madison, NJ

Javier Penalosa, Ph.D.
Diversity of Living Things, Plants
Associate Professor, Biology Department
Buffalo State College
Buffalo, NY

Raymond T. Pierrehumbert, Ph.D.
Earth's Atmosphere
Professor in Geophysical Sciences (Atmospheric Science)
The University of Chicago
Chicago, IL

Brian J. Skinner, Ph.D.
Earth's Surface
Eugene Higgins Professor of Geology and Geophysics
Yale University
New Haven, CT

Nancy E. Spaulding, M.S.
Earth's Surface, The Changing Earth, Earth's Waters
Earth Science Teacher (retired)
Elmira Free Academy
Elmira, NY

Steven S. Zumdahl, Ph.D.
Matter and Energy, Chemical Interactions
Professor Emeritus of Chemistry
University of Illinois
Urbana-Champaign, IL

Susan L. Zumdahl, M.S.
Matter and Energy, Chemical Interactions
Chemistry Education Specialist
University of Illinois
Urbana-Champaign, IL

Safety Consultant

Juliana Texley, Ph.D.
Former K–12 Science Teacher and School Superintendent
Boca Raton, FL

English Language Advisor

Judy Lewis, M.A.
Director, State and Federal Programs for reading proficiency
and high risk populations
Rancho Cordova, CA

Teacher Panel Members

Carol Arbour
Tallmadge Middle School,
Tallmadge, OH

Patty Belcher
Goodrich Middle School,
Akron, OH

Gwen Broestl
Luis Munoz Marin Middle School,
Cleveland, OH

Al Brofman
Tehipite Middle School,
Fresno, CA

John Cockrell
Clinton Middle School,
Columbus, OH

Jenifer Cox
Sylvan Middle School,
Citrus Heights, CA

Linda Culpepper
Martin Middle School,
Charlotte, NC

Kathleen Ann DeMatteo
Margate Middle School,
Margate, FL

Melvin Figueroa
New River Middle School,
Ft. Lauderdale, FL

Doretha Grier
Kannapolis Middle School,
Kannapolis, NC

Robert Hood
Alexander Hamilton Middle School,
Cleveland, OH

Scott Hudson
Covedale Elementary School,
Cincinnati, OH

Loretta Langdon
Princeton Middle School,
Princeton, NC

Carlyn Little
Glades Middle School,
Miami, FL

Ann Marie Lynn
Amelia Earhart Middle School,
Riverside, CA

James Minogue
Lowe's Grove Middle School,
Durham, NC

Joann Myers
Buchanan Middle School,
Tampa, FL

Barbara Newell
Charles Evans Hughes Middle School,
Long Beach, CA

Anita Parker
Kannapolis Middle School,
Kannapolis, NC

Greg Pirolo
Golden Valley Middle School,
San Bernardino, CA

Laura Pottmyer
Apex Middle School,
Apex, NC

Lynn Prichard
Booker T. Washington Middle Magnet
School, Tampa, FL

Jacque Quick
Walter Williams High School,
Burlington, NC

Robert Glenn Reynolds
Hillman Middle School,
Youngstown, OH

Stacy Rinehart
Lufkin Road Middle School,
Apex, NC

Theresa Short
Abbott Middle School,
Fayetteville, NC

Rita Slivka
Alexander Hamilton Middle School,
Cleveland, OH

Marie Sofsak
B F Stanton Middle School,
Alliance, OH

Nancy Stubbs
Sweetwater Union Unified School District,
Chula Vista, CA

Sharon Stull
Quail Hollow Middle School,
Charlotte, NC

Donna Taylor
Okeeheelee Middle School,
West Palm Beach, FL

Sandi Thompson
Harding Middle School,
Lakewood, OH

Lori Walker
Audubon Middle School & Magnet Center,
Los Angeles, CA

Teacher Lab Evaluators

Andrew Boy
W.E.B. DuBois Academy,
Cincinnati, OH

Jill Brimm-Byrne
Albany Park Academy,
Chicago, IL

Gwen Broestl
Luis Munoz Marin Middle School,
Cleveland, OH

Al Brofman
Tehipite Middle School,
Fresno, CA

Michael A. Burstein
The Rashi School,
Newton, MA

Trudi Coutts
Madison Middle School,
Naperville, IL

Jenifer Cox
Sylvan Middle School,
Citrus Heights, CA

Larry Cwik
Madison Middle School,
Naperville, IL

Jennifer Donatelli
Kennedy Junior High School,
Lisle, IL

Melissa Dupree
Lakeside Middle School,
Evans, GA

Carl Fechko
Luis Munoz Marin Middle School,
Cleveland, OH

Paige Fullhart
Highland Middle School,
Libertyville, IL

Sue Hood
Glen Crest Middle School,
Glen Ellyn, IL

William Luzader
Plymouth Community Intermediate School,
Plymouth, MA

Ann Min
Beardsley Middle School,
Crystal Lake, IL

Aileen Mueller
Kennedy Junior High School,
Lisle, IL

Nancy Nega
Churchville Middle School,
Elmhurst, IL

Oscar Newman
Sumner Math and Science Academy,
Chicago, IL

Lynn Prichard
Booker T. Washington Middle Magnet
School, Tampa, FL

Jacque Quick
Walter Williams High School,
Burlington, NC

Stacy Rinehart
Lufkin Road Middle School,
Apex, NC

Seth Robey
Gwendolyn Brooks Middle School,
Oak Park, IL

Kevin Steele
Grissom Middle School,
Tinley Park, IL

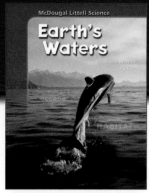

McDougal Littell Science

Earth's Waters

eEdition

Earth's Waters

Unit Features

SCIENTIFIC AMERICAN

1 The Water Planet 6

the BIG idea

Water moves through Earth's atmosphere, oceans, and land in a cycle.

2 Freshwater Resources 38

the BIG idea

Fresh water is a limited resource and is essential for human society.

In what ways do you depend on water? page 38

What causes these waves? page 72

Features

Visual Highlights

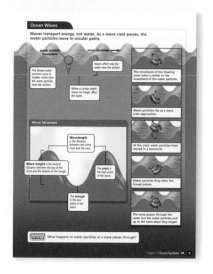

Internet Resources @ ClassZone.com

INVESTIGATIONS AND ACTIVITIES

EXPLORE THE BIG IDEA

Chapter Opening Inquiry

CHAPTER INVESTIGATION

Full-Period Labs

EXPLORE

Introductory Inquiry Activities

INVESTIGATE

Skill Labs

Standards and Benchmarks

Each chapter in **Earth's Waters** covers some of the learning goals that are described in the *National Science Education Standards* (NSES) and the Project 2061 *Benchmarks for Scientific Literacy.* Selected content and skill standards are shown below in shortened form. The following National Science Education Standards are covered on pages xii-xxvii in Frontiers in Science, and in Timelines in Science, as well as in chapter features and laboratory investigations: Understanding About Scientific Inquiry (A.9), Understanding About Science and Technology (E.6), Science and Technology in Society (F.5), Science as a Human Endeavor (G.1), Nature of Science (G.2), and History of Science.

Content Standards

1 The Water Cycle

National Science Education Standards

D.1.f | Water, which covers the majority of Earth's surface, circulates through Earth's atmosphere, surface, and crust in what is known as the "water cycle." Water evaporates from the surface, rises and cools as it moves to higher elevations, condenses as rain or snow, and falls to the surface.

D.3.d | The Sun is the major source of energy for phenomena on Earth's surface, such as the water cycle.

Project 2061 Benchmarks

4.B.2 | Three-fourths of Earth's surface is covered by a relatively thin layer of water, some of it frozen. The entire planet is surrounded by a relatively thin blanket of air.

4.B.7 | Water evaporates from Earth's surface, rises and cools, and condenses into rain or snow. The water falling on land as precipitation collects in rivers and lakes, soil, and porous layers of rock, and much of it flows back into the ocean.

2 Freshwater Resources

National Science Education Standards

F.3.b | Human activities can induce hazards through resource acquisition, urban growth, land-use decisions, and waste diposal. Such activities can speed up many natural changes.

F.4.b | Risks are associated with natural hazards such as floods—which can destroy habitats, damage property, and harm or kill people. Risks are also associated with chemical hazards such as pollution in air, water, and soil, as well as with biological hazards, such as bacteria and viruses.

Project 2061 Benchmarks

4.B.8 | Fresh water, limited in supply, is essential for life and also for most industrial processes. Rivers, lakes, and groundwater can be depleted or polluted, becoming unavailable or unsuitable for life.

4.B.11 | The benefits of Earth's resources—such as fresh water, air, soil, and trees—can be reduced by using them wastefully or by deliberately or inadvertently destroying them. Cleaning up polluted air, water, or soil or restoring depleted soil, forests, or fishing grounds can be very difficult or costly.

3 Ocean Systems

National Science Education Standards

D.1.g | Water is a solvent. As it passes through the water cycle, it dissolves minerals and gases and carries them to oceans.

D.1.j | Global patterns of atmospheric movement influence local weather. Oceans have a major effect on climate, because water in the oceans holds a large amount of heat.

D.3.c | Gravity is the force that keeps planets in orbit around the Sun and governs the rest of motion in the solar system. Gravity explains the phenomenon of the tides.

Project 2061 Benchmarks

4.B.6 | Climates have sometimes changed abruptly in the past. Even relatively small changes in atmospheric or ocean content can have widespread effects on climate if the change lasts long enough.

4.B.9 | Heat energy carried by ocean currents has a strong influence on climate around the world.

4.C.1 | The interior of Earth is hot. Heat flow and movement of material within Earth cause earthquakes and volcanic eruptions and create mountains and ocean basins.

4 Ocean Environments

National Science Education Standards

C.4.c | For ecosystems (such as the ocean) the major source of energy is sunlight. The energy passes from organism to organism in food webs.

C.4.d | The number of organisms an ecosystem can support depends on the resources available and on factors such as quantity of light and range of temperatures.

Project 2061 Benchmarks

4.B.11 | The atmosphere and oceans have a limited capacity to absorb waste and recycle materials naturally.

Process and Skill Standards

National Science Education Standards

A.1 | Identify questions that can be answered through investigation.

A.2 | Design and conduct a scientific investigation.

A.3 | Use appropriate tools and techniques to gather and interpret data.

A.4 | Use evidence to predict, explain, and model.

A.5 | Use critical thinking to find relationships between results and interpretations.

A.6 | Consider alternative explanations and predictions.

A.7 | Communicate procedures, results, and conclusions.

A.8 | Use mathematics in scientific investigations.

E.2 | Design a solution or product.

E.3 | Implement the proposed solution.

Project 2061 Benchmarks

1.A.3 | Some knowledge in science is very old and yet is still used today.

3.B.1 | Design requires taking constraints into account.

9.B.3 | Graphs can show the relationship between two variables.

9.C.4 | Graphs can show patterns and can be used to make predictions.

11.C.4 | Use equations to summarize observed changes.

12.B.1 | Find what percentage one number is of another.

12.C.1 | Compare amounts proportionally.

12.D.1 | Use tables and graphs to organize information and identify relationships.

12.D.2 | Read, interpret, and describe tables and graphs.

12.D.4 | Understand information that includes different types of charts and graphs, including circle charts, bar graphs, line graphs, data tables, diagrams, and symbols.

Introducing Earth Science

Scientists are curious. Since ancient times, they have been asking and answering questions about the world around them. Scientists are also very suspicious of the answers they get. They carefully collect evidence and test their answers many times before accepting an idea as correct.

In this book you will see how scientific knowledge keeps growing and changing as scientists ask new questions and rethink what was known before. The following sections will help get you started.

What Is Earth Science?

Earth science is the study of Earth's interior, its rocks and soil, its atmosphere, its oceans, and outer space. For many years, scientists studied each of these topics separately. They learned many important things. More recently, however, scientists have looked more and more at the connections among the different parts of Earth—its oceans, atmosphere, living things, and rocks and soil. Scientists have also been learning more about other planets in our solar system, as well as stars and galaxies far away. Through these studies they have learned much about Earth and its place in the universe.

The text and pictures in this book will help you learn key concepts and important facts about earth science. A variety of activities will help you investigate these concepts. As you learn, it helps to have a big picture of earth science as a framework for this new information. The four unifying principles listed below will give you this big picture. Read the next few pages to get an overview of each of these principles and a sense of why they are so important.

- **Heat energy inside Earth and radiation from the Sun provide energy for Earth's processes.**

- **Physical forces, such as gravity, affect the movement of all matter on Earth and throughout the universe.**

- **Matter and energy move among Earth's rocks and soil, atmosphere, waters, and living things.**

- **Earth has changed over time and continues to change.**

the **BIG** idea

Each chapter begins with a big idea. Keep in mind that each big idea relates to one or more of the unifying principles.

Heat energy inside Earth and radiation from the Sun provide energy for Earth's processes.

The lava pouring out of this volcano in Hawaii is liquid rock that was melted by heat energy under Earth's surface. Another, much more powerful energy source constantly bombards Earth's surface with energy, heating the air around you, and keeping the oceans from freezing over. This energy source is the Sun. Everything that moves or changes on Earth gets its energy either from the Sun or from the inside of our planet.

What It Means

You are always surrounded by different forms of energy, such as heat energy or light. **Energy** is the ability to cause change. All of Earth's processes need energy to occur. A process is a set of changes that leads to a particular result. For example, **evaporation** is the process by which liquid changes into gas. A puddle on a sidewalk dries up through the process of evaporation. The energy needed for the puddle to dry up comes from the Sun.

Heat Energy Inside Earth

Underneath the cool surface layer of rock, Earth's interior is so hot that the solid rock there is able to flow very slowly—a few centimeters each year. In a process called **convection,** hot material rises, cools, then sinks until it is heated enough to rise again. Convection of hot rock carries heat energy up to Earth's surface, where it provides the energy to build mountains, cause earthquakes, and make volcanoes erupt.

Radiation from the Sun

Earth receives energy from the Sun as **radiation**—energy that travels across distances in the form of certain types of waves. Visible light is one type of radiation. Radiation from the Sun heats Earth's surface, making bright summer days hot. Different parts of Earth receive different amounts of radiation at different times of the year, causing seasons. Energy from the Sun also causes winds to blow, ocean currents to flow, and water to move from the ground to the atmosphere and back again.

Why It's Important

Understanding Earth's processes makes it possible to

- know what types of crops to plant and when to plant them
- know when to watch for dangerous weather, such as tornadoes and hurricanes
- predict a volcano's eruption in time for people to leave the area

Physical forces, such as gravity, affect the movement of all matter on Earth and throughout the universe.

The universe is everything that exists, and everything in the universe is governed by the same physical laws. The same laws govern the stars shown in this picture and the page on which the picture is printed.

What It Means

What do the stars in a galaxy, the planet Earth, and your body have in common? For one thing, they are all made of matter. **Matter** is anything that has mass and takes up space. Rocks are matter. You are matter. Even the air around you is matter. Matter is made of tiny particles called **atoms** that are too small to see through an ordinary microscope.

Everything in the universe is also affected by the same physical forces. A **force** is a push or a pull. Forces affect how matter moves everywhere in the universe.

- One force you experience every moment is **gravity,** which is the attraction, or pull, between two objects. Gravity is pulling you to Earth and Earth to you. Gravity is the force that causes objects to fall downward toward the center of Earth. Gravity is also the force that keeps objects in orbit around planets and stars.

- **Friction** is the force that resists motion between two surfaces that are pressed together. Friction can keep a rock on a hillside from sliding down to the bottom of the hill. If you lightly rub your finger across a smooth page in a book and then across a piece of sandpaper, you can feel how the different surfaces produce different frictional forces. Which is easier to do?

- There are many other forces at work on Earth and throughout the universe. For example, Earth has a magnetic field. A compass needle responds to the force exerted by Earth's magnetic field. Another example is the contact force between a rock and the ground beneath it. A contact force occurs when one object pushes or pulls on another object by touching it.

Why It's Important

Physical forces influence the movement of all matter, from the tiniest particle to you to the largest galaxy. Understanding forces allows people to

- predict how objects and materials move on Earth
- send spacecraft and equipment into space
- explain and predict the movements of Earth, the Moon, planets, and stars

Matter and energy move among Earth's rocks and soil, atmosphere, waters, and living things.

When a wolf eats a rabbit, matter and energy move from one living thing into another. When a wolf drinks water warmed by the Sun, matter and energy move from Earth's waters into one of its living things. These are just two examples of how energy and matter move among different parts of the Earth system.

What It Means

Think of Earth as a huge system, or an organized group of parts that work together. Within this system, matter and energy move among the different parts. The four major parts of Earth's system are the

- **atmosphere,** which includes all the air surrounding the solid planet
- **geosphere,** which includes all of Earth's rocks and minerals, as well as Earth's interior
- **hydrosphere,** which includes oceans, rivers, lakes, and every drop of water on or under Earth's surface
- **biosphere,** which includes all the living things on Earth

Matter in the Earth System

It's easy to see how matter moves within the Earth system. When water in the atmosphere falls as rain, it becomes part of the hydrosphere. When an animal drinks water from a puddle, the water becomes part of the biosphere. When rainwater soaks into the ground, it moves through the geosphere. As the puddle dries up, the water becomes part of the atmosphere again.

Energy in the Earth System

Most of the energy you depend on comes from the Sun and moves among the four major parts of the Earth system. Think again about the puddle that is drying up. Sunlight shines through the water and heats the soil, or geosphere, beneath the puddle. Some of this heat energy goes into the puddle, moving into the hydrosphere. As the water evaporates and becomes part of the atmosphere, it takes the energy that came from the Sun with it. The Sun provides energy for all weather and ocean currents. Without the Sun, life could not exist on Earth's surface.

Why It's Important

Understanding how matter and energy move through the Earth system makes it possible to

- predict how a temperature change in ocean water might affect the weather
- determine how clearing forests might affect rainfall
- explain where organisms on the ocean floor get energy to carry out life processes

Earth has changed over time and continues to change.

You see Earth changing all of the time. Rain turns dirt to mud, and a dry wind turns the mud to dust. Many changes are small and can take hundreds, thousands, or even millions of years to add up to much. Other changes are sudden and can destroy in minutes a house that had stood for many years.

What It Means

Events are always changing Earth's surface. Some events, such as the building or wearing away of mountains, occur over millions of years. Others, such as earthquakes, occur within seconds. A change can affect a small area or even the entire planet.

Records of Change

What was the distant past like? Think about how scientists learn about ancient people. They study what the people left behind and draw conclusions based on the evidence. In a similar way, scientists learn about Earth's past by examining the evidence they find in rock layers and by observing processes now occurring.

By observing that water breaks down rocks and carries the material away to other places, people learned that rivers can slowly carve deep valleys. Evidence from rocks and fossils along the edges of continents shows that all continents were once joined and then moved apart over time. A **fossil** is the trace of a once-living organism. Fossils also show that new types of plants and animals develop, and others, such as dinosaurs, die out.

Change Continues Today

Every year, earthquakes occur, volcanoes erupt, and rivers flood. Continents continue to move slowly. The Himalayan Mountains of Asia push a few millimeters higher. **Climate**—the long-term weather patterns of an area—may also change. Scientists are studying how changes in climates around the world might affect Earth even within this century.

Why It's Important

Understanding the changing Earth makes it possible to

- predict and prepare for events such as volcanic eruptions, landslides, floods, and climate changes
- design buildings to withstand shaking during earthquakes
- protect important environments for plants and animals

The Nature of Science

You may think of science as a body of knowledge or a collection of facts. More important, however, science is an active process that involves certain ways of looking at the world.

Scientific Habits of Mind

Scientists are curious. They ask questions. A scientist who finds an unusual rock by the side of a river would ask questions such as, "Did this rock form in this area?" or "Did this rock form elsewhere and get moved here?" Questions like these make a scientist want to investigate.

Scientists are observant. They look closely at the world around them. A scientist who studies rocks can learn a lot about a rock just by picking it up, looking at its color, and feeling how heavy it is.

Scientists are creative. They draw on what they know to form possible explanations for a pattern, an event, or an interesting phenomenon that they have observed. Then scientists put together a plan for testing their ideas.

Scientists are skeptical. Scientists don't accept an explanation or answer unless it is based on evidence and logical reasoning. They continually question their own conclusions as well as the conclusions suggested by other scientists. Scientists only trust evidence that can be confirmed by other people or other methods.

Scientists use seismographs to observe and measure vibrations that move through the ground.

This scientist is collecting a sample of melted rock from a hot lava flow in Hawaii.

Science Processes at Work

You can think of science as a continuous cycle of asking and seeking answers to questions about the world. Although there are many processes that scientists use, all scientists typically do the following:

- Observe and ask a question
- Determine what is known
- Investigate
- Interpret results
- Share results

Observe and Ask a Question

It may surprise you that asking questions is an important skill. A scientific investigation may start when a scientist asks a question. Perhaps scientists observe an event or a process that they don't understand, or perhaps answering one question leads to another.

Determine What Is Known

When beginning an inquiry, scientists find out what is already known about a question. They study results from other scientific investigations, read journals, and talk with other scientists. The scientist who is trying to figure out where an unusual rock came from will study maps that show what types of rocks are already known to be in the area where the rock was found.

Investigate

Investigating is the process of collecting evidence. Two important ways of doing this are experimenting and observing.

An **experiment** is an organized procedure to study something under controlled conditions. For example, the scientist who found the rock by the river might notice that it is lighter in color where it is chipped. The scientist might design an experiment to determine why the rock is a different color on the inside. The scientist could break off a small piece of the inside of the rock and heat it up to see if it becomes the same color as the outside. The scientist would need to use a piece of the same rock that is being studied. A different rock might react differently to heat.

A scientist may use photography to study fast events, such as multiple flashes of lightning.

Rocks, such as this one from the Moon, can be subjected to different conditions in a laboratory.

Observing is the act of noting and recording an event, characteristic, or anything else detected with an instrument or with the senses. A scientist makes observations while performing an experiment. However, some things cannot be studied using experiments. For example, streaks of light called meteors occur when small rocks from outer space hit Earth's atmosphere. A scientist might study meteors by taking pictures of the sky at a time when meteors are likely to occur.

Forming hypotheses and making predictions are two other skills involved in scientific investigations. A **hypothesis** is a tentative explanation for an observation or a scientific problem that can be tested by further investigation. For example, the scientist might make the following hypothesis about the rock from the beach:

The rock is a meteorite, which is a rock that fell to the ground from outer space. The outside of the rock changed color because it was heated up from passing through Earth's atmosphere.

A **prediction** is an expectation of what will be observed or what will happen. To test the hypothesis that the rock's outside is black because it is a meteorite, the scientist might predict that a close examination of the rock will show that it has many characteristics in common with rocks that are already known to be meteorites.

Interpret Results

As scientists investigate, they analyze their evidence, or data, and begin to draw conclusions. **Analyzing data** involves looking at the evidence gathered through observations or experiments and trying to identify any patterns that might exist in the data. Scientists often need to make additional observations or perform more experiments before they are sure of their conclusions. Many times scientists make new predictions or revise their hypotheses.

Scientists use computers to gather and interpret data.

Scientists make images such as this computer drawing of a landscape to help share their results with others.

Share Results

An important part of scientific investigation is sharing results of experiments. Scientists read and publish in journals and attend conferences to communicate with other scientists around the world. Sharing data and procedures gives scientists a way to test each others' results. They also share results with the public through newspapers, television, and other media.

The Nature of Technology

When you think of technology, you may think of cars, computers, and cell phones. Imagine having no refrigerator or radio. It's difficult to think of a world without the products of what we call technology. Technology, however, is more than just devices that make our daily activities easier. Technology is the process of using scientific knowledge to design solutions to real-world problems.

Science and Technology

Science and technology go hand in hand. Each depends upon the other. Even a device as simple as a thermometer is designed using knowledge of the ways different materials respond to changes in temperature. In turn, thermometers have allowed scientists to learn more about the world. Greater knowledge of how materials respond to changes in temperature helped engineers to build items such as refrigerators. They have also built thermometers that could be read automatically by computers. New technologies lead to new scientific knowledge and new scientific knowledge leads to even better technologies.

The Process of Technological Design

The process of technological design involves many choices. What, for example, should be done to protect the residents of an area prone to severe storms such as tornadoes and hurricanes? Build stronger homes that can withstand the winds? Try to develop a way to detect the storms long before they occur? Or learn more about hurricanes in order to find new ways to protect people from the dangers? The steps people take to solve the problem depend a great deal on what they already know about the problem as well as what can reasonably be done. As you learn about the steps in the process of technological design, think about the different choices that could be made at each step.

Identify a Need

To study hurricanes, scientists needed to know what happens inside the most dangerous parts of the storm. However, it was not safe for scientists to go near the centers of hurricanes because the winds were too strong and changed direction too fast. Scientists needed a way to measure conditions deep inside the storm without putting themselves in danger.

Design and Develop

One approach was to design a robotic probe to take the measurements. The probe and instruments needed to be strong enough to withstand the fast winds near the center of a hurricane. The scientists also needed a way to send the probe into the storm and to get the data from the instruments quickly.

Scientists designed a device called a dropsonde, which could be dropped from an airplane flying over the hurricane. A dropsonde takes measurements from deep inside the storm and radios data back to the scientists.

Test and Improve

Even good technology can usually be improved. When scientists first used dropsondes, they learned about hurricanes. They also learned what things about the dropsondes worked well and what did not. For example, the scientists wanted better ways to keep track of where the probe moved. Newer dropsondes make use of the Global Positioning System, which is a way of pinpointing any position on Earth by using satellite signals.

Using McDougal Littell Science

Reading Text and Visuals

This book is organized to help you learn. Use these boxed pointers as a path to help you learn and remember the **Big Ideas** and **Key Concepts**.

Read the Big Idea.

As you read **Key Concepts** for the chapter, relate them to **the Big Idea**.

Take notes.

Use the strategies on the **Getting Ready to Learn** page.

CHAPTER

3 Ocea

the **BIG** idea

The oceans are a connected system of water in motion.

Key Concepts

SECTION 3.1 The oceans are a connected system. Learn about ocean water and the ocean floor.

SECTION 3.2 Ocean water moves in currents. Learn about currents and how they interact with climate and weather.

SECTION 3.3 Waves move through oceans. Learn how waves form and move through the ocean.

SECTION 3.4 Waters rise and fall in tides. Learn how tides are relate to the Sun and the Moon.

Internet Preview

CLASSZONE.COM
Chapter 3 online resources: Content Review, Simulation, Visualization, three Resource Centers, Math Tutorial, Test Practice

c 72 Unit: Earth's Waters

CHAPTER 3

Getting Ready to Learn

CONCEPT REVIEW

- Water covers most of Earth.
- Earth's waters circulate in the water cycle.
- The water in the oceans is salt water.

VOCABULARY REVIEW

salt water p. 11
water cycle p. 12
evaporation p. 13
desalination p. 66

CONTENT REVIEW
CLASSZONE.COM
Review concepts and vocabulary.

TAKING NOTES

OUTLINE

As you read, copy the headings into your notebook in the form of an outline. Then add notes in your own words that summarize what you read.

VOCABULARY STRATEGY

Draw a **word triangle** for each new vocabulary term. At the bottom, write and define the term. Above that, write a sentence in which you use the term correctly. At the top, draw a small picture to represent the term.

See the Note-Taking Handbook on pages R45–R51.

c 74 Unit: Earth's Waters

SCIENCE NOTEBOOK

OUTLINE
I. The oceans are a connected system.
   A. Ocean water covers much of Earth.
   B. Ocean water contains salts and gases.
      1.
      2.
   C. Ocean temperatures vary.
      1.
      2.

The salinity of ocean water is about 35 grams of salt per 1000 grams of water

salinity: a measure of the saltiness of water

Read each heading.

See how it fits into the outline of the chapter.

KEY CONCEPT

The oceans are a connected system.

Remember what you know.

Think about concepts you learned earlier and preview what you'll learn now.

◀ **BEFORE, you learned**

- Most water on Earth is salt water
- The ocean plays an important role in the water cycle

▶ **NOW, you will learn**

- What ocean water contains
- What the ocean floor looks like
- How people explore the ocean

VOCABULARY

salinity p. 76
density p. 76
continental shelf p. 80
sonar p. 82

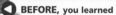

EXPLORE Density

Why do liquids form layers?

PROCEDURE

① Insert the straw into one of the solutions. Cover the top of the straw with your finger and then remove the straw from the solution. The liquid should stay in the straw.

② Using this technique, try to layer the three liquids in your straw so that you can see three distinct layers.

③ Experiment with the order in which you place the liquids into the straw. Between trials, empty the contents of the straw into the waste cup.

WHAT DO YOU THINK?
Did it matter in what order you layered the liquids? If so, can you explain why?

MATERIALS

- 3 solutions— A, B, and C—provided by your teacher
- clear straw
- waste cup

Try the activities.

They will introduce you to science concepts.

Ocean water covers much of Earth.

As land animals, we naturally think of our planet as a rocky and solid place. We even named our planet Earth, which means "land" or "soil." But look at a globe and you will see that oceans cover most of Earth. In fact, 71 percent of Earth is covered in seawater.

Looking at a map of the world, you can see the seven continents spread over our planet. These landmasses divide Earth's global ocean into connected sections. Different sections of the ocean have different names, such as Atlantic, Indian, and Pacific. However, all the sections are connected.

OUTLINE
Remember to start an outline for this section.

I. Main idea
  A. Supporting idea
    1. Detail
    2. Detail
  B. Supporting idea

Learn the vocabulary.

Take notes on each term.

Reading Text and Visuals

The Water Cycle

Water on Earth moves in a continual cycle.

② Condensation
Water vapor changes into liquid water, forming clouds.

③ Precipitation
Frozen or liquid water falls to the surface.

① Evaporation
Water rises as vapor from the surface into the atmosphere.

Liquid water flows on Earth and collects in puddles, ponds, lakes, rivers, and oceans. It also sinks into the ground.

❶ The process in which water changes from liquid to vapor is called **evaporation.** Heat energy from the Sun warms up the surface of the ocean or another body of water. Some of the liquid water evaporates, becoming invisible water vapor, a gas.

❷ The process in which water vapor in the atmosphere becomes liquid is called **condensation.** Condensation occurs as air cools. Because cold air can hold less water vapor than warm air, some of the vapor condenses, or turns into droplets of liquid water. These droplets form clouds. At high altitudes clouds contain ice crystals. Unlike water vapor, clouds are visible evidence of water in the atmosphere.

❸ Water that falls from clouds is **precipitation.** Inside a cloud, water droplets bump together and merge into larger droplets. They finally become heavy enough to fall as precipitation—rain, sleet, or hail. The water from precipitation sinks into the soil or flows into streams and rivers in the process called runoff. The force of gravity pulls the flowing water downward and, in most cases, eventually to the ocean.

 VISUALIZATION
CLASSZONE.COM

See how water moves through Earth's system in the water cycle.

CHECK YOUR READING Why does water vapor in air condense into liquid droplets?

Chapter 1: **The Water Planet 13**

Doing Labs

To understand science, you have to see it in action. Doing labs helps you understand how things really work.

① Read the entire lab first.

② Form a hypothesis.

③ Follow the procedure.

④ Record the data.

CHAPTER INVESTIGATION

Wave Movement

OVERVIEW AND PURPOSE The particles in liquid water are constantly moving. Surfers, boaters, and people in inner tubes enjoy the effects of this motion—even though they never see what is happening at the particle level. How do water particles move in waves? In this investigation you will
• observe the movements of a floating object as waves pass through water
• use your observations to draw conclusions about how water particles move in waves

MATERIALS
• small aquarium or clear, shoebox-size container
• water
• small plastic dropping bottle or plastic spice container, with cap
• salt

▶ **Problem**   Write It Up

What does the motion of a floating object reveal about the movement of water particles in a passing wave?

▶ **Hypothesize**   Write It Up

Write a hypothesis to explain what the motion of a floating object might reveal about how water particles move in a wave. Your hypothesis should take the form of an "If . . . , then . . . , because . . ." statement.

▶ **Procedure**

1. Fill the aquarium or clear container with cold tap water until it is three-quarters full.

2. Make the small bottle float with its top just below the surface of the water. You can accomplish this in several ways. First, try adding warm water to the bottle, then securely capping it without air bubbles. See if it will float. You can add salt to the bottle to move the bottle lower in the water. If the bottle is too low, you can trap a small air bubble under the cap to move the bottle higher in the water. Adjust these factors until you successfully float the bottle. The investigation will also work if the top of the bottle just touches the water's surface.

3. Remove the bottle from the water. Make sure the cap is tightly sealed.

step 2

4. Push your hand back and forth in the water at one end of the aquarium for about 30 seconds, to produce waves.

5. Gently place the small bottle back into the center of the aquarium. With your eyes level with the water surface, observe the motion of the waves and the bottle. Repeat as many times as needed until you notice the bottle behaving the same way with each passing wave.

▶ **Observe and Analyze**   Write It Up

1. **RECORD** Make a diagram showing the aquarium setup, including the water, the waves, and the small bottle. Use arrows to show how the bottle moved as waves passed. Or you may draw several diagrams of the aquarium, showing the bottle at different locations as waves passed. Label the various parts of the waves.

2. **ANALYZE** Did the bottle travel with the wave? Why or why not?

▶ **Conclude**   Write It Up

1. **INTERPRET** Compare your results with your hypothesis. Do your data support your hypothesis?

2. **INTERPRET** Answer the problem question.

3. **INFER** What do your observations tell you about particle movement in waves? Did the results surprise you? Explain.

4. **EVALUATE** Why was it necessary to float the bottle just under the surface of the water rather than letting it float right on top?

5. **PROVIDE EXAMPLES** What problems, if any, did you encounter in carrying out the procedure?

6. **IDENTIFY LIMITS** In what ways was this experiment limited in showing particle movement? Identify possible sources of error.

7. **PREDICT** How do you think particle motion in a wave with a tall wave height might differ from that in a wave with a short wave height?

8. **SYNTHESIZE** In this lab you made waves with your hand. In the ocean, most waves are caused by wind. Earthquakes, landslides, and other events also cause waves in the ocean. What do earthquakes, landslides, wind, and your hand have in common that allows all of them to make waves?

▶ **INVESTIGATE Further**

CHALLENGE Redesign this experiment in a way you think will better demonstrate the particle motion in a water wave. You need not limit yourself to the materials you used in this lab. Why will your version of the experiment work better?

Wave Movement
Problem What does the motion of a floating object reveal about the movement of water particles in a passing wave?
Hypothesize
Observe and Analyze
Table 1. Diagram of Setup

no wave	before crest	at crest	after crest	in trough

Conclude

⑤ Analyze your results.

⑥ Write your lab report.

Using Technology

The Internet is a great source of information about up-to-date science. The ClassZone Website and SciLinks have exciting sites for you to explore. Video clips and simulations can make science come alive.

Look for red banners.

Go to **ClassZone.com** to see simulations, visualizations, resources centers, and content review.

Watch the videos.

See science at work in the **Scientific American Frontiers** video.

Look up SciLinks.

Go to **scilinks.org** to explore the topic.

NSTA
scilinks.org

SCiLINKS

Water Cycle **Code: MDL018**

Earth's Waters
Contents Overview

Unit Features

1 The Water Planet   6

> (the **BIG** idea)
>
> Water moves through Earth's
> atmosphere, oceans, and land
> in a cycle.

2 Freshwater Resources   38

> (the **BIG** idea)
>
> Fresh water is a limited resource and
> is essential for human society.

3 Ocean Systems   72

> (the **BIG** idea)
>
> The oceans are a connected system
> of water in motion.

4 Ocean Environments   110

> (the **BIG** idea)
>
> The ocean supports life and contains
> natural resources.

Exploring the Water Planet

Technology allows scientists to see far below the ocean's surface, making exploration easier than ever before.

SCIENTIFIC AMERICAN FRONTIERS

View the video segment "Into the Deep" to learn how scientists explore mid-ocean ridges and deep-sea vents.

A crab encounters a research submersible.

Earth's Least-Known Region

What is the least-explored region on Earth? You might guess it's a small area where few things live, perhaps in a vast desert or in high mountains. But this region covers more than 50 percent of the planet and contains almost 98 percent of its living space. It is the deep sea, the part of the ocean sunlight cannot reach, where no plants grow. The deep sea was once thought to be of little interest. Now researchers are studying the organisms living in the deep sea and mapping the resources of the sea floor. Other parts of the ocean are getting more attention, too. For example, researchers are studying how surface water carries nutrients to new areas and how the ocean affects Earth's climate.

As people explore the ocean more thoroughly, they frequently discover new organisms. Many of these organisms are being found in the deep sea. Some, though, are being found in water that is only a few meters deep. One octopus that lives in shallow tropical water was first described in 1998. This brown octopus avoids being eaten by predators by mimicking the appearances and colors of poisonous organisms. For example, the octopus slips six of its arms and much of its body into a hole on the sea floor. Then it waves its other two arms in opposite directions, which makes it look like a banded sea snake. The octopus's colors change to yellow and black, matching the snake's bands. Another organism the octopus mimics is a multicolored lionfish with its poisonous fins spread out.

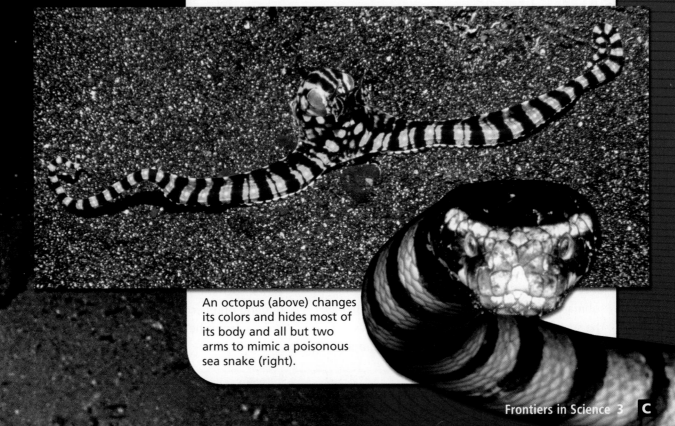

An octopus (above) changes its colors and hides most of its body and all but two arms to mimic a poisonous sea snake (right).

These scale worms, first described in 1988, live only around deep-sea vents and are thought to feed on the larger tubeworms.

Exploring Deep-Sea Vents

Deep-sea vents support astonishing life forms. These organisms depend on materials dissolved in scalding hot vent water, not on sunlight, for their ultimate source of energy. The superheated vent water contains many dissolved minerals. The minerals become solid as the vent water mixes with cold ocean water. Earth's richest deposits of minerals like copper, silver, and gold may be around some of these vents. To study the minerals that lie beneath thousands of meters of water, researchers use remotely operated devices to collect data and samples.

Exploring the Ocean and Climate

The ocean moves large amounts of heat energy between areas of Earth, affecting the atmosphere and climate. Consider that even though some parts of Alaska and Great Britain are equally close to the North Pole, Great Britain is warmer. Air over the Atlantic Ocean gains heat energy from a warm ocean current, and winds carry this warmth toward Great Britain. In addition to moving across the surface, water also mixes vertically in the ocean. The ocean contains many layers of water, with the warmest generally at the top. But the middle layers of the ocean may now be heating up quickly. Researchers are working to understand how the mixing of water in the ocean affects Earth's atmosphere and climate.

SCIENTIFIC AMERICAN FRONTIERS

View the "Into the Deep" segment of your *Scientific American Frontiers* video to learn how scientists are exploring the deep sea.

IN THIS SCENE FROM THE VIDEO ▶ a deep-sea vent spews out superheated water that is rich in dissolved minerals.

THE DEEPEST DIVES Robert Ballard has made dozens of expeditions in *Alvin,* a three-person submarine. This small vessel can dive deep below the surface to underwater mountain ranges called mid-ocean ridges. Ballard's photographs helped prove that the mountains in a mid-ocean ridge are volcanoes.

While exploring a valley that runs along the top of a mid-ocean ridge, Ballard discovered deep-sea vents. Water that flows out of the vents is very hot and rich in minerals. Ballard was also one of the first scientists to see the giant clams, tubeworms, and other animals that live around the vents. Such life forms are unusual because they depend on energy from within Earth instead of energy from the Sun.

Exploring Ocean Nutrients

Some water masses move in circular or spiral patterns, as you can see in the photograph below. These spinning water masses are called eddies. Water in eddies mixes slowly with the surrounding water. An eddy that contains nutrient-rich water can drift great distances, mixing with nutrient-poor water over a long time, sometimes years. The added nutrients allow populations of tiny plantlike organisms to grow quickly. These organisms are the base of the ocean food chain, and almost all other ocean organisms depend on them. Researchers are studying how changes in the sizes and numbers of eddies affect ocean organisms. Nutrient-rich eddies may be important to fish, such as salmon, that many people eat.

Eddies are mixing seawater from the coast of Japan with water farther from shore.

? UNANSWERED Questions

Scientists who study the ocean know that much of it is yet to be explored and that many questions remain.

- How many, and what types of, ocean organisms will be discovered in the next decades?
- How do changes in ocean surface temperatures affect weather?
- What is the best way to maintain populations of fish that people depend on for food?

UNIT PROJECTS

As you study this unit, work alone or with a group on one of the projects listed below.

Track a Drop of Water

Suppose you could follow a drop of surface water as it journeys from your hometown to the ocean.

- Find out which rivers and lakes the drop would travel through, and which ocean it would join.
- Present your findings. You might make a travelogue, a map, or both.

Life in the Water

Investigate the different life forms that live in the water in your area.

- Collect water samples from different sources, such as indoor taps, fountains, puddles, marshes, lakes, and streams.
- Examine a drop from each sample under a microscope. Sketch any living organisms you see.
- Write a lab report to present your findings about the water samples.

Ocean News Report

Imagine that you are part of a news group assigned to report on major discoveries made about the world's oceans over the past 25 years.

- Research the most important or unusual facts uncovered about the oceans. Note what technology was used to gather the data.
- Prepare a special TV or Web-site report about your investigation. Where possible, include photographs or illustrations.

CAREER CENTER
CLASSZONE.COM

Learn more about careers in oceanography.

CHAPTER

1

The Water Planet

the **BIG** idea

Water moves through Earth's atmosphere, oceans, and land in a cycle.

In what forms does water exist on Earth?

Key Concepts

SECTION

1.1 **Water continually cycles.**
Learn about how water on Earth moves in a world-wide system.

SECTION

1.2 **Fresh water flows and freezes on Earth.**
Learn about fresh water in rivers, lakes, and ice.

SECTION

1.3 **Fresh water flows underground.**
Learn about water under the land surface and how it is used.

Internet Preview

CLASSZONE.COM

Chapter 1 online resources: Content Review, Simulation, Visualization, four Resource Centers, Math Tutorial, Test Practice

EXPLORE (the BIG idea)

Where Can You See Water?

Look in your home or school for examples of frozen and liquid water. Go outside and look for the same, plus evidence of water in the air. Record your observations.

Observe and Think
What did you find inside? outside? Did you see evidence of water in the air?

Does the Ice Float?

Place an ice cube in a glass of tap water. Does it float at all? Now add two spoonfuls of salt to the water and stir it in. What happens to the ice cube?

Observe and Think What might the salt do to the water that affects the way the ice cube floats?

Internet Activity: Water

Go to **ClassZone.com** to learn what different forms of water exist on Earth and how water is a part of Earth's systems.

Observe and Think What are the different ways that water exists on Earth?

NSTA
scilinks.org
SCiLINKS

Water Cycle **Code: MDL018**

Getting Ready to Learn

◀ CONCEPT REVIEW

- Water built up on Earth's surface over time.
- Water is essential for life.
- Earth has an atmosphere of gases.

◀ VOCABULARY REVIEW

See Glossary for definitions.

atmosphere

glacier

system

 CONTENT REVIEW
CLASSZONE.COM
Review concepts and vocabulary.

▶ TAKING NOTES

MAIN IDEA AND DETAIL NOTES

Make a two-column chart. Write the main ideas, such as those in the blue headings, in the column on the left. Write details about each of those main ideas in the column on the right.

VOCABULARY STRATEGY

Write each new vocabulary term in the center of a **four-square** diagram. Write notes in the squares around the term. Include a definition, some characteristics, and some examples. If possible, write some things that are not examples.

See the Note-Taking Handbook on pages R45–R51.

SCIENCE NOTEBOOK

MAIN IDEAS	DETAIL NOTES
1. Water is a unique substance.	1. Only substance in three forms at normal temperatures
	1. Can be solid, liquid, gas
	1. As liquid, can fit any container

Definition	Characteristics
Water that is not salty	Little or no taste, color, or smell

FRESH WATER

Examples	Nonexamples
Liquid in rivers, lakes	Liquid in oceans

Water continually cycles.

 BEFORE, you learned

- The force of running water causes erosion
- Water can be solid

▶ **NOW, you will learn**

- What makes water important
- How much of Earth's water is salt water
- How water moves throughout Earth and its atmosphere

VOCABULARY

fresh water p. 11
salt water p. 11
water cycle p. 12
evaporation p. 13
condensation p. 13
precipitation p. 13

EXPLORE Water Vapor

Where does the water come from?

PROCEDURE

① Put the ice in the glass and fill it with water.

② Observe what happens to the outside of the glass.

WHAT DO YOU THINK?

- Where did the water on the outside of the glass come from?
- What does this activity tell you about the air surrounding you? What conclusion can you draw?

MATERIALS
- clear glass
- ice
- water

MAIN IDEA AND DETAILS
Make a two-column chart to start organizing information about water.

Water is a unique substance.

Seen from outer space, Earth glistens like a beautiful blue and white marble. Welcome to the "water planet," the only planet in our solar system with a surface covered by a vast amount of liquid water. Because of water, a truly amazing substance, life can exist on Earth.

What is so amazing about water? In the temperature ranges we have on Earth, it exists commonly as a solid, a liquid, and a gas. At a low temperature, water freezes. It becomes a solid, which is ice. At a higher temperature, it flows easily in liquid form. Liquid water can become a gas, especially at higher temperatures. If you have ever noticed how something wet dries out in the hot sunlight, you have observed the effect of liquid water changing into a gas. The gas form is the invisible water vapor in our atmosphere.

Liquid water can fit any container. It can hold its shape in a raindrop, then merge with other drops to flow down a hill or slow down and sit for centuries in a lake.

Water covers most of Earth.

Earth looks bluish from space because most of Earth's surface is ocean. If you look at a globe or a world map, you will see the names of four oceans—Atlantic, Pacific, Indian, and Arctic. If you look more closely or trace the four named oceans with your finger, you will see that they are connected to one another. Together they form one huge ocean. Any part of this ocean is called the sea.

The global ocean covers 71 percent, or almost three-quarters, of Earth's surface. Most of the ocean is in the Southern Hemisphere. The ocean is, on average, 3.8 kilometers (2.4 mi) deep. Although most of the water covering Earth is ocean, water also covers some land areas, as rivers, lakes, and ice.

 CHECK YOUR READING Where is most of Earth's water?

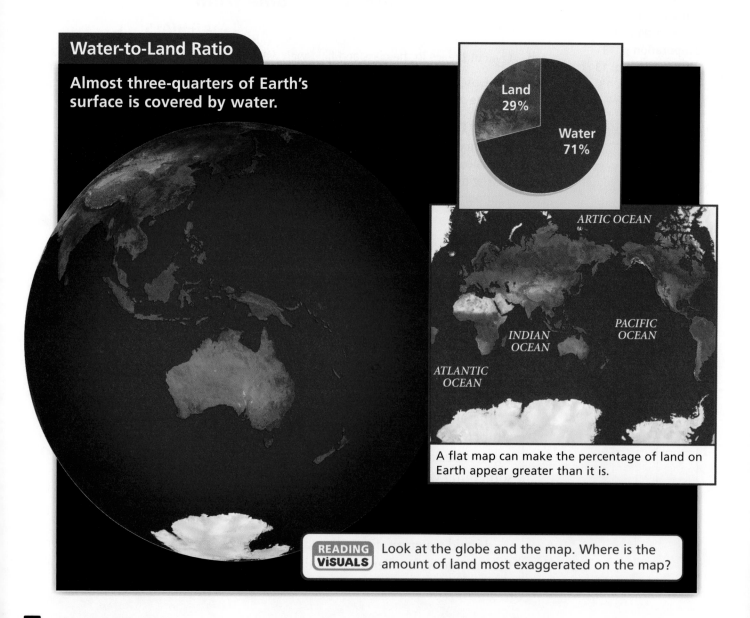

Water-to-Land Ratio

Almost three-quarters of Earth's surface is covered by water.

Land 29%

Water 71%

ARTIC OCEAN

PACIFIC OCEAN

INDIAN OCEAN

ATLANTIC OCEAN

A flat map can make the percentage of land on Earth appear greater than it is.

READING VISUALS Look at the globe and the map. Where is the amount of land most exaggerated on the map?

Water and Life

Without water, nothing would live on Earth. Living things need water to function. Your own body is two-thirds water. In your body, your blood—which is mostly water—carries nutrients that give you energy and flushes wastes away. Many forms of life live in water. Oceans, lakes, and rivers are home to fish, mammals, plants, and other organisms. Even a single drop of water may contain tiny forms of life.

Fresh Water and Salt Water

When you hear the word *water*, you might imagine a cool drink that quenches your thirst. The water that you drink and depend on for survival is fresh water. **Fresh water** is water that is not salty and has little or no taste, color, or smell. Most rivers and lakes are fresh water.

The water in the ocean is salt water. **Salt water** is water that contains dissolved salts and other minerals. Human beings and most other land animals cannot survive by drinking salt water, although many other forms of life can live in salt water.

You may be surprised to learn that even though fresh water is important for life, fresh water is actually scarce on Earth. Because most of Earth's water is in the ocean, most of the water on Earth is salt water. The illustration below compares the amounts of fresh water and salt water on Earth. Almost all—about 97 percent—of Earth's water is salt water in the ocean. Only about 3 percent of Earth's water, at any given time, is fresh water.

VOCABULARY
Remember to write the terms *fresh water* and *salt water* in four-square diagrams in your notebook.

 CHECK YOUR READING What is the difference between fresh water and salt water?

Salt Water vs. Fresh Water

Most water on Earth is salt water.

3% fresh water

97% salt water

Forms of Fresh Water

- ■ Free flowing 30%
- ▣ Frozen 70%

Ice on land and in oceans

Water underground and in rivers, lakes, atmosphere, and plants and animals

Imagine that this glass of water represents all of the water on Earth.

Water moves in a worldwide cycle.

MAIN IDEA AND DETAILS
Record in your notes this main idea and important details about the water cycle.

Water continually moves and changes form. Water from clouds falls over the oceans and on land. Water flows in rivers and collects in lakes and under the ground. Water can be a solid in the form of ice, or it can be an invisible vapor in the atmosphere.

The Water Cycle

Water's movement on Earth is a cycle, or continually repeating process. The **water cycle** is the continuous movement of water through the environment of Earth. In the water cycle, water is constantly changing form, from a liquid on land, to a vapor in the atmosphere, and again to a liquid that falls to the surface. The flow of water on land and underground is also part of the water cycle. As water moves in the water cycle, the total amount of water in Earth's system does not change very much. The water cycle involves three major processes: evaporation, condensation, and precipitation.

INVESTIGATE The Water Cycle

How does water cycle through an environment?

DESIGN —YOUR OWN—

PROCEDURE

1. Construct an environment in a jar with a lid. You can use plants, soil, water, and containers.

2. Find the mass of your closed jar after you construct it.

3. Draw a detailed, colored picture of your jar.

4. Let your jar sit for several days.

5. Find the mass of your jar again, and draw another picture of it.

WHAT DO YOU THINK?

- How did the jar's appearance change over several days?
- How did its mass change?
- What can you conclude about how water cycles through an environment?

CHALLENGE How could you change your environment so that the jar's appearance would change at a faster rate?

SKILL FOCUS
Modeling

MATERIALS
- jar with lid
- soil
- rocks or pebbles
- sand
- smaller containers
- water
- small plants
- triple-beam balance

TIME
30 minutes (for construction; 20 minutes for analysis)

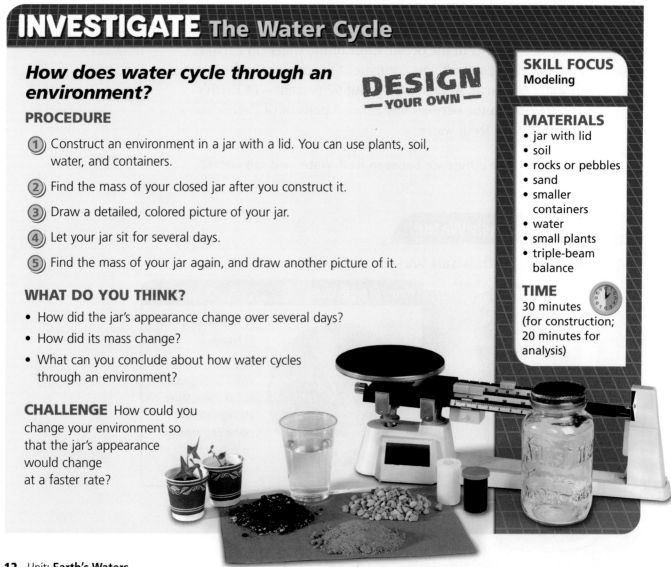

The Water Cycle

Water on Earth moves in a continual cycle.

2 Condensation
Water vapor changes into
liquid water, forming clouds.

3 Precipitation
Frozen or liquid
water falls to
the surface.

1 Evaporation
Water turns into vapor
in the atmosphere and
rises from the surface.

Liquid water flows on Earth and collects
in puddles, ponds, lakes, rivers, and
oceans. It also sinks into the ground.

❶ The process in which water changes from liquid to vapor is called
evaporation. Heat energy from the Sun warms up the surface of
the ocean or another body of water. Some of the liquid water
evaporates, becoming invisible water vapor, a gas.

❷ The process in which water vapor in the atmosphere becomes
liquid is called **condensation.** Condensation occurs as air cools.
Because cold air can have less water vapor than warm air, some
of the vapor condenses, or turns into droplets of liquid water.
These droplets form clouds. At high altitudes clouds are made of
ice crystals. Unlike water vapor, clouds are visible evidence of
water in the atmosphere.

❸ Water that falls from clouds is **precipitation.** Inside a cloud, water
droplets bump together and merge into larger droplets. They finally
become heavy enough to fall as precipitation—such as rain or sleet.
The water from precipitation sinks into the soil or flows into streams
and rivers in the process called runoff. The force of gravity pulls the
flowing water downward and, in most cases, eventually to the ocean.

VISUALIZATION
CLASSZONE.COM

See how water moves
through Earth's system
in the water cycle.

CHECK YOUR READING   Why does water vapor in air condense into liquid droplets?

Most of the water that evaporates on Earth—85 percent of it—evaporates from the ocean. (About 75 percent of this condenses into cloud droplets and falls right back into the ocean.) The remaining 15 percent of evaporating water comes from such sources as damp ground, lakes, wet sidewalks, rivers, and sprinklers. Plants are also part of the water cycle. They pull up water from the ground and then release much of it into the air through their leaves.

Even though the water that evaporates into the atmosphere comes from both the salty ocean and from fresh water on land, all the precipitation that falls back to the surface is fresh water. When salt water evaporates, the salt is left behind. Through the water cycle the ocean water that human beings cannot drink becomes a source of fresh water for human beings and other life on Earth.

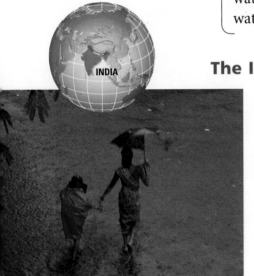

The Impact of the Water Cycle

The action of the water cycle is easy to spot. When it rains or snows, you can see precipitation in action. When you look at a flowing stream, you see the water cycle returning water to the sea. When a stream dries up, you know that the water cycle in the area has slowed down for a while.

Wet weather can fill reservoirs with drinking water and pour needed water on crops. Wet weather can also bring too much rain. For example, during the wet season in India, winds blow moist air inland from the Indian Ocean. Tremendous rains fall over the land for months. The rain is usually welcome after a long and hot dry season. However, these seasonal rains frequently cause devastating floods, covering acres and acres of land with water.

Flooding usually occurs during India's annual rainy season.

1.1 Review

KEY CONCEPTS

1. Name three things about water that make it unique or important.

2. How much of Earth's water is fresh water?

3. Explain the three processes that make up the water cycle.

CRITICAL THINKING

4. **Apply** How can a drop of salt water once have been a drop of fresh water?

5. **Compare and Contrast** What are two differences between salt water and fresh water?

⬤ CHALLENGE

6. **Infer** In 1996, the *Galileo* space probe sent back photographs that showed ice on the surface of one of the moons of Jupiter. Scientists suspected there was water under the ice. Why did this discovery excite some people who thought there was a chance of finding life on that moon?

Does Mars Have a Water Cycle?

Mars once had water flowing on its surface. Today, it is a frozen desert. Astronomers think that most of the water on Mars has been frozen for the past 3.9 billion years. But there is growing evidence that Mars has had flowing water recently—in the last 10 million years. Some astronomers suggest that Mars may have a multimillion-year water cycle. According to their hypothesis, occasional volcanic activity melts ice, releasing floods of water. After the water evaporates, condenses, and falls as rain, it becomes ice again. And if Mars does have a water cycle, it could have something else that goes with water on Earth: life.

Mars has features that appear to be like those created by water on Earth.

▶ Issues

For Mars to have this water cycle, it would need several features.

- a source of energy for melting ice into water
- conditions for water to evaporate
- conditions for water vapor to condense

▶ Observations

Astronomers have observed several facts about Mars.

- Mars has water ice at its north and south poles and underground.
- Mars has had very large volcanoes in the past, although it seems to have no active volcanoes today.
- Mars takes about 687 Earth days to orbit the Sun.
- Mars has an atmosphere that is 100 times thinner than the atmosphere of Earth.
- Mars has an average surface air temperature of –55°C (–67°F).
- Mars has features that look like ones shaped by water on Earth: ocean shorelines, river valleys, and gullies.
- Mars has rocks that were probably formed in the presence of liquid water.

Icecaps cover the poles of Mars.

▶ Determine the Relevance of Each Observation

On Your Own Decide whether each observation is relevant in determining whether Mars has a water cycle.

As a Group Discuss the relevance of each observation to the idea of a water cycle on Mars. List other information that might be helpful.

CHALLENGE Research information about Mars. Identify facts that support or oppose the idea of a Martian water cycle.

RESOURCE CENTER

Learn more about evidence that Mars may or may not have a water cycle.

Fresh water flows and freezes on Earth.

 BEFORE, you learned

- Water covers most of Earth's surface
- Water continually cycles
- Water falls to Earth's surface as precipitation

 NOW, you will learn

- How fresh water flows and collects on land
- How surface water forms lakes
- How frozen water exists on Earth

VOCABULARY

divide p. 17
drainage basin p. 17
turnover p. 19
eutrophication p. 20
iceberg p. 22

EXPLORE Water Collection

How does water flow and collect?

PROCEDURE

① With the open egg carton on a level tray, pour water slowly into the center of the carton until the cups are three-quarters full.

② Empty the carton. Tip it slightly, as shown in the photograph, and pour water into the higher end. Stop pouring when the carton is about to overflow.

WHAT DO YOU THINK?

- How did the water flow when you poured it into the level carton? into the tilted carton? Where did it collect in the carton? Where did it not collect?
- What might your observations tell you about how water flows when it falls on land?

MATERIALS

- plastic-foam egg carton
- tray or pan
- plastic bottle
- water

MAIN IDEA AND DETAILS
Record in your notebook this main idea and details about it.

Water flows and collects on Earth's surface.

Imagine you are in a raft on a river, speeding through whitewater rapids. Your raft splashes around boulders, crashing its way downriver. Then the raft reaches a lake. You glide across the surface, slowing down. At the end of the lake, your raft enters a river again and floats down it.

In your raft you are following the path a water drop might take on its way to the ocean. All over the planet, the force of gravity pulls water downhill. Fresh water flows downhill in a series of streams and rivers, collects in lakes and ponds, and eventually flows into the ocean. All of this water flows between high points called divides, in areas called drainage basins.

Divides and drainage basins affect the way water flows on land. A **divide** is a ridge, or continuous line of high land, from which water flows in different directions. If you were on a skateboard and began at the top of a hill, you would ride in one general direction down the hillside. On the other side of the hill, you would ride downhill in a completely different direction. The top of the hill is like a divide. A divide can be a continuous ridge of high mountains. On flatter ground, a divide can simply be the line of highest ground.

A **drainage basin,** or watershed, is an area into which all of the water on one side of a divide flows. If you pour water into the basin of your bathroom sink, it will flow down the side from high points to low, and eventually down the drain, which is at the lowest point. In mountainous areas, hills and mountains form the sides of basins, and valleys form the low points. Flatter regions also have basins. The basins may not be obvious in these regions, but they still drain water.

When it rains in a drainage basin, the water forms streams and rivers or sinks into the ground. Every stream, river, and lake is in a basin. In most places, the water eventually flows to the sea. In a bowl-shaped basin, the water may collect at the bottom of the basin or evaporate.

Divides and Drainage Basins

Divides separate drainage basins.

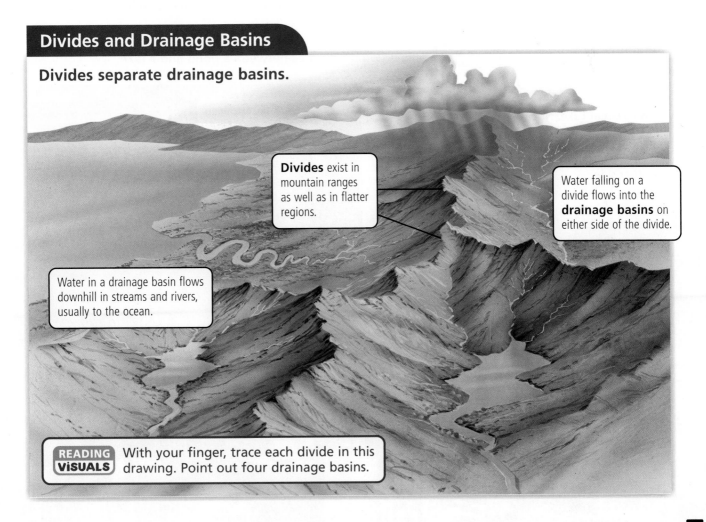

Divides exist in mountain ranges as well as in flatter regions.

Water falling on a divide flows into the **drainage basins** on either side of the divide.

Water in a drainage basin flows downhill in streams and rivers, usually to the ocean.

READING VISUALS With your finger, trace each divide in this drawing. Point out four drainage basins.

Surface water collects in ponds and lakes.

Lakes and ponds form where water naturally collects in low parts of land. Some lakes were formed during the last ice age. For example, the Great Lakes were formed when huge sheets of ice scraped out a series of giant depressions. Other lakes, such as Crater Lake in Oregon, were formed when water collected inside the craters of inactive volcanoes.

Water can fill a lake in several ways. Where the land surface dips below the level of underground water, the low land area fills with water. Rainfall and other precipitation contribute water to all lakes. Water may flow through a lake from a stream or river. Water may also flow away from a lake through a stream running downhill from the lake. Many lakes maintain fairly steady levels because of the balance of flow in and flow out.

The main difference between a pond and a lake is in their overall size. A pond is smaller and shallower than a lake, and there are many plants, such as water lilies and cattails, rooted in its muddy bottom. A lake may have water so deep that sunlight can't reach the bottom. In the deeper part of the lake, plants can't take root, so they grow only around the lake's edges. Ponds and lakes provide homes for many kinds of fish, insects, and other wildlife. They also provide resting places for migrating birds.

CHECK YOUR READING Name two differences between a pond and a lake.

Chicago, Illinois, at the southwest corner of Lake Michigan, is the largest city on a Great Lake. Note that the lake is so wide that from Chicago you cannot see Michigan on the other side.

Lake Michigan is the third largest of the five Great Lakes, which border eight states and Canada's Ontario province.

Lake Turnover

The water in a lake is not as still as it might appear. The changing temperatures of the seasons affect the water and cause it to move within the lake in a yearly cycle.

In a place with cold winters, ice may form on a lake, so that the wind cannot ruffle the surface. The water temperature in the lake remains steady, and the water stops moving. The water just below the surface ice is near freezing, so the fish move to the bottom, where the water is a bit warmer.

In many lakes the water temperatures at different levels vary as the seasons change. In the spring and summer, sunlight can warm a layer of water at the top of a lake. Because the colder water beneath the top layer is denser than the warmer water above it, the water levels do not mix easily. The warm water contains more oxygen, so fish may be more plentiful in the upper part of the lake.

READING TiP

Cold water is denser than (has more mass than the same amount of) warm water.

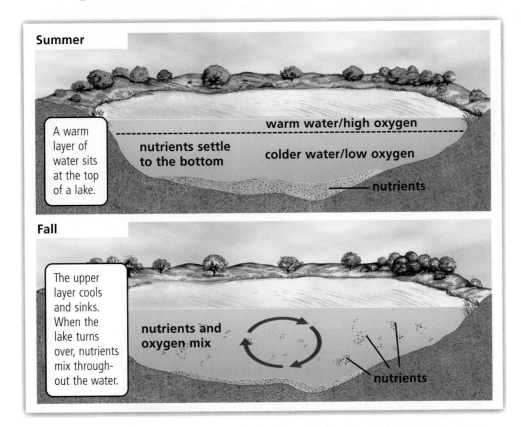

Summer

A warm layer of water sits at the top of a lake.

warm water/high oxygen

nutrients settle to the bottom

colder water/low oxygen

nutrients

Fall

The upper layer cools and sinks. When the lake turns over, nutrients mix throughout the water.

nutrients and oxygen mix

nutrients

In the fall, days cool and the surface water cools too. The upper layer becomes heavy and sinks, so that the lake water "turns over." Nutrients from minerals and from dead plants and organisms are stirred up from the bottom. These nutrients are used by many life forms in the lake. The rising and sinking of cold and warm water layers in a lake is called **turnover.** Turnover occurs twice each year as the seasons change.

CHECK YOUR READING What happens to surface water when the weather cools in the fall?

Eutrophication

A lake does not remain a lake forever. Through natural processes that take thousands of years, most lakes eventually are filled in and become meadows—fields covered with grass and other plants. A lake can become filled in as sediments, including the remains of dead fish, plants, and other organisms, pile up on the bottom.

READING TiP

Eutrophication comes from the Greek word *eutrophos,* meaning "well-nourished."

The activity of life in a lake is affected by nutrients. Nutrients are the foods and chemicals that support living things. When the amounts of such nutrients as phosphorus and nitrogen in a lake increase, algae and other organisms in the water grow more rapidly. An increase of nutrients in a lake or pond is called **eutrophication** (yoo-TRAHF-ih-KAY-shuhn). As eutrophication occurs, algae form a thick scum on the water. The amount of oxygen in the water decreases, until fish and other organisms that require oxygen cannot survive. The illustration below shows what happens to a lake when nutrient levels increase.

1. When the amounts of such nutrients as nitrogen and phosphorus increase, algae grow faster and form a scum layer at the surface.

2. Dead algae, plants, and fish pile up. Plants grow more quickly, leaving more debris as they die. Water evaporates, and the lake becomes shallower.

3. The lake becomes a soggy marsh, then finally a completely filled-in meadow.

The process of eutrophication is usually slow. In some cases, however, eutrophication happens more quickly than it normally would because of pollution from human activities. Nitrogen in fertilizers used on farms and gardens may be washed into lakes. Phosphates from laundry detergents may be present in wastewater that reaches lakes. The extra nutrients cause algae and plants in lakes to grow faster and more thickly than they normally would grow. Eutrophication from pollution causes clear lakes to become clogged with algae and plants.

CHECK YOUR READING How does human activity contribute to eutrophication?

Most fresh water on Earth is frozen.

If you want fresh water, take a trip to Greenland or the South Pole. Two-thirds of the world's fresh water is locked up in the ice covering land near the poles.

The ice sheet that covers Antarctica is almost one and a half times as big as the United States and is in places more than a kilometer thick. Ice on Earth's surface contains more than 24 million cubic kilometers of fresh water. Just how much water is that? Imagine that you have three glasses of lemonade. If you take one sip from one of the glasses of lemonade, you have drunk the water in all the lakes and rivers on Earth. The rest of the glass represents liquid ground water. The other two glasses of lemonade represent all the frozen water on the planet.

Ice on Land

In Earth's coldest regions—near both poles and in high mountains—more snow falls each year than melts. This snow builds up to form glaciers. A glacier is a large mass of ice and snow that moves over land. There are two types of glaciers. The ice sheets of Antarctica and Greenland are called continental glaciers because they cover huge landmasses. The other type of glacier is a valley glacier, which builds up in high areas and moves slowly down between mountains.

RESOURCE CENTER
CLASSZONE.COM

Find out more about frozen fresh water.

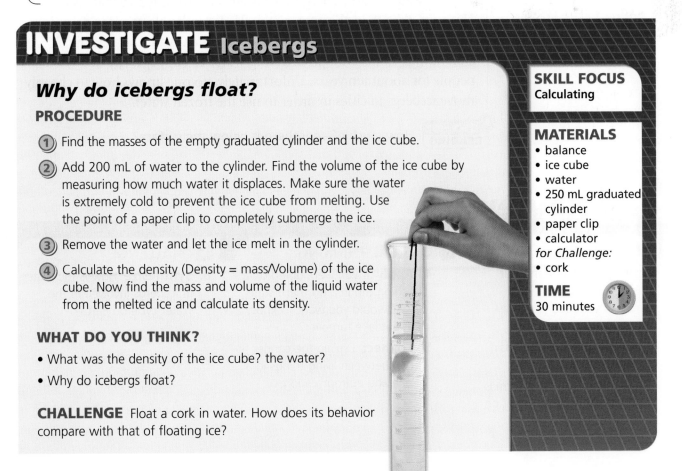

INVESTIGATE Icebergs

Why do icebergs float?

PROCEDURE

1. Find the masses of the empty graduated cylinder and the ice cube.

2. Add 200 mL of water to the cylinder. Find the volume of the ice cube by measuring how much water it displaces. Make sure the water is extremely cold to prevent the ice cube from melting. Use the point of a paper clip to completely submerge the ice.

3. Remove the water and let the ice melt in the cylinder.

4. Calculate the density (Density = mass/Volume) of the ice cube. Now find the mass and volume of the liquid water from the melted ice and calculate its density.

WHAT DO YOU THINK?

• What was the density of the ice cube? the water?

• Why do icebergs float?

CHALLENGE Float a cork in water. How does its behavior compare with that of floating ice?

SKILL FOCUS
Calculating

MATERIALS
• balance
• ice cube
• water
• 250 mL graduated cylinder
• paper clip
• calculator
for Challenge:
• cork

TIME
30 minutes

Icebergs

An **iceberg** is a mass of ice floating in the ocean. An iceberg starts out as part of a glacier. In places such as Antarctica and Greenland, glaciers form ice shelves that extend out over the ocean. When a large chunk of a shelf breaks off and floats away, it becomes an iceberg.

Thousands of icebergs break off from ice sheets each year. In the Northern Hemisphere, ocean currents push icebergs south into the warmer Atlantic Ocean. It may take an iceberg two to three years to float down to the area off the coast of Canada. In that region, it breaks apart and melts in the sea. A North Atlantic iceberg sank the *Titanic*.

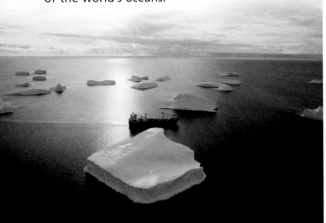

Icebergs are masses of frozen fresh water floating in the salt water of the world's oceans.

How big is an iceberg? One iceberg that recently broke off an Antarctic ice shelf was the size of Connecticut. Off the coast of eastern Canada, some icebergs tower 46 meters (150 ft) above the surface of the ocean. This is impressive, because most of a floating iceberg is below the surface. Only about one-eighth of the total weight and volume of the iceberg can be seen above the surface of the sea. When people say "It's only the tip of the iceberg," they mean that a lot of something is unrevealed.

The water in an iceberg may have been frozen for 15,000 years. However, the ice in the center, if melted, can be clean, clear drinking water. And an iceberg can hold a lot of water. An iceberg as big as a city block holds enough drinking water to supply a city of 50,000 people for about ten years. Unfortunately, no one knows how to cheaply move icebergs to cities in order to use the frozen water.

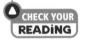

CHECK YOUR READING How much of an iceberg is below the surface?

1.2 Review

KEY CONCEPTS

1. Why is it important that fresh water flows over Earth's surface?

2. Explain the relationship between a drainage basin and a divide.

3. Where and in what form is most of the fresh water on Earth?

CRITICAL THINKING

4. **Apply** If you were going on a fishing trip in a northern state, why would you want to know about lake turnover?

5. **Connect** Explain the connection between living things in a lake and eutrophication.

CHALLENGE

6. **Synthesize** How is the water in icebergs involved in the water cycle on Earth?

MATH TUTORIAL
CLASSZONE.COM

Click on Math Tutorial for help multiplying fractions and whole numbers.

SKILL: MULTIPLYING FRACTIONS AND WHOLE NUMBERS

How Big Is an Iceberg?

In salt water, the part of an iceberg that is visible above water is only 1/8 of the whole iceberg. The remaining 7/8 of the iceberg is hidden under the water's surface. You can use fractions to estimate how much ice is underwater.

Example

An iceberg is made of 1000 cubic meters of ice. How much of the ice is underwater?

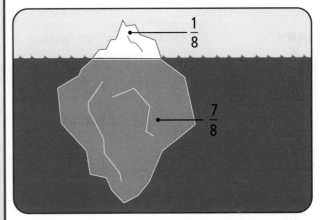

Solution

(1) Write a word equation.

$$\text{Volume of ice underwater} = \text{volume of iceberg} \cdot \text{fraction underwater}$$

(2) Substitute.

$$\text{Volume of ice underwater} = 1000 \text{ m}^3 \cdot \frac{7}{8}$$

(3) Multiply the numerator by the total volume.

$$= \frac{1000 \text{ m}^3 \cdot 7}{8}$$

(4) Calculate and simplify.

$$= \frac{7000 \text{ m}^3}{8} = 875 \text{ m}^3$$

ANSWER About 875 cubic meters of ice are underwater.

Calculate how much ice is underwater.

1. The iceberg is made of 1600 cubic meters of ice.

2. The iceberg is made of 1800 cubic meters of ice.

3. The iceberg is made of 12,000 cubic meters of ice.

CHALLENGE About 500 cubic meters of an iceberg is visible above the water. Estimate the total volume of the iceberg.

KEY CONCEPT

Fresh water flows underground.

◀ **BEFORE**, you learned

- Water flows in river systems on Earth's surface
- Water collects in ponds and lakes on Earth's surface

▶ **NOW**, you will learn

- How water collects and flows underground
- How underground water reaches the surface in springs and by wells

VOCABULARY

groundwater p. 24
permeable p. 24
impermeable p. 25
water table p. 25
aquifer p. 26
spring p. 28
artesian well p. 28

EXPLORE Flow of Water

What does water flow through?

PROCEDURE

① Fill the cup with water.

② Have a partner hold the filter open over a sink, bucket, or pan while you pour water into it.

WHAT DO YOU THINK?

- Why did the water remain in the cup before you poured it?
- What route did the water take to pass through the filter?

CHALLENGE What other materials might hold water? allow water to flow through?

MATERIALS

- water
- cup
- paper coffee filter
- bucket, dishpan, or sink

Water fills underground spaces.

After a rainstorm, water does not stay on the ground for long. What happens to this water? It flows along Earth's surface into a river or reservoir, evaporates, or sinks into the soil. Plants use some of the water that sinks into the ground, and the rest of it sinks deeper into Earth. Water held underground is called **groundwater.** The ground under your school may seem too solid to hold water, but it is likely that groundwater sits or moves under the surface.

To understand how groundwater collects, you need to know the difference between permeable and impermeable materials. The ground beneath your feet is made of both permeable and impermeable materials.

A **permeable** substance is a substance that liquids can flow through. Liquids flow through a coffee filter because the filter is permeable. Soil,

VOCABULARY
In your notebook make four-square diagrams for the terms *groundwater* and *permeable.*

sand, and gravel are permeable because there are spaces between the particles. Water flows into and through these spaces. The bigger the particles, the more easily water can flow. Gravel and larger rocks have large spaces between them, so water flows quickly through. Sandy soil also has many pores, or spaces. Some rocks, such as sandstone, are permeable although the spaces in these rocks are extremely small.

An **impermeable** substance is a substance that liquids cannot flow through. A drinking glass holds orange juice because the material of the glass is impermeable. Rocks such as granite are impermeable. Unless granite has cracks, it has no spaces for water to go through. Many impermeable materials are hard, but not all of them. Clay is soft, but it is nearly impermeable. Water can get between its particles, but the overlapping of the particles stops the water from flowing through.

READING **TiP**

The prefix *im* in *impermeable* means "not."

How does groundwater collect? Gravity causes rainwater to sink into the soil. If it rains heavily, all the spaces in the soil fill with water. Eventually the water reaches impermeable rock. There it is held in place or forced to flow in a different direction.

Even when the soil on Earth's surface is dry, huge amounts of groundwater may be stored below. The top of the region that is saturated, or completely filled with water, is called the **water table.** The saturated region below the water table is called the saturation zone.

CHECK YOUR READING What prevents groundwater from sinking farther down?

Groundwater

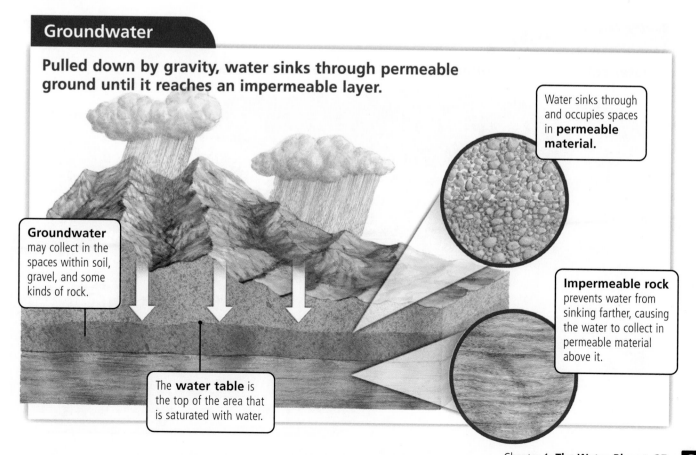

Pulled down by gravity, water sinks through permeable ground until it reaches an impermeable layer.

Water sinks through and occupies spaces in **permeable material.**

Groundwater may collect in the spaces within soil, gravel, and some kinds of rock.

Impermeable rock prevents water from sinking farther, causing the water to collect in permeable material above it.

The **water table** is the top of the area that is saturated with water.

Aquifers

An **aquifer** is an underground layer of permeable rock or sediment that contains water. Some aquifers lie deep under layers of impermeable rock. Other aquifers lie just beneath the topsoil.

SIMULATION
CLASSZONE.COM

Explore how groundwater fills in aquifers.

Aquifers can be found all over the world. They lie under deserts as well as wet regions. As the map below shows, they are found in many areas of the United States. An aquifer might be a bed of sand or gravel only a few meters thick. Or it might be an enormous layer of sandstone, several hundred meters thick, holding water in countless pore spaces. The Ogallala Aquifer is the largest aquifer in North America. It covers 450,000 square kilometers (176,000 mi^2), from South Dakota to Texas.

For an aquifer to form, three things are needed:

- A layer of permeable material holds the water. Groundwater is stored in the pore spaces of gravel, sand, or rock.

- A neighboring area of impermeable rock keeps the water from draining away. Sometimes impermeable rock lies both above and below an aquifer.

- A source of water replenishes or refills the aquifer. Like any body of water, an aquifer can be emptied.

You know that fresh water on land flows toward the ocean. Water that is underground acts like slow-motion streams, rivers, and lakes. Underground water moves slowly. The water is under pressure

Aquifers

Water collects underground in layers of permeable material.

water table

permeable rock

water table

impermeable rock

aquifer

Aquifers in the United States

Aquifer

from all sides, and it must go around endless tiny corners and passageways in rock. Unlike the water in an aboveground river, groundwater moves sideways, down, and even up. In some areas, groundwater is pushed upward so that it flows from a hillside. Because it moves so slowly, much of the water in an aquifer may have been there for thousands of years.

The Importance of Aquifers

When water sinks into land, the ground acts like a giant filter. Stones and sand in the ground can filter out bacteria and other living organisms. This ground filter also removes some harmful chemicals and minerals. The filtering process can make groundwater clear and clean and ready to drink. If it is not polluted, groundwater may not need expensive treatment. It is one of our most valuable natural resources.

Many big cities collect water from rivers and store it in reservoirs above the ground. However, about one-fifth of the people in the United States get their fresh water from underground. Most people who live in rural areas pump groundwater from wells. In many desert regions people depend on sources of underground water.

INVESTIGATE Aquifer Filtration

How can the ground filter water?
PROCEDURE

1. Cap the top of the bottle. Invert it and add to it a layer of gravel, then a layer of sand, then a layer of soil.

2. Slowly pour water onto the soil until a water table becomes visible in the sand beneath it.

3. Add the pollutants pepper, cocoa, and food coloring to the bottle top. Slowly unscrew the cap so that water trickles into the bucket.

4. Observe the water that filtered through.

5. Pour more water onto the soil and let water trickle out.

WHAT DO YOU THINK?

- Which pollutants were filtered out before reaching the "aquifer"? Which ones reached the aquifer?

- What effect does pollution have on drinking water that comes from aquifers?

CHALLENGE What could you do to clean up an aquifer?

SKILL FOCUS
Making models

MATERIALS
- water
- 1L plastic bottle with bottom cut off
- gravel
- sand
- soil
- pepper
- cocoa
- food coloring
- bottle bottom or bucket

TIME
30 minutes

Underground water can be brought to the surface.

MAIN IDEA AND DETAILS
In your notebook, fill out a chart for this main idea.

If you had lived in colonial America or in ancient Greece, your daily chore might have been to haul water home from a well. You would have lowered a bucket into a pit until it reached the water table, then pulled the filled bucket up with a rope. Or you might have worked at digging a well, hacking away at the ground with a shovel until water flowed into the hole you dug.

Today's technology makes it easier to bring groundwater to the surface. Powerful drills bore through rock, and motors pump groundwater to the surface and to kitchen sinks. Scientists study the sizes and areas of aquifers. They know where to get water and how much to expect.

Springs and Wells

Groundwater can be collected from springs and wells. A **spring** is a flow of water from the ground at a place where the surface of the land dips below the water table. In some springs, the water bubbles up, then sinks back into the soil. In others, the water flows into a stream or lake. Spring water has a fresh clean taste, and many water companies bottle this water to sell.

Underground pressure causes this artesian well to shoot water 18 meters (60 ft) into the air.

A well is a hole in the ground that reaches down to the saturation zone—the wet region below the water table. Usually, a pump is used to draw the water out of the ground, and a screen is used to filter out particles of sand and gravel. If the water table is near the surface, a well can be dug by hand. The part of the well beneath the water table will fill with water.

Most modern wells are dug with motorized drills. A drill digs through soil and rock into the saturation zone; then a pipe is lowered into the drill hole. A pump is used to raise the water from the ground. Some wells are more than 300 meters (1000 ft) deep.

One kind of well does not need a pump. An **artesian well** is a well in which water flows to the surface naturally because it is under pressure. In places where impermeable rock dips into an aquifer, the water directly below the rock is pushed to a lower level than the water on either side. When a well is drilled into the water beneath the rock, the weight of the surrounding water pushes the water upward.

 CHECK YOUR READING What makes water flow upward out of an artesian well?

Springs and Wells

Water is brought up from the ground in various ways.

Water flows from an **artesian well** because the water underground is under pressure.

A **spring** occurs where the water table meets the ground surface.

well dug for home

water table

aquifer

How to Make a Well

aquifer

water table

1 Drill into the ground with special machinery.

2 When the drill hole reaches below the water table, lower a pipe into it.

3 At the top of the well, install a pump powered by a motor or human effort to pull up water.

READING VISUALS Look at the top illustration. What would happen if the water table dropped below the bottom end of the well?

The depth of the water table in a particular place can vary from season to season, depending on how much rain falls and how much water is used. When water is taken from an aquifer, the water table might drop. When it rains or snows, some of the water filters back into the aquifer, replacing what has been taken. If water is used faster than it is replaced, wells may run dry. Low groundwater levels can also cause the ground to settle and damage the environment.

As more and more people live on Earth, the amounts of groundwater used to irrigate crops increase. In some states where crops are grown in dry areas, as much as 70 percent of all the groundwater brought to the surface is used for irrigation. Water used for irrigation is recycled back into the water cycle. In some places it sinks back into the ground and filters into aquifers. In other regions much of the water evaporates or flows away, and the groundwater levels are lowered.

Hot Springs

Yellowstone National Park sits atop the remains of an ancient volcano. The rain and melted snow that sink into the ground there eventually reach depths of more than 3000 meters (10,000 feet), where the rocks are extremely hot. The water heats up and reaches the boiling point. Then it becomes even hotter while remaining liquid because it is under such great pressure from the rocks pushing on it from all sides.

The hot water deep underground is like water in an enormous boiling pot—with a lid 3000 meters thick. The water expands the only way that it can, by pushing upward through weak places in the rocks. A place where the water surfaces is a hot spring. A hot spring has a continual flow of hot water.

Vapor rises from these hot springs in Yellowstone National Park in Wyoming.

In a geyser, water heats underground. The diagram shows the underground "plumbing" of a geyser in Iceland.

Hot water and steam are pushed up to the surface where they erupt.

A geyser is a kind of hot spring. The illustrations above show how a geyser works. Beneath the surface, there are underground channels in the rock. The rising hot water is forced to travel through these narrow passages. Like water in a garden hose, the water moves with force because it is under pressure. When it finally reaches Earth's surface, the pressure makes it burst out. It shoots into the air as a dramatic fountain of water and steam. In Yellowstone National Park there are more than 300 geysers. One of the largest, Old Faithful, shoots a jet of hot water and steam about 20 times a day. The eruptions last from 1.5 to 5 minutes, and reach heights of 30 to 55 meters (106 to 184 ft).

RESOURCE CENTER
CLASSZONE.COM

Learn more about geysers and hot springs.

CHECK YOUR READING Why does water shoot out of Old Faithful with such great force?

1.3 Review

KEY CONCEPTS

1. Draw a diagram that shows how water collects underground.

2. What is the difference between a spring and a well?

3. What causes water to rise out of the ground in hot springs and geysers?

CRITICAL THINKING

4. **Connect** Is a T-shirt permeable or impermeable? How about a raincoat? Explain why.

5. **Infer** Would you expect to find a spring on the very top of a hill? Why or why not?

⬥ CHALLENGE

6. **Sequence** On a blank sheet of paper, draw a cartoon strip that shows how aquifers collect and store water and how people bring the water to the surface. Show at least five steps in the process. Write captions for your drawing to explain the steps.

CHAPTER INVESTIGATION

Water Moving Underground

OVERVIEW AND PURPOSE

Many people rely on underground aquifers for their drinking water. Some aquifers are small and localized. Others can supply water to huge regions of the United States. Perhaps your own drinking water comes from an underground aquifer. In this investigation you will

DESIGN —YOUR OWN— EXPERIMENT

- design an experiment to determine what types of materials best hold and transport water
- infer which types of Earth materials make the best aquifers

▶ Problem

Write It Up

What types of materials will best hold and transport water?

▶ Hypothesize

Write It Up

Write a hypothesis that answers the problem question in "If . . . , then . . . , because . . ." form.

▶ Procedure

1. Design a procedure to test the materials samples to determine which will best hold and transport water. Your procedure should be designed to identify both which material absorbed the most water and which material absorbs water the fastest.

2. Record your procedure in your **Science Notebook.**

MATERIALS
- granite sample
- sandstone sample
- sand
- square piece of cotton muslin or cotton knit, measuring 30 cm per side
- rubber band
- golf ball
- scale
- large jar
- water

WATER

3 Create a data table to organize the data you will collect.

4 Be sure that you make both qualitative and quantitative observations.

5 Be sure to include a calculations section in your **Science Notebook.**

▶ Observe and Analyze

1. **RECORD OBSERVATIONS** Draw a diagram of your experimental setup.

2. **CALCULATE** Which item absorbed the most water?

3. **SCIENTIFIC METHOD** How did you use the golf ball? What did it represent?

▶ Conclude

1. **INTERPRET** Answer the problem question.

2. **COMPARE** Compare your results with your hypothesis. Do your data support your hypothesis?

3. **IDENTIFY LIMITS** In what ways was this activity limited in demonstrating how water moves underground? How might your experimental setup lead to incorrect conclusions?

4. **APPLY** Look over your data table. Your results should indicate both which material absorbed the most water and which material absorbed water the fastest. How do these two characteristics compare in terms of their importance for an aquifer?

5. **INFER** Which types of Earth materials make the best aquifers?

▶ INVESTIGATE Further

CHALLENGE The data you gathered in this investigation reflect the permeability of each Earth material tested. What qualities and characteristics determine their permeabilities?

Water Moving Underground
Problem What types of materials will best hold and transport water?
Hypothesize
Procedure
Observe and Analyze
Table 1.

Conclude

the BIG idea

Water moves through Earth's atmosphere, oceans, and land in a cycle.

CONTENT REVIEW
CLASSZONE.COM

◀ **KEY CONCEPTS SUMMARY**

1.1 Water continually cycles.
Water moves through Earth's environment in a continuous cycle.

1 Evaporation Water becomes vapor.

2 Condensation Vapor changes into liquid.

3 Precipitation Water falls to the surface.

VOCABULARY
fresh water p. 11
salt water p. 11
water cycle p. 12
evaporation p. 13
condensation p. 13
precipitation p. 13

1.2 Fresh water flows and freezes on Earth.

Water on land collects and flows in rivers and lakes. Much of Earth's fresh water is frozen.

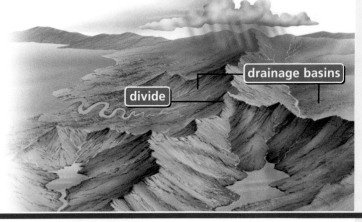

divide

drainage basins

VOCABULARY
divide p. 17
drainage basin p. 17
turnover p. 19
eutrophication p. 20
iceberg p. 22

1.3 Fresh water flows underground.
Water collects and moves beneath the land surface.

Gravity pulls water down through **permeable** materials until it reaches an impermeable layer.

Water collects in open spaces in soil, gravel, or rock.

The **impermeable** layer prevents water from sinking farther down.

VOCABULARY
groundwater p. 24
permeable p. 24
impermeable p. 25
water table p. 25
aquifer p. 26
spring p. 28
artesian well p. 28

Reviewing Vocabulary

Use the terms in the box below to answer the next nine questions.

evaporation	precipitation	water cycle
turnover	eutrophication	artesian
iceberg	groundwater	permeable

1. Which word describes an increase in nutrients in a lake or pond?

2. Which kind of well does not need a pump?

3. Which term describes a seasonal change in a lake?

4. Which term describes a substance through which water can pass?

5. Which term names the continuous movement of water through Earth's environment?

6. What is the name for an enormous chunk of floating ice?

7. What word means the turning of liquid water into a gas?

8. What is the name of water stored in an aquifer?

9. What word is another name for rain, snow, sleet, and hail?

Reviewing Key Concepts

Multiple Choice *Choose the letter of the best answer.*

10. What are the three forms of water on Earth?
   a. groundwater, lakes, and clouds
   b. liquid water, frozen water, and water vapor
   c. gas, steam, and vapor
   d. groundwater, oceans, and ice

11. How much of Earth's water is fresh water?
   a. almost all
   b. about half
   c. very little
   d. none

12. Which process forms clouds?
   a. evaporation
   b. precipitation
   c. condensation
   d. dehydration

13. What ice formation covers Greenland and Antarctica?
   a. iceberg
   b. landmass
   c. valley glacier
   d. continental glacier

14. Which is a characteristic of a pond?
   a. rooted plants covering the entire bottom
   b. plants only near shore
   c. a layer of impermeable rock
   d. water heated by underground rock

15. How are glaciers like rivers?
   a. They are made of liquid water.
   b. Their water sinks into the ground.
   c. They flow downhill.
   d. They are a mile thick.

16. How is water stored in an aquifer?
   a. in an open underground lake
   b. in cracks and spaces in rocks
   c. in impermeable rock
   d. in wells and springs

Short Answer *Write a short answer to each question.*

17. Explain why most of the water cycle takes place over the ocean.

18. How does an iceberg form?

19. Why are aquifers valuable?

20. What is the difference between a valley glacier and a continental glacier?

Thinking Critically

Use the photograph to answer the next four questions. There are four liters of water in the jug. The hose has been overflowing for about ten seconds.

21. **OBSERVE** Describe what the water in the hose is doing.

22. **IDENTIFY EFFECTS** Explain what effect the water in the jug has on the water in the hose. Why does the water rise in the hose?

23. **PREDICT** When will the water stop flowing from the hose? Why?

24. **COMPARE AND CONTRAST** How is what is happening in the hose like and unlike what happens in an artesian well?

25. **EXPLAIN** Explain why the water cycle matters to humans and animals.

26. **CONNECT** In a mountainous area, temperatures are lower at higher altitudes. Explain the connection between this fact and the existence of valley glaciers.

27. **COMPARE AND CONTRAST** Explain the difference between clouds and water vapor in the atmosphere.

28. **INFER** Explain why water in a bowl-shaped drainage basin does not eventually flow to the ocean.

29. **APPLY** Name at least two things that you think people could do to lessen eutrophication caused by pollution.

30. **APPLY** Explain why even though evaporation draws water but not salt from the ocean, the ocean does not become saltier.

   PREDICT Fill in the chart with predictions of how water will collect under the stated conditions.

Conditions	Prediction
31. A bed of permeable rock lies atop a bed of impermeable rock; rainfall is plentiful.	
32. Heavy snows fall in a region that has year-round freezing temperatures.	
33. A large depression is left in impermeable rock by a glacier.	
34. Water from farm fields and gardens runs off into ponds.	

the BIG idea

35. **SYNTHESIZE** Explain why a raindrop that falls on your head may once have been water in the Pacific Ocean.

36. **MODEL** Draw a diagram of two drainage basins, showing how water flows and collects on the surface of Earth. Label the divide, as well as the bodies of water into which water flows.

UNIT PROJECTS

If you are doing a unit project, make a folder for your project. Include in your folder a list of the resources you will need, the date on which the project is due, and a schedule to keep track of your progress. Begin gathering data.

Analyzing Data

In an experiment to study the effect of heating on evaporation, identical pans of water were placed for two hours under different types of lights. The temperature of the air just above each pan was measured with a thermometer every 30 minutes. The amount of evaporation was determined by subtracting the amount of water in the pan at the end of two hours from the amount that was in the pan at the beginning. The data table shows the results. Study the data and answer the questions below.

Pan	Description	Average Air Temperature Above the Water	Evaporation
1	under regular light	22°C (72°F)	30 mL (1.0 oz)
2	under heat lamp on low	25°C (78°F)	40 mL (1.4 oz)
3	under heat lamp on high	28°C (83°F)	50 mL (1.7 oz)

1. What is the relationship between the air temperature and the evaporation rate?

   a. There is no relationship between the temperature and the rate.

   b. As the temperature increases, the rate decreases.

   c. As the temperature increases, the rate stays the same.

   d. As the temperature increases, the rate increases.

2. If the air temperature averaged 27°C (80°F), about how much water would evaporate in two hours?

   a. 28 mL   **c.** 48 mL

   b. 38 mL   **d.** 58 mL

3. The constants in this experiment are the factors that stay the same for all three pans. Which of the following is a constant?

   a. the type of light

   b. the size of the pans

   c. the air temperature above the water

   d. the amount of evaporation

4. The dependent variable in an experiment is the factor that is measured to gather results. Which is the dependent variable in this experiment?

   a. the amount of evaporation

   b. the amount of water in each pan in the beginning

   c. the type of light

   d. the air temperature

5. Which change would make the results of this experiment more reliable?

   a. conducting the experiment for four hours

   b. decreasing the amount of water in the pans

   c. increasing the air temperature for one pan

   d. using a fan to blow air on one of the pans

Extended Response

Answer the two questions below in detail. Include some of the terms shown in the word box. In your answers, underline each term you use.

low	eutrophication	meadow
water table	saturation zone	

6. Kori notices that a pond at his summer camp is filled with more soil and plants each year. Explain how this change fits into the pattern of how ponds change over time.

7. Juanita's family gets water from a well on their ranch. Each time a well has gone dry, they have had to dig a new one that was deeper than the old one. Explain why they have needed to go deeper.

Freshwater Resources

the **BIG** idea

Fresh water is a limited resource and is essential for human society

In what ways do you depend on water?

Key Concepts

SECTION 2.1
Fresh water is an essential resource.
Learn how water is needed for life and how water is used for human activities.

SECTION 2.2
Society depends on clean and safe water.
Learn how water is made safe for drinking and how wastewater is treated.

SECTION 2.3
Water shortages threaten society.
Learn about the causes of water shortages and about ways to conserve water.

Internet Preview

CLASSZONE.COM

Chapter 2 online resources: Content Review, Simulation, Visualization, two Resource Centers, Math Tutorial, Test Practice

EXPLORE (the BIG idea)

How Much Water Do You Drink?

From the time you get up to when you finish dinner, keep a list that notes each time you drink a liquid—including water, juice, milk, and soda. Write down what you drank and how much you think you drank.

Observe and Think
How many times did you drink something? From your list, estimate in numbers of medium glassfuls the total amount you drank.

What Happens When Salt Water Evaporates?

Dissolve a spoonful of salt in a cup of water. Put the cup in a warm place, such as a sunny windowsill. Leave it there until the water completely evaporates.

Observe and Think Examine the cup. If you could capture the water that evaporated, would that water be salty? Explain your answer.

Internet Activity: Aquifers

Go to **ClassZone.com** to explore the limits of an aquifer. Review past water usage and try to determine how long the water in an aquifer will last.

Observe and Think
What can be done to slow the use of underground water?

NSTA
scilinks.org
SCiLINKS

Water Pollution **Code: MDL019**

Getting Ready to Learn

◀ CONCEPT REVIEW

- Water can be a solid, a liquid, or a gas.
- Water continually cycles on Earth.
- Water flows underground.

◀ VOCABULARY REVIEW

fresh water p. 11

water cycle p. 12

groundwater p. 24

aquifer p. 26

ⓘ CONTENT REVIEW
CLASSZONE.COM
Review concepts and vocabulary.

▶ TAKING NOTES

SUPPORTING MAIN IDEAS

Make a chart to show main ideas and the information that supports them. Write each blue heading from the chapter in each box. In boxes below it, add supporting information, such as reasons, explanations, and examples.

VOCABULARY STRATEGY

Place each vocabulary term at the center of a **description wheel**. Write some words describing it on the spokes.

See the Note-Taking Handbook on pages R45–R51.

SCIENCE NOTEBOOK

Fresh water supports life.

The human body is more than one-half water.

Living cells need water.

Water is a limited resource.

can be sprayed

can be in canals

water drawn is from aquifers, lakes, and rivers

IRRIGATION

process of supplying water

used in dry areas

used for crops

2.1 Fresh water is an essential resource.

 BEFORE, you learned

- Fresh water is found on Earth's surface and underground
- People use wells to bring ground water to the surface

 NOW, you will learn

- How water is required for life
- How water is used for many human activities

VOCABULARY

irrigation p. 43
aquaculture p. 45
dam p. 46
lock p. 46

THINK ABOUT

How valuable is water?

In the United States, fresh water seems plentiful. When you want water for a drink or to wash, you can go to a drinking fountain or turn on the tap to get all the water you want. In some parts of the world, water is scarce and difficult to get. In Port-au-Prince, Haiti, this girl is getting her bucket filled with fresh water so that she can take water home. If you had to get your water this way, how might that change the way you think of water? Would you use water differently than you do now?

Fresh water supports life.

Close your eyes and imagine a beautiful place in nature that is full of life. Maybe you think of trees, flowers, and a waterfall and pools where animals come to drink. Water is important in any scene that involves life.

People have always lived near clean, fresh water. Why is water so important to humans? One reason is that our bodies are more than one-half water. Without the water in your blood, your cells would not receive the nutrients they need. Your skin and tissues hold water in your body, but some water is lost every day. As a result, you get thirsty and drink water or something that contains mostly water, such as milk or juice. Without water, a person cannot live for more than a few days. And without water, people wouldn't be able to grow food.

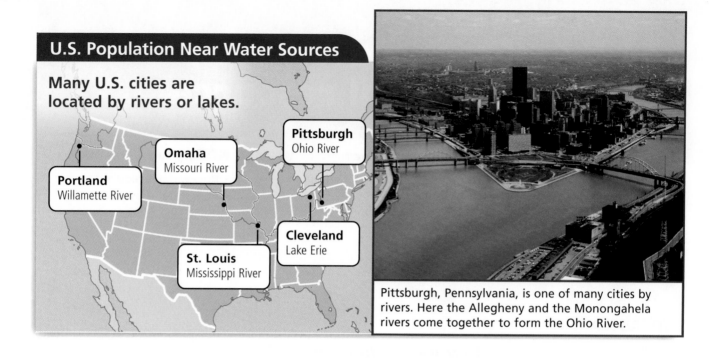

U.S. Population Near Water Sources

Many U.S. cities are located by rivers or lakes.

Portland
Willamette River

Omaha
Missouri River

Pittsburgh
Ohio River

Cleveland
Lake Erie

St. Louis
Mississippi River

Pittsburgh, Pennsylvania, is one of many cities by rivers. Here the Allegheny and the Monongahela rivers come together to form the Ohio River.

You have read that fresh water on Earth is a limited resource. A fixed amount cycles through the atmosphere, flows in rivers, is held in lakes and glaciers, and is stored in aquifers deep under the ground. As more and more people live on the planet every year, our water sources become more precious. If too much water is taken from aquifers, the supply will eventually run out. If the water in rivers and lakes becomes polluted, we can no longer use it.

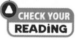 **CHECK YOUR READING** What can happen to water as the world population grows?

Most human activities require water.

 SUPPORTING MAIN IDEAS Record details about how water is important to human activities.

Almost everything you do requires water. When you take a shower or brush your teeth, you use water. Your dishes and clothes are washed with water. You might exercise in water at a pool.

Some of the ways you use water might surprise you. Let's say you do your homework after school. You grab a slice of pizza from the refrigerator, switch on the light, and sit down to read a book in your favorite chair. Have you used any water so far? The answer is yes, many gallons of water.

On farms water was needed to grow the tomatoes and wheat for your pizza. The cheese topping came from a cow that drank water and ate grain grown with water. The paper in your book was produced at a paper plant that used vast amounts of water to wash and mix wood pulp. When you switch on a light, you are probably using energy that was generated by some form of moving water. And the metal in the lamp was mined from underground, using—you guessed it—water.

INVESTIGATE Water Usage

How much water do you use in a week?

PROCEDURE

1. Write down all the ways you use water in a day. Start with the time you get up in the morning. Include things such as brushing your teeth, flushing the toilet, using ice, and taking a shower.

2. Look at the Water Use sheet, and from it, identify other ways that you and others in your household use water.

3. Add up how many liters of water you use in a day, and multiply that by 7. This is how much water you use in a week.

WHAT DO YOU THINK?

• Which of your activities used the most water?
• What are some ways that you could reduce the amount of water you use weekly?

CHALLENGE Based on your weekly water usage, how much water is used by the United States annually? **Hint:** Find the population of the United States in a reference source.

Farming

In the United States, about 40 percent of the water that is used goes to growing crops and raising livestock. Any kind of farm depends on water to grow plants for food and to raise animals. To grow oranges, a farm needs about 0.25 centimeters (0.1 in.) of rainfall a day. To produce one hamburger can require 5000 liters (1300 gal.) of water or more because animals not only drink water but also eat grass and grain that use water.

In many areas, rainfall does not provide enough water to support crops and animals. In these drier areas, farmers draw water from aquifers, rivers, or lakes to grow crops. The process of supplying water to land to grow crops is **irrigation.**

A common method of irrigation pours water through canals and waterways so that it flows through the fields. A little more than half of U.S. farms that are irrigated use this method, which is called flood irrigation. Most of the other farms that irrigate use spray irrigation, which sprays water onto the fields. You can think of lawn sprinklers as an example of spray irrigation for grass. On farms, the water often is delivered by metal structures that roll around entire fields.

These green irrigated fields are circular because the metal sprinklers move like clock hands from a center point

Industry

The industries that make our cars, notebooks, jeans, sneakers, skateboards, and TVs are major water users. The manufacture of just about any item you can name probably uses water. Consider these examples.

- The process of making one car can require about 50 times the car's weight in water. This process begins with the mining of minerals and ends with the final washing as the car rolls out of the factory.
- In many industries, huge amounts of water are used to cool down machines.
- In a coal mine, water is used to separate chunks of coal from other clumps of dirt and rock.
- A paper mill uses 100 to 300 metric tons of water to manufacture one ton of paper.

Water used in industry can be used again. Factories can clean the water they use and return most of it to lakes and rivers.

 CHECK YOUR READING How is water used in industry?

A paper mill uses large quantities of water to process wood pulp.

Transportation and Recreation

Since the earliest times, rivers and lakes have helped people visit their neighbors and trade food and goods. In the United States, major rivers and the Great Lakes provide an efficient way to transport goods, especially cargo that is bulky and heavy, such as coal. For example, on the Great Lakes, large ships carry iron ore from Minnesota to cities where it is used to make steel. On the Mississippi River, barges haul grain to ports, where the grain may be processed or placed on ships to go overseas.

Great Lakes

This freighter carries cargo on the Great Lakes.

People also use rivers and lakes for recreation. Whitewater rafting, canoeing, and kayaking are popular activities. Many people also like to camp, picnic, swim, and fish along the shores of freshwater rivers and lakes.

Not every section of a river can be navigated by boat. A river may flow too fast or be too shallow for safe travel. To make water transportation easier, people dig channels called canals that bypass rough spots and connect waterways. For example, a 376-kilometer (234-mi) canal lets boats travel between the Tennessee and Tombigbee rivers in Mississippi and Alabama. In Canada, west of Buffalo, New York, the Welland Canal connects two Great Lakes, Ontario and Erie. It is part of the waterway known as the St. Lawrence Seaway, which connects the Great Lakes to the Atlantic Ocean.

Fisheries and Aquaculture

Fresh water is full of life—from tiny one-celled organisms to small shrimp and worms, to trout and salmon. Rivers and lakes provide fish for our food, a living resource that people depend upon. They also provide food for frogs, insects, birds, and larger animals.

When people talk about livestock, do you think of fish? Probably not, but fish farming is a thriving business all over the world. **Aquaculture** is the science and business of raising and harvesting fish in a controlled situation. Freshwater fish farms provide a cheap, ready source of catfish, trout, and salmon. However, aquaculture also causes some problems. The farms can cause excess nutrients and pollution to flow into rivers and lakes.

To help maintain the population of fish in rivers and lakes, fish hatcheries are used to raise fish to release into lakes and rivers. Hatcheries give people who fish something to catch and also help threatened species survive.

An aquaculture worker tends to a fish farm in Nepal.

NEPAL

Energy

Not so long ago, water wheels could be seen dotting the rivers of America. The force of the river turned the water wheel, which powered machinery in factories such as grain mills. In dams, electricity is generated in a similar way. A **dam** is a structure that holds back and controls the flow of water in a river or other body of water.

At a hydroelectric dam built across a river, water rushing through the dam turns machines called turbines, generating electricity. Even electric plants that are not powered by rivers use water. For example, many plants use coal or nuclear power to heat water, creating steam that turns the turbines. Nuclear power stations also use water to cool the system.

At a hydroelectric plant, water flowing through a dam spins turbines to produce electricity.

Dams and other structures alter rivers.

When a dam is built on a river, the landscape and the shape of a river are greatly changed. Below the dam, the speed and volume of water flow may change, making a new ecosystem. Behind the dam, water may collect and form a lake covering what once had been a river valley.

In some locations, a lake behind a dam is used as a source of fresh water. A lake that is used to store water is called a reservoir (REHZ-uhr-VWAHR). Some dams are built solely for the purpose of creating a reservoir, and many communities rely on reservoirs for their water needs. Some reservoirs provide opportunities for boating and other recreational activities.

Dams have purposes in addition to providing hydroelectric power and forming reservoirs. Dams may also be built to control rivers that flow too fast or too unpredictably for boats to use them. These dams might separate a river into sections of different elevations, like steps in a staircase. To allow boats to climb or descend these steps and move to the next river section, locks are built at the dams. A **lock** is a section of waterway, closed off by gates, in which the water level is raised or lowered to move ships through.

In addition to rivers with dams, locks are used in canals and rivers that connect lakes of different elevations. Locks are also used in canals that slope upward and then downward, such as the Panama Canal. The Panama Canal is dug into a strip of land between the Atlantic and Pacific oceans, allowing ships a handy shortcut.

VOCABULARY
Add a description wheel for *lock* in your notebook.

● **CHECK YOUR READING** Why do ships need to use locks?

In some cases dams cause problems as well as solve them. For example, in Egypt's Nile valley the giant Aswan Dam stopped floods that happened every year. However, the dam also blocked the flow of rich soil to the valley below the dam. The soil in the Nile valley was fertile for more than 4000 years. Yet today farmers need to add chemical fertilizers to grow their crops.

Dams can also cause problems for fish. When a dam blocks a river, salmon and steelhead cannot reach their breeding grounds. People have tried to solve this problem by installing fish ladder structures along dams that allow fish to climb up the river.

RESOURCE CENTER
CLASSZONE.COM
Learn more about dams.

Locks and Dams

Locks and dams control the flow of rivers and allow boats to pass through.

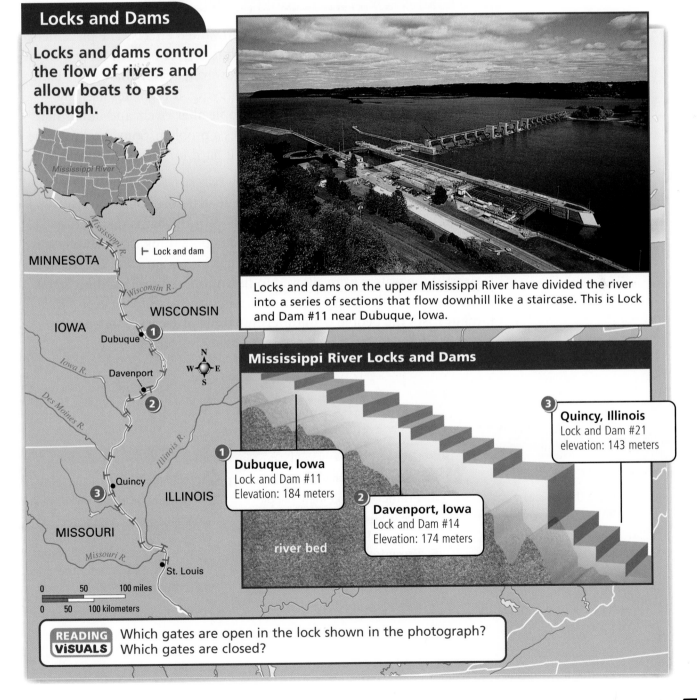

⊢ Lock and dam

MINNESOTA

WISCONSIN

IOWA

Dubuque ➊

Davenport ➋

Quincy ➌

ILLINOIS

MISSOURI

St. Louis

| 0 | 50 | 100 miles |
| 0 | 50 | 100 kilometers |

Locks and dams on the upper Mississippi River have divided the river into a series of sections that flow downhill like a staircase. This is Lock and Dam #11 near Dubuque, Iowa.

Mississippi River Locks and Dams

➌ **Quincy, Illinois**
Lock and Dam #21
elevation: 143 meters

➊ **Dubuque, Iowa**
Lock and Dam #11
Elevation: 184 meters

➋ **Davenport, Iowa**
Lock and Dam #14
Elevation: 174 meters

river bed

READING VISUALS Which gates are open in the lock shown in the photograph? Which gates are closed?

This dammed-up waterway in Texas spilled around its dam during a flood. It formed a new channel that flows to the left of the dam.

Other changes to rivers can have unwanted effects. The placement of locks and the digging of a channel into a river bottom force a river to follow a constant path. In nature, however, a river changes its path depending on how much water it is carrying. It regulates itself by flooding during the wet season. As people alter rivers and build their homes closer to them, flooding becomes a problem. Some people argue that changing the natural flow makes it hard for a river to regulate itself, causing even more flooding.

People have different opinions about structures on rivers. In some places with hydroelectric dams, people want the dams removed so that salmon can swim upstream. Some people think that habitats for wildlife would be improved on the upper Mississippi and the Missouri rivers if the waters were allowed to flow more naturally. Others stress the value of hydroelectricity and the importance of navigation. In many cases the people with differing points of view try to reach compromises so that rivers can serve many purposes.

2.1 Review

KEY CONCEPTS

1. What are three ways that you directly use fresh water daily?

2. Identify a benefit and a possible disadvantage of aquaculture.

3. Explain why dams are both helpful to people and harmful to a river.

CRITICAL THINKING

4. **Predict** Do you think people will need more or less fresh water in the future? Why?

5. **Provide Examples** Explain how water is used in the manufacture of three products that you use every day.

○ CHALLENGE

6. **Connect** In some towns near rivers, the federal government is buying houses and paying people to move to a different location. Explain why the government might be doing this.

MATH TUTORIAL
CLASSZONE.COM

Click on Math Tutorial for more help finding the volume of a rectangular prism.

SKILL: VOLUME OF RECTANGULAR PRISMS

Fish in an Aquarium

A fish requires a certain minimum amount of water to survive. If you plan to keep fish in an aquarium, you can calculate the volume of the aquarium to be sure it will contain enough water.

Example

An aquarium is 50 centimeters long, 30 centimeters wide, and 40 centimeters high. How many liters of water will it hold?

40 cm

50 cm **30 cm**

Solution

Use the formula for the volume of a rectangular prism.

Volume = length × width × height	Write a word equation.
$V = lwh$	Replace the words with variables.
= 50 cm × 30 cm × 40 cm	Substitute 50 for l, 30 for w, and 40 for h.
= 60,000 cm^3	Multiply. Note that cm^3 is a cubic centimeter.
= 60,000 mL	Each cubic centimeter holds a milliliter.
= 60 L	Because there are 1000 milliliters in one liter, divide 60,000 by 1000.

ANSWER The aquarium holds 60 liters of water.

Find the volume of each aquarium. Give your answer in liters.

1. The aquarium is 100 centimeters long, 50 centimeters wide, and 80 centimeters high.

2. The aquarium is 50 centimeters long, 20 centimeters wide, and 40 centimeters high.

3. The aquarium is 50 centimeters long, 40 centimeters wide, and 50 centimeters high.

CHALLENGE You are designing an aquarium to house several fish of different species. The aquarium must hold 300 liters of water and fit in a space that is 100 centimeters long and 50 centimeters wide. How high should the aquarium be?

2.2 Society depends on clean and safe water.

◀ **BEFORE, you learned**

- Water supports life
- Water is used in many ways

▶ **NOW, you will learn**

- How drinking water and wastewater are treated
- How fresh water can become polluted
- How water pollution can be prevented

VOCABULARY

concentration p. 51
sewage system p. 53
septic system p. 54
point-source pollution p. 54
nonpoint-source pollution p. 54

EXPLORE Concentration

What is one part per million?

PROCEDURE

1. Pour 50 mL of water into the graduated cylinder. This is equal to 1000 drops of water.

2. Add one drop of food coloring to the water in the cylinder. This represents one drop of food coloring to 1000 drops of water, or one part per thousand.

3. Fill the eyedropper from the cylinder.

4. Empty the cylinder and pour 50 mL of new water into the cylinder. Add one drop from the eyedropper to the cylinder. The mixture now contains one part food coloring per thousand thousand parts water, or one part per million (ppm).

MATERIALS

- water
- graduated cylinder
- eyedropper
- food coloring

WHAT DO YOU THINK?
The amount of sodium found in clean spring water is five parts per million. How would you conduct this experiment to make a mixture of food coloring in water of five parts per million?

Treatment makes water safe for drinking.

SUPPORTING MAIN IDEAS
Remember to start a new chart for each main idea.

When you wash your face or brush your teeth, do you ever wonder where the water comes from? It depends on where you live. In many places, water is pumped from a nearby well dug into an underground aquifer. If you live in a big city such as New York City or San Francisco, the water may travel a great distance to arrive at your sink. It is piped to the city from reservoirs that may be many miles away. Then it is stored in tanks or in a local reservoir before flowing through pipes to your home.

Water comes from many different sources, so it may contain impurities or organisms that cause disease. For this reason, drinking water in larger systems is cleaned, or treated, before people can drink it.

Quality Standards

Fresh water can contain a variety of harmful substances and organisms. Certain substances and organisms may be present naturally, but others get into water because of pollution from human activity. Some of the impurities in water are safe for humans to drink in small quantities. However, when impurities reach high concentrations, they can harm people. A **concentration** is the amount of a substance that is in another substance. For example, soft drinks have a high concentration of sugar in water. Concentrations are often expressed in parts per million.

A government agency called the Environmental Protection Agency (EPA) sets standards for safe, clean drinking water. The EPA standards are guidelines for the protection of our natural water sources and the quality of the water that reaches our homes. Government agencies in states and local communities enforce laws based on the EPA standards.

The EPA lists standards for harmful organisms that can cause disease. It also lists safe levels for copper and certain other metals that can be found in water. In addition, the EPA checks for a variety of chemicals and harmful radioactive materials.

Your local water provider regularly tests the water to make sure it meets the EPA requirements. If any concentrations are higher than the EPA standards, the water must be treated. As a result, the United States has one of the safest, cleanest water supplies in the world.

CHECK YOUR READING How does a water provider know that it must treat water?

Students test river water in West Virginia for pollutants.

EPA Standards for Substances in Water		
Substance	**Common Source**	**Maximum Allowed, in Parts per Million**
Copper	Natural deposits; household pipes	1.3
Cyanide	Various factories	0.2
Lead	Natural deposits; household pipes	0.015
Mercury	Natural deposits; refineries and factories; landfills; crop fields	0.002
Nitrite	Water running off fertilized fields; sewage leaks; natural deposits	1

Treatment of Drinking Water

VISUALIZATION
CLASSZONE.COM

See a water treatment plant in action.

In a water treatment plant, thousands of gallons of water flow through a series of tanks, where the water is filtered and treated with chemicals to remove harmful substances and kill organisms. The major steps are chemical disinfection and the removal of dirt.

Water Treatment and Distribution

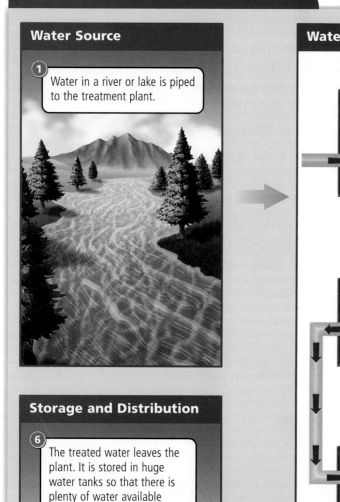

Water Source

1. Water in a river or lake is piped to the treatment plant.

Storage and Distribution

6. The treated water leaves the plant. It is stored in huge water tanks so that there is plenty of water available when people need it.

Water Treatment Plant

2. The water flows through mixers, where clumping agents and disinfecting chemicals are added. A clumping agent is a substance that makes dirt and bacteria clump together.

3. The water flows into a clarifying pool so that it can clarify, or become clearer. Here, the heavy lumps of dirt sink to the bottom and are scraped away.

4. Water flows through layers of coal, sand, and gravel, which filter out tiny particles of dust and dirt.

5. Now the water looks clear and clean. Chlorine is added to kill the last of the bacteria.

Wastewater is treated and released.

Wastewater is the water that runs down the drain. Before wastewater can be released back into the environment, it needs to be treated. Sewage and septic systems are two ways of treating wastewater.

Sewage System

A **sewage system** is a system that collects and treats wastewater from a city or a town. Sewage pipes carry wastewater from homes and businesses to a water treatment plant.

In the first part of treatment, wastewater is strained to remove large objects. Then the water is pumped into a tank, where it sits until the heaviest sludge sinks to the bottom. The sludge is taken away to decompose in another tank. Then chlorine is added to the water to kill the harmful bacteria. This process removes about half of the pollutants.

During the second part of the process, extra oxygen is pumped into the wastewater. The oxygen causes certain kinds of bacteria to grow in great numbers. These bacteria consume much of the sludge and oil that is still in the water. In other words, these tiny organisms help clean the water. More sludge also settles out, and grease is skimmed off the top. Chemicals clean the water one more time and remove any extra chlorine.

Water Use Cycle

water treatment

wastewater treatment

Wastewater Treatment

A sewage system collects and treats wastewater.

urban

residential

industrial

street drains

sewer pipes

sewer pipes

street drain treatment

sewage treatment

river

treated water

Septic System

A **septic system** is a small wastewater system used by a home or a business. Septic systems are more common in lightly populated areas that do not have central sewage treatment centers. In a house with a septic system, wastewater is carried out through a pipe to an underground tank away from the house. The sludge, or thicker material, in the wastewater settles to the bottom. Much of this sludge is consumed naturally by bacteria, just as in the large sewage treatment plants. Sludge that remains has to be removed from the tank every few years.

Septic tank

inlet pipe
from house

floating material

ground surface

wastewater

Solids in the water are broken down by bacteria or sink to the tank bottom.

Cleaner water flows out and spreads and sinks in the ground.

sludge

Water pollution comes from many sources.

You have learned how fresh water is treated before we drink it. Unfortunately, treatment only works for water that has fairly low concentrations of harmful substances. Sometimes human activities add far too many minerals, chemicals, or organisms to a water supply. Then a lake or a river becomes polluted. No amount of treatment can make the water safe to drink. Pollution can come from one known source, or point, or it can come from many points.

- **Point-source pollution** is pollution that enters water from a known source. It might be sewage flowing from a pipe or chemicals spewing out of a factory. This pollution is easy to spot, and laws can be enforced to stop it.

- **Nonpoint-source pollution** is pollution whose source is hard to find or is scattered. Rain and gravity cause water to wash off streets, lawns, construction sites, and farms. This water, called runoff, can carry oil, gas, pesticides, chemicals, paints, and detergents into storm drains or over land and then to rivers and lakes. If you don't know exactly where pollution comes from, it is hard to enforce laws against it. For this reason, nonpoint-source pollution causes most water pollution.

VOCABULARY
Add a description wheel for *point-source pollution* to your notebook.

Sources of Water Pollution

Human activity can pollute the water supply.

Homes

- Improper disposal of household batteries, chemicals, and motor oil
- Use of fertilizers and pesticides
- Poorly functioning septic systems

Cities

- Illegal dumping of toxic chemicals
- Water and pollutants running off from streets
- Unsafe disposal of motor oil and other products

Sewage

- Improper disposal of factory wastewater
- Poorly functioning sewage systems
- Dumping of raw wastewater when sewage systems cannot handle heavy rainfall

Farms

- Heavy use of fertilizers and pesticides
- Leaks and spills of animal waste
- Animals grazing near rivers and lakes

Shipping, Boating, and Oil Transport

- Spills of oil or other cargo from barges and ships
- Fuel spills and leakage from small boats
- Illegal dumping
- Illegal release of sewage

READING VISUALS Identify three examples of point-source pollution.

Water pollution can be prevented.

Water pollution is a serious problem because water is a limited resource. When water is polluted, there is less water available for use. Water pollution can also endanger people's health. People and businesses can do a number of things to prevent or reduce pollution of water.

Industry and Transportation Operators of factories and of vehicles that haul cargo can take a number of steps to prevent or reduce water pollution. For example, factories can maintain their pipelines and equipment to ensure that harmful chemicals are not leaking into the ground and contaminating groundwater. Transportation companies can inspect and repair their trucks, planes, and ships to prevent oil and fuels from leaking onto pavement or into water.

Industry can prevent or reduce pollution by reducing the amount of toxic waste it generates. Factories can reuse and recycle chemicals and materials used in manufacturing. Companies can also provide ways for their customers to recycle or return certain products—such as used motor oil or batteries—that can pollute water if they are disposed of improperly.

In the construction industry, builders can design their projects to reduce the pollution that new construction can cause. Builders can use less pavement when they build parking areas for malls and office buildings. Less pavement reduces the amount of water that may run off and carry pollutants from cars and other sources to rivers and lakes. And measures to preserve open land, especially wetland areas, can protect a natural water cleansing system and reduce runoff.

READING TiP

A toxic substance is one that is capable of causing harm to health.

CHECK YOUR READING How does pavement contribute to water pollution?

Pollution can make a lake or river dangerous or unusable. In many places, people are cleaning up and restoring freshwater resources.

Agriculture Farming generates chemical and natural waste that can contaminate water. Farmers can follow practices that prevent or reduce pollution from agriculture. On farms with livestock, pastures used by cows and other grazing animals can be fenced off to keep animals away from streams and lakes. Keeping livestock away from water reduces pollution from animal waste. Farms that keep animals in structures can keep waste out of the water supply by storing and disposing of manure properly.

New techniques in farming can reduce pollution. Many farmers grow food without pesticides, which can be toxic and pollute water. The farmers fight insects and other pests by bringing in their natural enemies, such as ladybugs. To fertilize soil, the use of natural substances and the planting of certain crops can take the place of manufactured chemicals. Farming that does not use such chemicals is known as organic.

At home There are a number of things most people can do in their daily lives to prevent or reduce water pollution. People can take their old household chemicals to hazardous waste collection sites. Toxic chemicals should not be poured down the drain or onto the ground. Proper disposal and recycling of electronic devices such as computers can prevent toxic metals contained in them from reaching the water supply.

In shopping for food, consumers can choose organic products to support farming methods that don't use toxic pesticides. People can try to use nontoxic products in their homes. They can also stop using toxic pesticides and weed killers, as well as chemical fertilizers, on lawns and gardens.

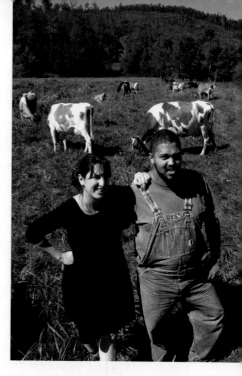

These farmers in Vermont use organic methods to produce milk and ice cream.

2.2 Review

KEY CONCEPTS

1. How are EPA standards used to ensure a clean, safe supply of water?

2. What are two ways that wastewater is treated before it can be released?

3. What is the difference between point-source pollution and nonpoint-source pollution?

CRITICAL THINKING

4. **Compare and Contrast** How are sewage systems and septic systems alike? How are they different?

5. **Categorize** Categorize the following as point- or non-point-source pollution: small boat leaking oil; fish farm releasing wastes into a river; person dumping motor oil onto the ground.

⚫ CHALLENGE

6. **Compare** What parts of sewage and septic systems are similar to the way water is naturally cleaned by Earth's water cycle?

CHAPTER INVESTIGATION

Monitoring Water Quality

OVERVIEW AND PURPOSE Water pollution in some amount seems to happen wherever people live. That's why water for home drinking is almost always treated. Proper water treatment depends on knowing what forms of pollution water contains. This two-part activity models the process of monitoring for water quality. In this investigation you will

- perform systematic testing procedures similar to those used to test the water supply
- test known samples for common "pollutants," and then identify unknown water samples based on those tests

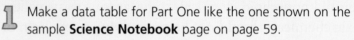

▶ Procedure

PART ONE

1. Make a data table for Part One like the one shown on the sample **Science Notebook** page on page 59.

2. Test the three different known contaminated water samples with the three types of indicator strips. Dip one of each strip into the solution and instantly remove it. A positive result causes a color change. Make your observations of color changes exactly 30 seconds after dipping the strip. Observe and note the results in your table so you know what a positive result looks like for each contaminant. Do not reuse test strips. You need fresh strips for each water sample.

3. Test the pure distilled water with the three types of indicator strips and note your results.

step 2

PART TWO

1. A water-testing company has mixed up four water samples taken from the following locations: a runoff stream from an agricultural field, a river near a factory, a pond on a dairy farm, and a mountain stream. You will test the four unknown samples using the same procedures as above to determine which sample has which contaminant. You will then determine which location the sample most likely came from.

MATERIALS
- 8 each of three types of indicator strips
- watch with second hand
- "pesticide-contaminated" water sample
- "bacteria-contaminated" water sample
- "chemical-contaminated" water sample
- pure distilled water sample
- 4 unknown water samples

2. Make a data table for Part Two like the one shown on the sample **Science Notebook** below.

3. Test each water sample as in step 2, Part One. Record your observations as you test each unknown sample with each indicator strip. Note all color changes you observe.

4. Consult the chart you completed in Part One as you perform tests to determine which type of contaminant each unknown sample contains. From this information determine which location the sample probably came from.

Observe and Analyze

1. **IDENTIFY CONTROLS** Why was it necessary to test the distilled water in Part One?

2. **IDENTIFY** Use what you have learned in this chapter to determine which location corresponds to the types of pollution you learned to identify in Part One.

3. **ANALYZE** Compare your testing results from the unknown water samples with your testing results from the known water samples. Are your results similar?

Conclude

1. **COMPARE** How did your results in Part One compare with your results in Part Two?

2. **EVALUATE** What part of this investigation was the most difficult? Why?

3. **IDENTIFY LIMITS** What limitations does this type of testing pose for real-life water-quality technicians?

4. **APPLY** A runoff pool is contaminated with bacteria, chemicals, and pesticides. How would your water-testing results appear for a sample from this pool?

▶ INVESTIGATE Further

CHALLENGE Design a procedure to test unknown water samples that have numerous contaminants.

Monitoring Water Quality

Table 1. Positive Test Results of Known Water Samples

	Pure distilled water	Chemical-contaminated water	Bacteria-contaminated water	Pesticide-contaminated water
Indicator A				
Indicator B				
Indicator C				

Table 2. Test Results of Unknown Samples with Probable Locations

	Unknown #1	Unknown #2	Unknown #3	Unknown #4
Indicator A				
Indicator B				
Indicator C				
Type of Contaminant				
Location				

KEY CONCEPT

2.3
Water shortages threaten society.

 BEFORE, you learned

- Water is treated for drinking
- Wastewater is treated and released
- Pollutants contaminate the water supply

▶ **NOW, you will learn**

- How overuse causes water shortages
- How water can be conserved
- How governments and organizations manage water use

VOCABULARY

drought p. 61
desalination p. 66

EXPLORE The Value of Fresh Water

Does water cost more than gasoline?

PROCEDURE

1. Find out the current price of a liter of bottled water.

2. Find out the current price of a gallon of gasoline.

3. To calculate the price of gasoline in liters, multiply the price per gallon by 0.26.

WHAT DO YOU THINK?

- How do the prices of bottled water and gasoline compare?
- What do your results tell you about the value of drinking water?

MATERIALS
calculator

Water shortages are a global problem.

SUPPORTING MAIN IDEAS
Support the main idea of global water shortages with details and examples.

Most nations in the deserts of northern Africa and in the Middle East have severe water shortages. These are some of the driest regions on Earth, but their populations require more and more water as cities grow. Water that could be used to grow food is piped instead to the growing cities, where it is needed in homes and factories.

So how do people in these regions grow enough food? For the most part, they cannot. There is simply not enough water. Jordan imports, or brings in from other countries, about 91 percent of its grain. Israel imports about 87 percent, and Egypt, once a center of agriculture, imports 40 percent.

All over the world, the water supply is dwindling. Populations are growing everywhere, and people must be fed. Farmers draw water from underground aquifers faster than the water can be replaced.

Even places that normally get regular rainfall can face water shortages. **Drought** (drowt) is a long period of abnormally low rainfall. Drought can destroy crops and dry up water supplies. Usually, trees can survive a dry period because their roots reach into the ground for water. However, severe drought can dry out entire forests. Dry trees are more vulnerable to disease, and wildfires are harder to control.

Overuse can cause water shortages.

As the world's population grows, usable fresh water is becoming scarcer in many places. Agriculture uses two-thirds of the world's available fresh water. Unfortunately, only half of that water reaches the roots of the plants. The other half is lost to evaporation and runoff.

Overuse of underground water can cause an aquifer to be depleted, or consumed faster than its water is replaced. In most places where crops require irrigation, farmers water their fields with groundwater. India is using twice as much water from its aquifers as can be replaced. In the United States, farmers are taking so much water that they are draining the huge Ogallala Aquifer. The problem is that underground stores of water can take thousands of years to refill. Draining an aquifer can also destroy it. When water is removed, the ground may settle and close up the storage space.

River water is also being overused in many places. So much water is being taken out that many major rivers now run dry for a large part of the year. These rivers include the Ganges River in South Asia, the Indus River in Pakistan, and the Colorado River in the southwestern United States. People in seven western states use water from the Colorado. As cities in these states have grown, the demand for the river water has increased.

MARYLAND

A bridge stands over a dried-out part of a reservoir during a drought in Maryland.

CHECK YOUR READING How has overuse of water affected some rivers?

Fresh water can be conserved.

Although water shortages are a serious problem, the situation is not entirely hopeless. Conserving can solve a big part of the problem. Conservation is action taken to protect and preserve the natural world. To conserve water means to use less of it.

U.S. Household Water Usage

Americans use an average of 168 liters per person each day.

- toilet flushes 29%
- washing machine 21%
- shower 21%
- toilet leaks 5%
- dishwashing 3%
- bath 9%
- tap 12%

SOURCE: *U.S. Environmental Protection Agency*

The chart above shows how Americans use water each day. The amount that each American uses on average—168 liters—is higher than in most parts of the world. Note that 5 percent of the amount—more than 8 liters—is wasted by leaking toilets.

The Need for Conservation

Think about what you already know about the water cycle. When aquifers, lakes, and rivers are depleted—or used up faster than the water in them can be replaced naturally—available fresh water from those water supplies decreases. Because water supplies in many regions are being depleted, conservation is an urgent issue.

These water-catching devices are used to collect and store rainwater in Hawaii.

Much of the western United States is mostly desert, and yet the population in dry parts of the West is growing each year. What will happen if the aquifers and rivers that supply this region with water dry up? The less water that people use today, the more water there will be to use in the future.

Water shortages are an increasing problem around the world as the population grows in many regions. About half a billion people in 31 countries—mostly in the Middle East and Africa—currently face water shortages. By 2025, the number of people without enough water will increase five times, to about 2.8 billion people.

Conservation Practices

People conserve water in three ways. The first way is to use less water. Some cities conserve their supply of water simply by repairing leaks in underground pipes. The second way is to reuse water. Many cities reuse treated wastewater for landscaping. The third method is to recycle water, or use water again for the same purpose.

Farmers can conserve water by using drip irrigation instead of spraying water. They can change the grooves in their fields so the water stays in the soil longer. Most industries can use water at least twice before returning it to a river or lake. For example, water used to cool machines can be recycled back through the same system.

At home, people can change their plumbing and their habits. Low-flow toilets and showerheads can cut water use in half. People conserve water by turning off the faucet while brushing their teeth, taking shorter showers, and running the dishwasher only when it is full. Leaking pipes and dripping faucets in homes cause huge amounts of water to be wasted. Repair and maintenance of plumbing systems would reduce water use greatly.

RESOURCE CENTER
CLASSZONE.COM

Learn more about water conservation.

CHECK YOUR READING What are the three main ways in which people conserve water?

INVESTIGATE Water Conservation

How much water does a dripping faucet use?

1. Adjust a faucet so that water drips slowly.

2. Set a container under the faucet and collect the dripping water for five minutes.

3. Turn off the faucet. Use the graduated cylinder to measure how much water dripped. Record your results in milliliters.

4. Multiply the amount by 12 to determine how much water would drip in an hour. Then divide that number by 1000 to convert your result to liters.

WHAT DO YOU THINK?

- How much water would one leaky faucet waste in a day?

- In a town with 2000 houses with one leaky faucet in each, how much water would be wasted each day?

CHALLENGE How could you combine your results with those of your classmates to make the results more reliable?

SKILL FOCUS
Measuring

MATERIALS
- water faucet
- container
- funnel
- 100 mL graduated cylinder

TIME
20 minutes

People can balance water needs and uses.

People around the world have different views about how water should be used. Americans in the hot Southwest might want water for swimming pools and lawns. Developing countries need water to prevent disease and grow food. In some places, farmers use river water before it can reach others downstream. Some industries want water to make products.

As water becomes scarcer, the arguments become more serious. Public officials and experts can help manage water use and enforce fair laws. For example, what happens when a river flows from one state into another or across a national border? In such a situation, people must agree to share the water rights.

The Rio Grande flows through two states and then between Texas and Mexico. The water in this river is an international issue. In 1939 a legal agreement was made between the states of Colorado, New Mexico, and Texas, and between the United States and Mexico. It listed how much water each region could take.

In the past, water from the Rio Grande was used for farming. However, cities along the river are growing rapidly. All the cities need more water from the Rio Grande, and every year they will need more. The international agreement no longer solves this urgent problem. American and Mexican officials are looking for new solutions.

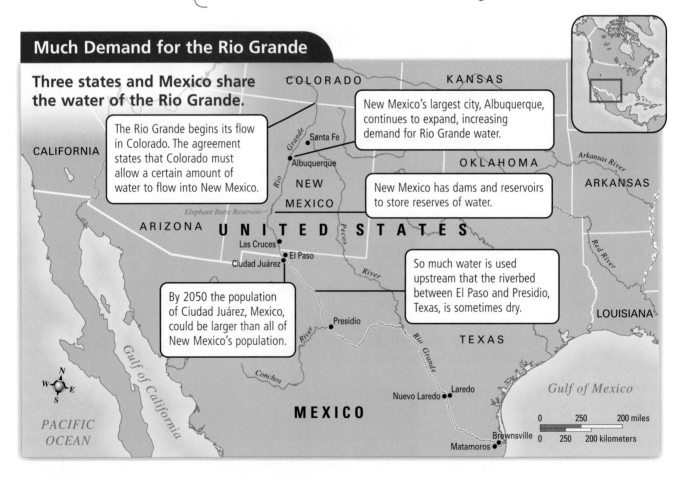

Much Demand for the Rio Grande

Three states and Mexico share the water of the Rio Grande.

The Rio Grande begins its flow in Colorado. The agreement states that Colorado must allow a certain amount of water to flow into New Mexico.

New Mexico's largest city, Albuquerque, continues to expand, increasing demand for Rio Grande water.

New Mexico has dams and reservoirs to store reserves of water.

So much water is used upstream that the riverbed between El Paso and Presidio, Texas, is sometimes dry.

By 2050 the population of Ciudad Juárez, Mexico, could be larger than all of New Mexico's population.

Shortages

When there is not enough water, crops will not grow. And when the crops fail to grow, there is not enough food to eat. The Middle East countries that import most of their grain are, in a way, importing water. Billions of tons of water are used to grow the imported grain.

International organizations help out countries where drought and floods have destroyed the crops. For example, in 2002 the World Food Programme alerted the world to a serious lack of food in southeast Africa. The United Nations agencies arranged for food aid. The shrinking of Lake Chad has also caused hardship for many Africans.

In the future, people may solve some of the problems by sharing water around the world. The governor of Alaska has suggested an undersea pipeline. This line would be between 2200 kilometers (1360 mi) and 3400 kilometers (2100 mi) long. Through this pipe, thousands of liters of fresh water would flow from Alaska to California. Some people have also suggested selling Great Lakes water to Japan. Many people in states and Canadian provinces around the lakes have strongly objected, because they think removing water could damage the lakes.

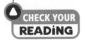 How can Alaska help solve a water shortage in California?

This satellite photograph of Lake Chad in Africa was taken in 1973.

A recent photograph shows how much the lake has shrunk.

Pollution

Where water flows across the boundaries of nations, pollution can flow across as well. One example of this problem is the Danube River in Europe. This river begins in the Black Forest in Germany. It empties into the Black Sea on the coast of Romania. As it flows through the cities of Vienna, Budapest, and Belgrade, more and more pollution is added to the water. Seventeen countries border either the Danube River or the Black Sea. To protect the river and the sea, as well as to manage use of the river water, 11 nations made an agreement among themselves and the European Union. They agreed to cooperate to prevent pollution of the water and to conserve and use water from the Danube sensibly. They also agreed to conserve and protect groundwater.

Some national and international water pollution problems are hard to solve. States in the northeastern United States are concerned about acid rain. Particle pollution from factories to the west is collected in clouds. Then the wind blows the clouds across the Eastern states, and acid rain falls in lakes and rivers that are far from the source. The acid rain can kill plants, as well as fish and other animals.

Desalination by Evaporation

① Sunlight heats up seawater.

② Heated water evaporates, and salt is left behind.

seawater →

③ Water vapor saturates air and condenses. Fresh water falls into collection troughs. Salt is removed periodically.

collection trough

fresh water

seawater

fresh water

New Sources

VOCABULARY
Add a description wheel for *desalination* in your notebook.

Can people find new sources of fresh water? The answer, at first, seems obvious. Just remove the salt from seawater. In dry regions, such as Israel, Lebanon, and some coastal towns in California and Florida, people are trying to obtain fresh water this way. The process of removing salt from ocean water is called **desalination** (dee-SAL-ih-NAY-shun). Some treatment plants use a method similar to the natural water cycle. Salt water is evaporated, and salt is left behind. Then water vapor is condensed, or returned to liquid form, as fresh water.

If this process were easy and inexpensive, water shortages might never happen. However, desalination can cost five times as much as normal water treatment. Therefore, it is not a solution that will work for most countries. As technology improves, the cost may go down.

Another possible source of fresh water is icebergs. Icebergs contain millions of liters of fresh water. However, the process of towing an iceberg to a city before it melts is too expensive to be practical.

2.3 Review

KEY CONCEPTS

1. What is drought and what problems does it cause?

2. How are aquifers and rivers being depleted?

3. Name two ways to help prevent water shortages.

CRITICAL THINKING

4. **Connect** Draw up a plan that suggests three ways to conserve water at your school. Be sure your ideas are practical, and explain how you might convince people to make the changes.

5. **Infer** Why do you think some people object to building a water pipeline from Alaska to California?

⬡ CHALLENGE

6. **Synthesize** Think about what you have learned about national and international water issues. Then think about what you know about aquifers. What usage problems might occur when one aquifer lies under two countries? How might people solve any problems that arise?

FARMER

Water and Farming

Farmers have used irrigation, the process of supplying water to crops, for at least 7000 years. Today, about 60 percent of the fresh water used in the world goes for irrigation. However, about one-third of this water does not reach the crops. Some of it runs off the field. By building ditches and ponds, farmers can capture runoff water and pump it back into a field.

Irrigation water can also evaporate before crops can use it. Farmers can reduce this loss by understanding how changes in air temperature, relative humidity, and wind speed affect the evaporation rate. Then farmers can adjust when and how much they irrigate.

Spray Irrigation

In some systems, sprinklers as much as 400 meters (1300 ft) long spray water on crops. Since the water is sprayed into the air, evaporation loss can be high. Spray irrigation is used for many crops in the western United States. Spraying at night can reduce evaporation loss.

Drip Irrigation

In drip irrigation, water bubbles out of pipes lying on or just above the ground throughout a field or orchard. The water reaches the ground quickly and in small amounts, so little is lost to runoff or evaporation. Farmers growing fruits and vegetables frequently use this system.

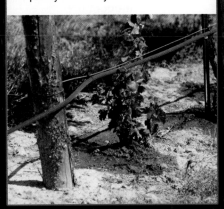

Flood Irrigation

Many farmers send water through small ditches between rows of crops, or sometimes farmers flood entire fields. Compared with other systems, flooding results in higher losses from runoff. Flooding is commonly used by rice farmers in eastern Asia.

EXPLORE

1. **ANALYZING** Compare the amounts of labor, machinery, and water used in each irrigation system. Which system uses water most efficiently? In what climate regions is this most important? Why would farmers choose a system that uses water less efficiently?

2. **CHALLENGE** Create a model of a flood irrigation system. Use dirt in a pan, with toothpicks to represent crops. Make ditches that send water evenly throughout the "field." As you pour water into your system, note any soil loss that may occur. How can you fix this problem?

the BIG idea

Fresh water is a limited resource and is essential for human society.

CONTENT REVIEW
CLASSZONE.COM

◄ KEY CONCEPTS SUMMARY

2.1 Fresh water is an essential resource.
Fresh water is essential for life and is used for many human activities.

- farming
- industry
- transportation and recreation
- fisheries and aquaculture
- energy
- living organisms

fresh water

VOCABULARY
irrigation p. 43
aquaculture p. 45
dam p. 46
lock p. 46

2.2 Society depends on clean and safe water.
Water is treated for safe drinking. Pollution can harm the water supply.

Water is drawn from a river or lake. → Water is treated. → Water is stored and distributed.

VOCABULARY
concentration p. 51
sewage system p. 53
septic system p. 54
point-source pollution p. 54
nonpoint-source pollution p. 54

2.3 Water shortages threaten society.
Drought and overuse can cause water shortages.

Lake Chad

Americans use an average of 168 liters per person each day.

- toilet flushes 29%
- washing machine 21%
- shower 21%
- toilet leaks 5%
- dishwashing 3%
- bath 9%
- tap 12%

SOURCE: *U.S. Environmental Protection Agency*

VOCABULARY
drought p. 61
desalination p. 66

Reviewing Vocabulary

Use words from the box below to answer the next nine questions.

septic system	nonpoint-source pollution	desalination
concentration	sewage system	point-source pollution
aquaculture	drought	irrigation

1. Which word means "fish farming"?

2. What is the term for a method farmers use to bring water to their fields from rivers and aquifers?

3. Which term can be used to describe the amount of a harmful substance in fresh water?

4. Which term would be used for waste flowing from a factory pipe?

5. Select the term for what a city uses to collect and treat wastewater.

6. Which term would describe oil running off from a parking lot during a rainstorm?

7. What word describes a period when there is little or no rainfall?

8. What process is used to obtain fresh water from seawater?

9. Which term describes a method for treating home wastewater in an underground tank?

Reviewing Key Concepts

Multiple Choice *Choose the letter of the best answer.*

10. Which type of irrigation pours water through canals and waterways?
    - **a.** flood irrigation
    - **b.** spray irrigation
    - **c.** drip irrigation
    - **d.** reservoir irrigation

11. A channel dug to allow boats to travel from one river to another is an example of a
    - **a.** canal
    - **b.** lake
    - **c.** reservoir
    - **d.** sewage system

12. A section of a waterway in which ships are raised or lowered is called a
    - **a.** turbine
    - **b.** fish ladder
    - **c.** dam
    - **d.** lock

13. Concentrations of substances are often expressed as
    - **a.** whole parts
    - **b.** parts per million
    - **c.** parts per thousand
    - **d.** parts per hundred

14. In a sewage plant, sludge and oil are consumed by
    - **a.** chlorine
    - **b.** sand
    - **c.** bacteria
    - **d.** filters

15. In a sewage system, what is added to kill harmful bacteria?
    - **a.** chlorine
    - **b.** sand
    - **c.** bacteria
    - **d.** soap

16. The term for pollution that can be traced to a specific location is
    - **a.** water pollution
    - **b.** point-source pollution
    - **c.** nonpoint-source pollution
    - **d.** runoff pollution

Short Answer *Write a short answer to each question.*

17. How are aquifers depleted?

18. How are EPA standards used to protect fresh water?

19. How does the practice of organic farming help prevent water pollution?

20. What problems do people have sharing water from the Rio Grande?

Thinking Critically

Use the map to answer the next five questions.

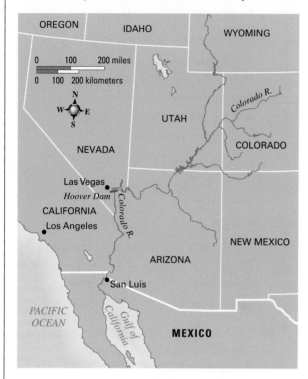

The Colorado River runs from Colorado to the Gulf of California. In California water is needed for 17 million people and also to irrigate 3642 square kilometers (900,000 acres) of farmland. The Colorado provides 60 percent of this water.

21. OBSERVE Through which states and countries does the Colorado River flow?

22. EXAMPLES What are three ways in which water from the Colorado is probably used?

23. INFER What conflicts probably exist between the states of California and Arizona?

24. PREDICT As populations grow in Las Vegas, southern California, and San Luis, Mexico, what problems will arise? How can they be solved?

25. CONNECT Do you think states should receive equal shares of the water in the Colorado River? Explain your answer.

26. IDENTIFY CAUSE Copy the concept map below, and complete it by adding two causes of, and two solutions to, the problem of the water level of an aquifer sinking.

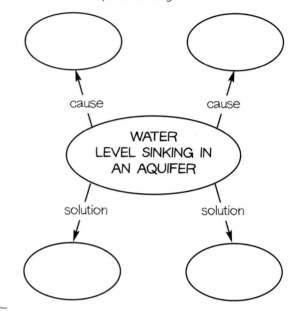

the BIG idea

27. PROVIDE EXAMPLES Look again at the photograph on pages 38–39. Now that you have finished the chapter, how would you change your response to the question on the photograph?

28. SEQUENCE Draw a diagram of the path that fresh water travels before and after humans use it. Show where freshwater comes from, how it is treated, how it arrives at our homes, how it leaves our homes as wastewater, how it is treated again, and how it reenters the water cycle.

UNIT PROJECTS

If you need to do an experiment for your unit project, gather the materials. Be sure to allow enough time to observe results before the project is due.

Analyzing a Graph

The line graph below shows the amount of a chemical found in a stream. During the period shown, a factory opened and released water into the stream. Later, a wastewater treatment plant opened and treated water from the factory before it entered the stream. Study the graph and use it to answer the first six questions below.

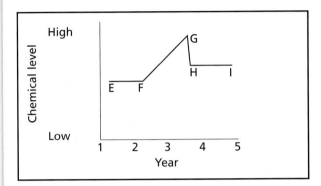

1. Which phrase best describes the concentration of the chemical at Point E?

  a. low   **c.** somewhat high

  b. medium   **d.** very high

2. A new factory opens during year 2. What immediately happens to the concentration of the chemical?

  a. It does not change.   **c.** It decreases slightly.

  b. It decreases sharply.   **d.** It increases sharply.

3. Which point probably marks when a new wastewater treatment plant opened?

  a. E   **c.** G

  b. F   **d.** I

4. Point-source pollution comes from a known source. Which amount is point-source pollution?

  a. the difference between E and F

  b. the difference between F and G

  c. the difference between G and H

  d. the difference between H and I

5. How do the concentrations of E and I compare?

  a. I is higher.

  b. I is lower.

  c. I and E are equal.

  d. The graph does not include enough data to compare concentrations.

6. Which statement best explains the data on the graph?

  a. The factory has less impact than the treatment plant does.

  b. The factory and the treatment plant have little influence on the water.

  c. The factory and the treatment plant balance each other out.

  d. The factory adds more of the chemical than the treatment plant removes.

Extended Response

Answer the two questions below in detail. Include some of the terms shown in the word box. Underline each term you use in your answers.

| evaporate | condense | precipitation |
| groundwater | irrigation | rain |

7. Describe the parts of the water cycle that are involved at a desalination plant.

8. For a science fair project, Anthony compared the growth of plants that got their water in different ways. One group grew in soil that he kept moist by providing water through a tube under the surface. For a second group, he poured water on top of the soil each day. In the third group, he sprayed water from a bottle on the plants. How are the three methods Anthony used similar to ways that farmers irrigate crops?

Ocean Systems

the **BIG** idea

The oceans are a connected system of water in motion.

Key Concepts

SECTION

3.1 The oceans are a connected system.
Learn about ocean water and the ocean floor.

SECTION

3.2 Ocean water moves in currents.
Learn about currents and how they interact with climate and weather.

SECTION

3.3 Waves move through oceans.
Learn how waves form and move through the ocean.

SECTION

3.4 Waters rise and fall in tides.
Learn how tides are related to the Sun and the Moon.

Internet Preview

CLASSZONE.COM

Chapter 3 online resources: Content Review, Simulation, Visualization, three Resource Centers, Math Tutorial, Test Practice

What causes these waves?

EXPLORE (the BIG idea)

What Makes Things Float or Sink?

Fill two clear cups with water. Add a heaping spoonful of salt to one cup and stir until it dissolves. Gently squeeze two drops of food coloring into each cup.

Observe and Think What happened to the drops of food coloring in each cup?

How Does Moving Air Affect Water?

Fill a pan with water. Use a straw to blow over the surface of the water.

Observe and Think What happened to the water when you blew on it? Draw a diagram to show what happened.

Internet Activity: The Ocean Floor

Go to **ClassZone.com** to expose the ocean floor by draining all of the water out of the ocean.

Observe and Think How are the features of the ocean floor similar to features on land? How are they different?

NSTA scilinks.org SCI**LINKS**

Exploring Earth's Oceans **Code: MDL020**

Getting Ready to Learn

◀ CONCEPT REVIEW

- Water covers most of Earth.
- Earth's waters circulate in the water cycle.
- The water in the oceans is salt water.

◀ VOCABULARY REVIEW

salt water p. 11

water cycle p. 12

evaporation p. 13

desalination p. 66

 CONTENT REVIEW
CLASSZONE.COM
Review concepts and vocabulary.

▶ TAKING NOTES

OUTLINE

As you read, copy the headings into your notebook in the form of an outline. Then add notes in your own words that summarize what you read.

VOCABULARY STRATEGY

Draw a **word triangle** for each new vocabulary term. At the bottom, write and define the term. Above that, write a sentence in which you use the term correctly. At the top, draw a small picture to represent the term.

See the Note-Taking Handbook on pages R45–R51.

SCIENCE NOTEBOOK

OUTLINE

I. The oceans are a connected system.
   A. Ocean water covers much of Earth.
   B. Ocean water contains salts and gases.
      1.
      2.
   C. Ocean temperatures vary.
      1.
      2.

The salinity of ocean water is about 35 grams of salt per 1000 grams of water

salinity: a measure of the saltiness of water

The oceans are a connected system.

 BEFORE, you learned

- Most water on Earth is salt water
- The ocean plays an important role in the water cycle

 NOW, you will learn

- What ocean water contains
- What the ocean floor looks like
- How people explore the ocean

VOCABULARY

salinity p. 76
density p. 76
continental shelf p. 80
sonar p. 82

EXPLORE Density

Why do liquids form layers?

PROCEDURE

1. Insert the straw into one of the solutions. Cover the top of the straw with your finger and then remove the straw from the solution. The liquid should stay in the straw.

2. Using this technique, try to layer the three liquids in your straw so that you can see three distinct layers.

3. Experiment with the order in which you place the liquids into the straw. Between trials, empty the contents of the straw into the waste cup.

WHAT DO YOU THINK?
Did it matter in what order you layered the liquids? If so, can you explain why?

MATERIALS
- 3 solutions— A, B, and C—provided by your teacher
- clear straw
- waste cup

Ocean water covers much of Earth.

As land animals, we naturally think of our planet as a rocky and solid place. We even named our planet Earth, which means "land" or "soil." But look at a globe and you will see that oceans cover most of Earth. In fact, 71 percent of Earth is covered in seawater.

Looking at a map of the world, you can see the seven continents spread over our planet. These landmasses divide Earth's global ocean into connected sections. Different sections of the ocean have different names, such as Atlantic, Indian, and Pacific. However, all the sections are connected.

OUTLINE
Remember to start an outline for this section.

I. Main idea
  A. Supporting idea
    1. Detail
    2. Detail
  B. Supporting idea

The global ocean is one connected body of water, divided into sections by the continents.

How did Earth become covered by an ocean? Scientists have several theories. The most commonly accepted explanation has to do with how Earth formed. Earth formed about 4.6 billion years ago as a ball of molten rock. Heavier materials sank to the core, and lighter materials floated toward the surface—the same way oil and vinegar in salad dressing separate into layers. Water vapor, a very light substance, rose to the cooler surface. By about 4 billion years ago, Earth had cooled enough for the water vapor to become liquid. At that time, the vapor condensed—just as water vapor condenses into droplets on a cool glass of lemonade—forming liquid water that became the ocean.

Ocean water contains salts and gases.

Despite its name, the salt water that fills the ocean is much more than just salt and water. Ocean water contains many different dissolved substances. Sodium chloride, which is the same compound as ordinary table salt, is the most plentiful of these substances. The ocean also contains other dissolved solids, as well as dissolved molecules of the same gases found in the atmosphere. In fact, the ocean contains all 92 elements that occur in nature, although most are in very tiny amounts.

Salts

VOCABULARY
Add word triangles for *salinity* and *density* to your notebook.

One taste will convince you that ocean water is salty. Every 1000 grams of seawater contains an average of 35 grams of salt. **Salinity** (suh-LIHN-ih-tee) is a measure of the amount of dissolved salt contained in water. The ocean contains many different kinds of salts. However, sodium chloride accounts for most of the ocean's salinity.

The elements that make up salts are found in rocks and minerals. Over time, rain and rivers wash some of these elements into the sea. The elements that make up salts also enter the ocean when underwater volcanoes erupt. Natural processes also remove salt from the ocean. Because salt is added as well as removed, the ocean's overall salinity does not change much over time. The ocean's salinity has stayed constant for the past 1.5 billion years.

Water that contains dissolved solids, such as salts, is heavier than the same amount of water with no dissolved solids. In other words, salt water has a greater density than fresh water. **Density** is a measure of the amount of matter packed into a given volume.

The higher water's salt content, the greater its density. The denser the water, the more easily things float in it. As you can see in the photograph on page 77, the Dead Sea is so salty (and dense) that people can float easily on the surface.

Salt water has a greater density than fresh water.

Fresh Water	Ocean Water	Dead Sea Water

dissolved solids

Fresh water has fewer dissolved solids than salt water, so it is less dense than salt water.

Ocean water is more dense than fresh water because it has more dissolved solids.

The Dead Sea is about ten times saltier than the ocean, so Dead Sea water is more dense than ocean water.

Located between Israel and Jordan, the Dead Sea is actually a salty lake and not part of the ocean. Its high salinity, and therefore high density, allows people to float more easily in it than in fresh water or in the ocean.

Dead Sea

Some parts of the ocean are saltier than others. When water evaporates from the ocean, the salts are left behind, causing the remaining water to become even saltier. Ocean water is especially salty in places where water evaporates quickly, such as in shallow areas and warm climates. Salinity is also higher in very cold areas, where the ocean water freezes. When ice forms on the ocean, the salt is left in the water below.

Salinity is lower in areas where the ocean is diluted by fresh water. For example, seawater has lower salinity in places where rivers empty into the ocean. Similarly, the ocean's salinity is lower in areas where a lot of rain falls.

CHECK YOUR READING How are salinity and density related?

INVESTIGATE Density

How does dense water move?

PROCEDURE

1. Read the instructions below and predict what will happen in steps 3 and 4 before you begin. Record your predictions.

2. Fill one jar with tap water and color it blue. Fill another jar with salt water and color it red. Place an index card over the top of the jar of red salt water.

3. With your hand over the index card, turn the jar over and place it on top of the jar with the blue tap water. Pull out the index card and observe the water movement, if any.

4. Repeat steps 2 and 3, but with the blue tap water on the top.

WHAT DO YOU THINK?

- Describe any ways in which your observations differed from your predictions. On what did you base your predictions?

- Explain why the water moved, if it did, in each of the two setups.

CHALLENGE How do you think water in the ocean might be layered?

SKILL FOCUS
Predicting

MATERIALS
- 2 baby food jars
- blue and red food coloring
- tap water
- 10 percent salt solution
- index cards
- large pan or bucket

TIME
30 minutes

Oxygen and Other Gases

Fish, like other animals, need oxygen to live. Oxygen and other gases dissolve in water, just as sugar dissolves in tea. The ocean contains the same gases as the air, including oxygen, nitrogen, and carbon dioxide. Dissolved gases are essential to ocean life.

You know that when you breathe, you use oxygen and exhale carbon dioxide. Ocean animals also take in oxygen and give off carbon dioxide. Oxygen and carbon dioxide get mixed into the ocean from the air above the ocean surface. Oxygen is also added to the ocean by plants and algae that live near the surface. Plants and algae use sunlight to convert carbon dioxide and water into food, and release oxygen into the water. Besides being used by plants to make food, carbon dioxide is a building block of ocean animals' shells.

Algae use dissolved carbon dioxide to make food, and give off oxygen.

Sea horses take in dissolved oxygen and give off carbon dioxide through their gills.

CHECK YOUR READING Where does the oxygen in the ocean come from? Name two sources.

Ocean temperatures vary.

Oceanographers—people who study the ocean—divide ocean water into three layers on the basis of temperature.

1 **The surface layer,** heated by the Sun and mixed by winds and waves, is the warmest layer. Warm water is less dense than cold water, so the heated water stays at the surface.

2 **The thermocline** (THUR-muh-KLYN) lies below the surface layer. The temperature of the water in the thermocline drops fast with depth.

3 **The deep water** is cold all year. Almost anywhere on the globe—even in the tropics—the temperature of the water at the ocean's bottom is around 0°C–3°C (32°F–37°F), at or barely above freezing.

The temperature of the water at the surface of the ocean varies by location and season. As you can see in the map of satellite data below, the surface layer is warmer near the equator than near the poles. Over much of Earth, the surface layer is warmer in the summer and cooler in the winter.

Ocean Temperature by Depth

sunlight

Water depth (meters): 0, 200, 400, 600, 800, 1000, 1200

1 surface layer
2 thermocline
3 deep water

Water temperature (°C): 0, 5, 10, 15, 20, 25

CHECK YOUR READING Why doesn't the warm water at the ocean's surface sink to the bottom?

Surface Temperature

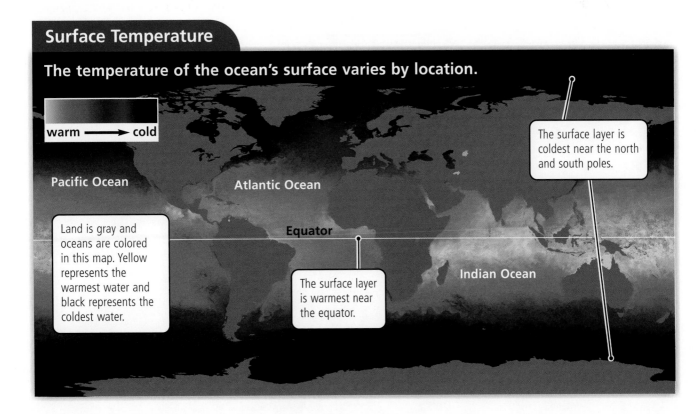

The temperature of the ocean's surface varies by location.

warm ⟶ cold

Pacific Ocean

Atlantic Ocean

The surface layer is coldest near the north and south poles.

Land is gray and oceans are colored in this map. Yellow represents the warmest water and black represents the coldest water.

Equator

The surface layer is warmest near the equator.

Indian Ocean

The ocean floor has many features.

People have sailed the ocean for thousands of years. However, the landscape of most of the ocean floor remained a mystery until the 1950s. Since then, exploration and improvements in mapping techniques have revealed many spectacular features on the ocean floor, including the tallest mountains and deepest canyons on Earth.

READING TiP

Abyss means "a very deep place." Abyssal plains are on the deep-ocean floor.

A **continental shelf** is the flat or gently sloping land that lies submerged around the edges of a continent and that extends from the shoreline out to a continental slope. Huge submarine canyons, some similar in size to the Grand Canyon, slice through continental shelves and slopes. Farther out, ocean trenches cut deep into the ocean floor. With a bottom over 11,000 meters (36,000 ft) below sea level, the Mariana Trench is the deepest place in the world. Flat abyssal (uh-BIHS-uhl) plains cover huge portions of the deep-ocean floor. Seamounts are undersea mountains. Tall volcanoes that poke above the surface are volcanic islands. Mid-ocean ridges, the world's longest mountain range, run throughout Earth's ocean like the seams on a baseball.

The Ocean Floor

The ocean floor has canyons, mountains, and many other features.

Submarine canyons cut through the continental shelf and slope.

An **abyssal plain** is a wide, flat area of the ocean floor that is covered with a thick layer of sediment.

A **continental shelf** is the flat or gradually sloping land that extends underwater from the edge of a continent to a continental slope.

A **continental slope** is land that drops down steeply at the edge of a continental shelf.

Ocean trenches are narrow, steep-sided clefts in the ocean floor.

Ocean Exploration

Because the majority of Earth's surface is underwater, until recently it remained largely unexplored. If your ears have ever hurt when you dived to the bottom of a pool, you have felt the effects of water pressure. That pressure is multiplied hundreds of times deep in the ocean. The deeper down you go, the more crushing the weight of the water.

Despite the pressure, darkness, lack of air, chilling cold, and other obstacles to ocean exploration, scientists have developed tools that help them discover what lies beneath the surface. Scuba equipment allows a diver to spend about an hour underwater, breathing air carried in a tank on his or her back. Scuba divers can safely reach depths as great as 40 meters (130 ft). To go even deeper, people use small submarines, such as the one pictured here. Robots equipped with cameras offer views of areas too deep or difficult for humans to reach.

Small submarines carry researchers to depths as great as 6500 meters (21,300 ft).

 CHECK YOUR READING What is one obstacle to ocean exploration?

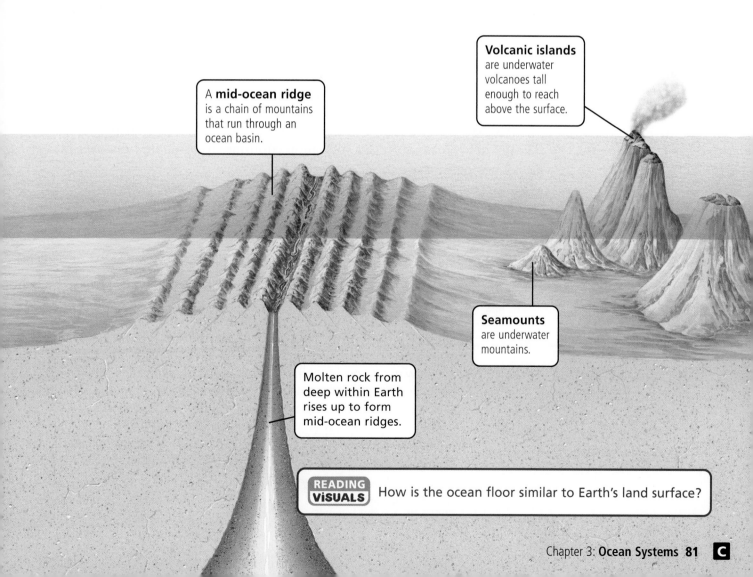

Volcanic islands are underwater volcanoes tall enough to reach above the surface.

A **mid-ocean ridge** is a chain of mountains that run through an ocean basin.

Molten rock from deep within Earth rises up to form mid-ocean ridges.

Seamounts are underwater mountains.

READING VISUALS How is the ocean floor similar to Earth's land surface?

Mapping the Ocean Floor

VOCABULARY Add a word triangle for *sonar* to your notebook.

Today's detailed maps of the ocean floor would amaze early scientists and sailors, who tested sea-floor depths by dropping weighted lines overboard. Now sailors find depths with **sonar,** a system that uses sound waves to measure distances and locate objects. Ships aim sound waves at the ocean's bottom and measure the time it takes to receive the echo. A fast echo means the bottom is shallow; a slow echo means the bottom is deep.

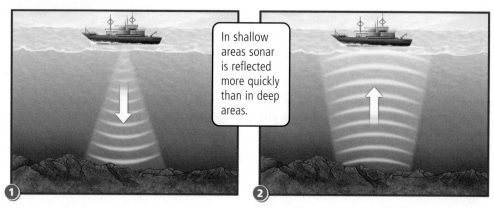

In shallow areas sonar is reflected more quickly than in deep areas.

1. To measure sea-floor depth, ships aim sound waves at the ocean floor.

2. The time it takes for the echo to return depends on the depth of the ocean floor.

Sonar can provide detailed images of small areas of the ocean floor. For mapping large areas, satellite imaging is much more efficient. Satellites can detect tiny bumps and dips in the ocean's height. These small surface differences reveal the shape of the ocean floor. For example, water levels are slightly higher over seamounts and lower over trenches. Because of its vast size and the challenges of exploring it, the ocean still holds many secrets. Exploration continues to bring new discoveries of geological formations and events.

CHECK YOUR READING What are two methods used in mapping the ocean floor?

3.1 Review

KEY CONCEPTS

1. What substances are contained in ocean water?

2. Describe or draw five features of the ocean-floor landscape.

3. Describe three kinds of technology or equipment used to explore the ocean.

CRITICAL THINKING

4. **Predict** A shallow pan and a deep bowl hold equal amounts of salt water. If you left both containers in the sun for a day and then measured the salinity of the water in each, which would be saltier? Why?

5. **Analyze** Where in the ocean do you think water pressure is greatest? Explain why.

CHALLENGE

6. **Synthesize** If you wanted to design a submarine to obtain the most information possible during a research voyage, what features would you include and why? First think about what types of information you would like to collect.

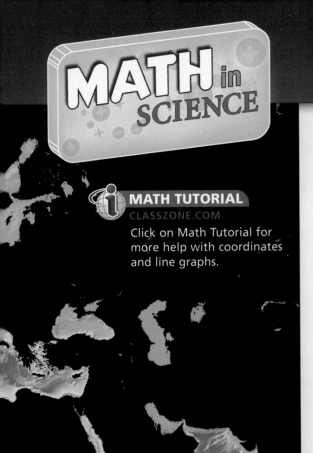

MATH TUTORIAL
CLASSZONE.COM

Click on Math Tutorial for more help with coordinates and line graphs.

Mapping the Ocean Floor

Before sonar and satellites, scientists used weighted lines to map the ocean floor. They tied a weight to a cable and dropped the weight overboard. When the weight landed on the ocean floor, the length of the cable indicated the depth of the ocean at that point. By combining many measurements, scientists could make approximate maps of sections of the ocean floor.

The table on the right gives depths at eight positions in the ocean off a coast. The positions are at regular intervals along a straight line. Depths are given as negative numbers.

Ocean-Floor Depths	
Position	Depth
1	−293
2	−302
3	−381
4	−485
5	−593
6	−624
7	−517
8	−204

Example

You can draw an approximate cross section of part of the ocean floor by making a line graph of the data. To graph the data, think of each column in the table as an ordered pair: **(Position, Depth)**.

(1) Copy the axes and labels.

(2) Graph each point. The first point has been graphed as an example.

(3) Connect the points with line segments.

Follow the steps above to graph points 2 through 8. Use the data and your graph to answer the following questions.

1. How deep is the ocean at position 2?

2. Which position is the deepest, and what is the depth there?

3. Shade the part of the graph that is underwater.

CHALLENGE Does your graph accurately represent the ocean floor between positions 5 and 6? Explain your reasoning.

The continents are shown in black and the ocean floor is colored in this satellite image. High points are orange and yellow, and the lowest points are deep blue-purple.

KEY CONCEPT

3.2 Ocean water moves in currents.

 BEFORE, you learned

- The ocean is explored with sonar and satellite imaging
- The ocean floor is a varied landscape
- The ocean contains dissolved salts and gases

NOW, you will learn

- What causes ocean currents
- How currents distribute heat around the globe
- How currents interact with climate and weather

VOCABULARY

ocean current p. 84
downwelling p. 86
upwelling p. 86
El Niño p. 88

EXPLORE Currents

How does cold water move?

PROCEDURE

① Stir together cold water, ice, and 3 drops of food coloring in the paper cup. Tape the cup to one inside corner of the plastic box.

② Fill the plastic box with enough room-temperature water to submerge the bottom of the cup.

③ Use a toothpick to carefully poke a hole in the bottom of the cup. Observe the movement of water.

WHAT DO YOU THINK?

How do you know the water is moving? What do you think is the reason for this movement?

MATERIALS

- cold water
- ice cubes
- food coloring
- paper cup
- masking tape
- clear plastic box
- toothpick
- room-temperature water

The oceans have major currents.

Would you ever want to go rafting on the ocean? Thor Heyerdahl of Norway did it in 1947 to demonstrate how early people might have migrated around the world. He floated on a wood raft from South America to Polynesia, without motor or paddles, powered only by an ocean current. An **ocean current** is a mass of moving water. There are many different currents that move water through the ocean. As they move water, ocean currents distribute heat and nutrients around the globe.

RESOURCE CENTER
CLASSZONE.COM

Learn more about the different types of ocean currents.

Surface Currents

Strong winds blowing over the ocean are set in motion by the uneven heating of Earth's surface. These winds cause surface currents to flow. The currents extend only about 100 to 200 meters (300–500 ft) down into the ocean, but they cover large areas. The map below shows the major surface currents.

Earth's rotation curls surface currents into giant clockwise whirlpools in the Northern Hemisphere. In the Southern Hemisphere, currents curl counterclockwise because of Earth's rotation. The shapes of continents also affect the paths of surface currents.

Use your finger to trace a few of the surface currents on the map. Surface currents carry warm water away from the equator and cool water away from the poles. In this way, surface currents moderate global temperatures.

This satellite image shows the Gulf Stream, a surface current that flows along the eastern coast of the United States. The colors indicate the temperature of the water.

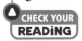 **CHECK YOUR READING** What causes surface currents?

Global Surface Currents

Surface currents are caused by winds. They move warm water away from the equator and cool water away from the poles.

→ **Warm currents**
→ **Cool currents**

READING VISUALS Which currents could be used for sailing east across the Atlantic Ocean?

Deep Currents

In addition to surface currents, there are also currents flowing deep in the ocean. Deep currents are driven by differences in water density. Dense water sinks in the ocean the same way that dense chocolate syrup sinks in a glass of milk.

Seawater can become more dense because of cooling, an increase in salinity, or both. The densest water is found in the polar regions. For example, as sea ice forms near Antarctica, the salinity of the cold water beneath the ice increases. The highly dense water sinks down the continental slope of Antarctica and then moves slowly across the ocean floor. It may take 1000 years for water from this current to resurface near the equator. Another deep current flows out from the Arctic Ocean.

The movement of water in deep currents involves two processes important to ocean life. **Downwelling** is the movement of water from the surface to greater depths. As the water sinks, it carries oxygen down from the surface. The oxygen allows animals to live in the deep ocean. **Upwelling** is the movement of water up to the surface. Because this process brings up nutrients from the deep ocean, large numbers of ocean animals live in areas where upwelling occurs.

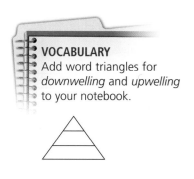

VOCABULARY
Add word triangles for *downwelling* and *upwelling* to your notebook.

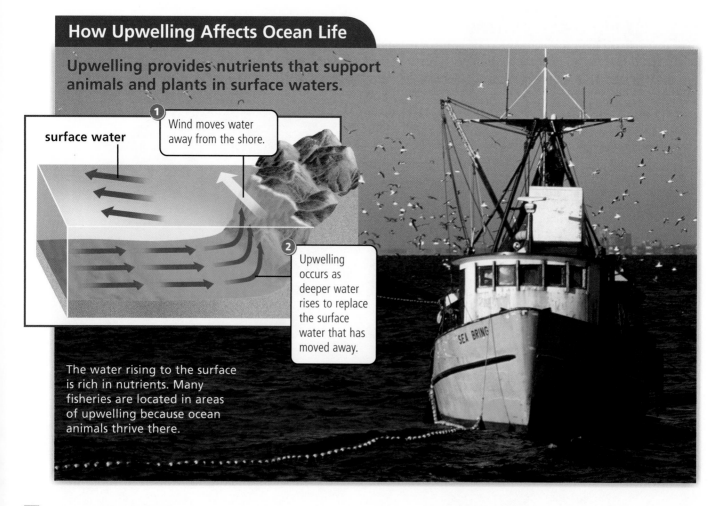

How Upwelling Affects Ocean Life

Upwelling provides nutrients that support animals and plants in surface waters.

surface water

1 Wind moves water away from the shore.

2 Upwelling occurs as deeper water rises to replace the surface water that has moved away.

The water rising to the surface is rich in nutrients. Many fisheries are located in areas of upwelling because ocean animals thrive there.

SEA BRING

INVESTIGATE Currents

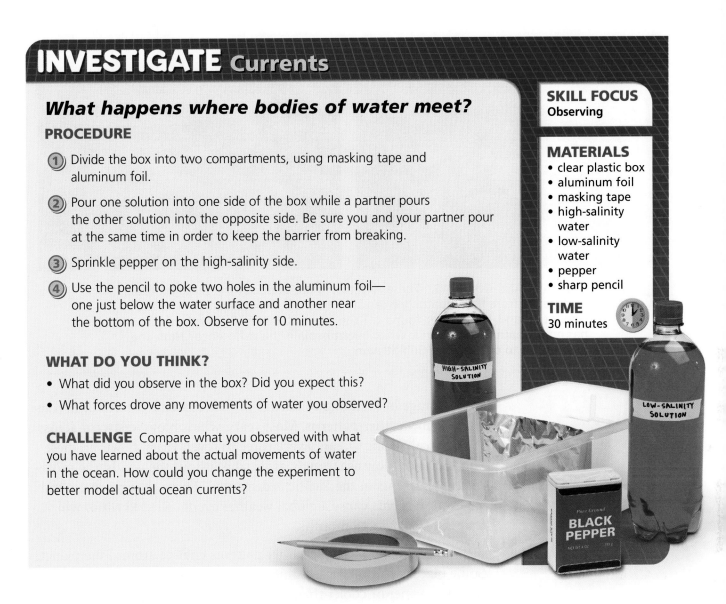

What happens where bodies of water meet?

PROCEDURE

1. Divide the box into two compartments, using masking tape and aluminum foil.

2. Pour one solution into one side of the box while a partner pours the other solution into the opposite side. Be sure you and your partner pour at the same time in order to keep the barrier from breaking.

3. Sprinkle pepper on the high-salinity side.

4. Use the pencil to poke two holes in the aluminum foil—one just below the water surface and another near the bottom of the box. Observe for 10 minutes.

WHAT DO YOU THINK?

- What did you observe in the box? Did you expect this?
- What forces drove any movements of water you observed?

CHALLENGE Compare what you observed with what you have learned about the actual movements of water in the ocean. How could you change the experiment to better model actual ocean currents?

SKILL FOCUS
Observing

MATERIALS
- clear plastic box
- aluminum foil
- masking tape
- high-salinity water
- low-salinity water
- pepper
- sharp pencil

TIME
30 minutes

Currents interact with climate and weather.

Imagine mixing red and blue paint in a cup by blowing through a straw. You can move some paint around, but you cannot predict exactly what pattern will result. Similarly, the ocean and the atmosphere interact in unpredictable ways. Moving air produces movement in the water while the water changes the air above it.

Remember that windblown surface currents help distribute heat around the globe by moving warm water away from the equator and cool water away from the north and south poles. The Gulf Stream, for example, is a surface current that moves warm water northeast-ward toward Great Britain and Europe. Because of the warm Gulf Stream waters, the British climate is mild. No polar bears wander the streets of Great Britain, as they might in places in Canada that are just as far north.

 CHECK YOUR READING How does the Gulf Stream affect Great Britain?

La Scie, Newfoundland

Fowey, England

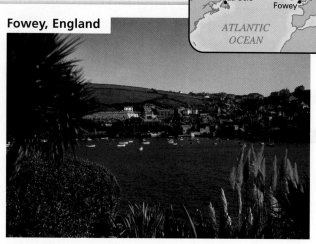

ATLANTIC OCEAN

La Scie

Fowey

READING VISUALS **COMPARE AND CONTRAST** These two towns are at about the same latitude, or distance from the equator. Ice can be found off the coast of La Scie, Newfoundland. Ice is never found off the coast of Fowey, England, which has mild weather year-round. What might explain this difference? **Hint:** the answer has to do with the Gulf Stream.

VOCABULARY
Remember to make a word triangle for *El Niño.*

A change in even one of Earth's surface currents can result in huge changes in weather patterns. Most years, winds blow westward across the tropical Pacific Ocean. Every three to seven years, however, these winds do not blow as strongly as usual. Without the winds, the movement of currents in the Pacific is disrupted. These changes in air and water movements cause a global weather event called **El Niño,** which may last for 12 to 18 months.

During El Niño years, weather patterns change around the planet. Some places get more or less rain or snow than usual. Temperatures may be warmer or cooler than in other years. By using satellite readings of ocean temperatures and floating measurement devices to study conditions in the Pacific, scientists can often predict when El Niño will occur and how severe, or strong, it will be.

3.2 Review

KEY CONCEPTS

1. What are two causes of currents in the ocean?

2. How do currents distribute heat around the globe?

3. How are climate and weather related to currents? Give two examples.

CRITICAL THINKING

4. **Infer** Describe at least two ways in which upwelled water might differ from the water around it.

5. **Infer** What factor do you think might cause a surface current to change direction?

◆ CHALLENGE

6. **Predict** What would happen if all ocean currents suddenly came to a halt? Describe some effects this change would have.

3.3 Waves move through oceans.

◀ **BEFORE, you learned**

- Currents are masses of moving water
- Surface currents are driven mainly by winds
- Deep currents are driven mainly by differences in density

 NOW, you will learn

- How waves form
- How waves move energy through water
- How wave action changes near the shore
- How waves can cause currents near the shore

VOCABULARY

longshore current p. 92
rip current p. 92

EXPLORE Waves

How does wave motion change with depth?

PROCEDURE

1. Fill an aquarium or another clear rectangular container about three-fourths full of water.

2. Tie several metal washers to each of four corks to make them float at different heights, as shown in the photograph.

3. Using your hand or a piece of cardboard, make steady waves in the water. Experiment with a variety of waves—some small and some large. Observe the cork movements.

MATERIALS

- aquarium or clear container
- corks
- string
- metal washers
- water

WHAT DO YOU THINK?
How does the movement of the corks change with depth?

OUTLINE
Remember to start an outline for this section.

I. Main idea
  A. Supporting idea
    1. Detail
    2. Detail
  B. Supporting idea

Waves form in the open ocean.

If you have ever blown across the surface of hot chocolate, you may have noticed ripples. Each of these ripples is a small wave. A wave is an up-and-down motion along the surface of a body of water. The vast ocean surface is covered with waves of various sizes, which are usually caused by winds. Moving air drags across the water's surface and passes energy to the water, causing waves. Other disturbances—such as earthquakes, landslides, and underwater volcanic eruptions—can also cause waves.

 What can cause waves to form in the ocean?

Wave Action at the Water's Surface

READING TiP

As you read about wave action at the water's surface, look at the illustrations on page 91.

RESOURCE CENTER
CLASSZONE.COM

Explore ocean waves.

A wave in the ocean has the same basic shape as many other waves.

- The **crest** is the high point of the wave.
- The **trough** (trawf) is the low point of the wave.
- **Wave height** is the vertical distance between the top of the crest and the bottom of the trough.
- **Wavelength** is the distance between one wave crest and the next.

You have read that currents move water from one place to another. In contrast, waves do not transport water. Waves move energy. They move through water, but the water stays more or less in the same place. Follow the drawings on page 91 to see how water particles move in a circle as a wave passes through. If waves do not transport water, how do surfers zip toward shore on waves? Surfers are powered by the energy traveling in the waves. Waves transport energy, not water.

Most waves affect only the water near the surface of the ocean. Water particles farther down move in smaller circles than particles near the surface. Below a certain depth, the waves no longer affect the water.

Wave Action near Shore

Waves may pass through the ocean for hundreds or thousands of kilometers before moving into shallow water. Then the waves lose speed and eventually topple over, losing their energy as they break on shore.

1 Wind passes energy to the water, causing waves.

2 In shallow water, waves begin to "feel" the sea bottom, causing them to lose speed. As the waves slow down, the wavelength shortens and the wave height increases.

3 When a wave gets too tall, it begins to fall over on itself and then crashes onto shore.

4 After waves break on shore, the water runs down the beach back into the ocean.

wave direction

When waves break on a beach, the water runs back down the sand into the ocean. If the shore is steeply sloped toward the water, the water may rush back to sea forcefully. An undertow is the pull of the water as it runs back to sea. Undertows may be dangerous. Some are strong enough to knock a person off his or her feet and into the waves.

Ocean Waves

Waves transport energy, not water. As a wave crest passes, the water particles move in circular paths.

water particle movement

wave direction →

Waves affect only the water near the surface.

The deeper water particles move in smaller circles than the water particles near the surface.

Below a certain depth, waves no longer affect the water.

The movement of the floating inner tube is similar to the movement of the water particles.

Water particles rise as a wave crest approaches.

At the crest, water particles have moved in a semicircle.

Water particles drop after the trough passes.

The wave passes through the water but the water particles end up in the same place they began.

Wave Structure

Wavelength is the distance between one wave crest and the next.

Wave height is the vertical distance between the top of the crest and the bottom of the trough.

The **crest** is the high point of the wave.

The **trough** is the low point of the wave.

READING VISUALS What happens to water particles as a wave passes through?

Waves cause currents near shore.

Sometimes swimmers notice that without trying, they have drifted far down a beach. Their drifting is due to a **longshore current,** which moves water parallel to the shore. Longshore currents occur in places where waves meet the land at an angle rather than head-on. Since waves rarely meet the land exactly head-on, or perpendicular to the shore, there is a longshore current along almost every shore. The waves hit the shore at an angle and then wash back straight down the beach into the ocean. This zigzag motion moves sand along the beach, piling it up at one end.

Longshore Current

longshore current

1. Incoming waves push sand up the beach at an angle.

2. The sand washes back straight down the beach.

wave direction

With each wave, the zigzag motion repeats, causing sand and water to move along the shoreline.

direction of longshore current

The movement of waves and longshore currents can build up sandbars in the waters near a shore. Sandbars are long ridges or piles of sand that can form parallel to the coastline. As waves wash over the sandbars and onto shore, water may collect behind the sandbars. Eventually, the pooled water will break through. **Rip currents** are narrow streams of water that break through sandbars and drain rapidly back to sea. Rip currents occur when high winds or waves cause a larger-than-usual amount of water to wash back from the shore.

CHECK YOUR READING What role does a sandbar play in the formation of a rip current?

Rip Current

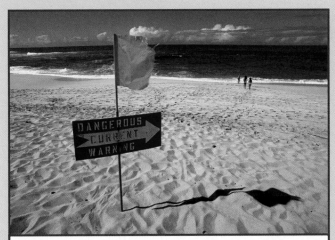

Signs such as this one on a beach in Hawaii warn swimmers of dangerous currents.

sandbar

1 High winds or waves cause a larger-than-usual amount of water to collect behind a sandbar.

2 The water breaks through the sandbar and washes rapidly out to sea in a rip current.

3 Swimmers can escape a rip current by swimming parallel to shore, out of the narrow current.

Like undertows, rip currents can be dangerous for swimmers. In the United States, around 100 people drown in rip currents each year. Most rescues made by lifeguards on U.S. beaches involve swimmers caught in rip currents.

Rip currents are too strong to swim against, but as you can see in the diagram, they are narrow. Swimming parallel to the shore is the best way to escape a rip current. Of course, it is better to avoid rip currents altogether! Many beaches offer daily rip-current forecasts based on information about wind and wave conditions.

3.3 Review

KEY CONCEPTS

1. How does moving air form waves in water?

2. Describe the movement of a water particle as a wave passes through.

3. What happens to waves near shore?

4. Name and describe two kinds of currents that wave action can cause near shore.

CRITICAL THINKING

5. **Compare and Contrast** Describe the similarities and differences between surface currents and waves.

6. **Apply** Imagine you find a piece of wood on the beach. The next day, the wood is 100 meters farther north. How might it have moved? Your answer should refer to currents.

⬥ CHALLENGE

7. **Infer** Some coastlines are more steeply sloped than others. How might wave action on a steeply sloped coastline differ from that on a gently sloped coastline?

CHAPTER INVESTIGATION

Wave Movement

OVERVIEW AND PURPOSE The particles in liquid water are constantly moving. Surfers, boaters, and people in inner tubes enjoy the effects of this motion—even though they never see what is happening at the particle level. How do water particles move in waves? In this investigation you will

- observe the movements of a floating object as waves pass through water
- use your observations to draw conclusions about how water particles move in waves

▶ Problem
Write It Up

What does the motion of a floating object reveal about the movement of water particles in a passing wave?

▶ Hypothesize
Write It Up

Write a hypothesis to explain what the motion of a floating object might reveal about how water particles move in a wave. Your hypothesis should take the form of an "If . . . , then . . . , because . . ." statement.

▶ Procedure

1. Fill the aquarium or clear container with cold tap water until it is three-quarters full.

2. Make the small bottle float with its top just below the surface of the water. You can accomplish this in several ways. First, try adding warm water to the bottle, then securely capping it without air bubbles. See if it will float. You can add salt to the bottle to move the bottle lower in the water. If the bottle is too low, you can trap a small air bubble under the cap to move the bottle higher in the water. Adjust these factors until you successfully float the bottle. The investigation will also work if the top of the bottle just touches the water's surface.

step 2

3. Remove the bottle from the water. Make sure the cap is tightly sealed.

MATERIALS
- small aquarium or clear, shoebox-size container
- water
- small plastic dropping bottle or plastic spice container, with cap
- salt

4. Push your hand back and forth in the water at one end of the aquarium for about 30 seconds, to produce waves.

5. Gently place the small bottle back into the center of the aquarium. With your eyes level with the water surface, observe the motion of the waves and the bottle. Repeat as many times as needed until you notice the bottle behaving the same way with each passing wave.

▶ Observe and Analyze [Write It Up]

1. **RECORD** Make a diagram showing the aquarium setup, including the water, the waves, and the small bottle. Use arrows to show how the bottle moved as waves passed. Or you may draw several diagrams of the aquarium, showing the bottle at different locations as waves passed. Label the various parts of the waves.

2. **ANALYZE** Did the bottle travel with the wave? Why or why not?

▶ Conclude [Write It Up]

1. **INTERPRET** Compare your results with your hypothesis. Do your data support your hypothesis?

2. **INTERPRET** Answer the problem question.

3. **INFER** What do your observations tell you about particle movement in waves? Did the results surprise you? Explain.

4. **EVALUATE** Why was it necessary to float the bottle just under the surface of the water rather than letting it float right on top?

5. **IDENTIFY PROBLEMS** What problems, if any, did you encounter in carrying out the procedure?

6. **IDENTIFY LIMITS** In what ways was this experiment limited in showing particle movement? Identify possible sources of error.

7. **PREDICT** How do you think particle motion in a wave with a tall wave height might differ from that in a wave with a short wave height?

8. **SYNTHESIZE** In this lab you made waves with your hand. In the ocean, most waves are caused by wind. Earthquakes, landslides, and other events also cause waves in the ocean. What do earthquakes, landslides, wind, and your hand have in common that allows all of them to make waves?

▶ INVESTIGATE Further

CHALLENGE Redesign this experiment in a way you think will better demonstrate the particle motion in a water wave. You need not limit yourself to the materials you used in this lab. Why will your version of the experiment work better?

Wave Movement

Problem What does the motion of a floating object reveal about the movement of water particles in a passing wave?

Hypothesize

Observe and Analyze

Table 1. Diagram of Setup

no wave	before crest	at crest	after crest	in trough

Conclude

3.4 Waters rise and fall in tides.

◀ **BEFORE,** you learned

- Wind provides the energy to form waves in the ocean
- Ocean waves change near shore
- The ocean is a global body of water

▶ **NOW,** you will learn

- What causes tides
- How tides affect coastlines
- How tides can be used to generate electricity

VOCABULARY

tide p. 96
tidal range p. 98
spring tide p. 99
neap tide p. 99

THINK ABOUT

What causes water levels to change in the ocean?

These two photographs were taken on the same day at the boat harbor in Lympstone, England. The change in water level in the harbor occurs every day on a regular and predictable basis. What forces cause shifts in such huge volumes of water? How can we explain the clocklike regularity of the flow?

VOCABULARY
Add a word triangle for *tide* to your notebook.

Coastal waters rise and fall each day.

Have you ever spent a day at a beach along the ocean? Perhaps you placed your blanket and beach chairs in the sand close to the water's edge. An hour later, you may have needed to move your blanket and chairs to keep the advancing waves from washing them away. The water level on coastlines varies with the time of day. This periodic rising and falling of the water level of the ocean is called the **tide.** The water level along a coast is highest at high tide, submerging parts of the coastline. The water level is lowest at low tide, exposing more of the coastline.

What in the world could cause such dramatic changes in the ocean's level? The answer is, nothing in this world. Read on to find out how out-of-this-world objects cause tides.

 CHECK YOUR READING How does the water level along a coast differ at high tide and at low tide?

The gravity of the Moon and the Sun causes tides.

Over 2000 years ago, people knew that the Moon and the tide were related. But 1700 years passed before the connection was explained in the terms of modern science. In 1687, Sir Isaac Newton developed his theories of gravity and linked the tide to the Moon's gravitational pull. Gravity is a force of attraction between objects. Earth's gravity pulls things toward its center—including you.

The gravity of the Sun and the gravity of the Moon also pull on objects on Earth. In response to the Moon's gravitational pull, Earth's water bulges on the side facing the Moon. The Moon's gravity also pulls on Earth itself. Earth gets pulled toward the Moon, leaving a second bulge of water on the side of Earth facing away from the Moon. The Sun's gravity pulls too, but with less effect because the Sun is so far away.

Daily Tides

The diagram below shows the two bulges of ocean water: one on the side of Earth closest to the Moon, and the other on the opposite side of Earth. At these bulges, it is high tide. Between the two bulges are dips. At these dips, it is low tide. As Earth rotates, different parts of it pass through the bulges and the dips. As a result, most places experience two high tides and two low tides each day.

VISUALIZATION
CLASSZONE.COM

Watch daily tides in action.

Daily Tides

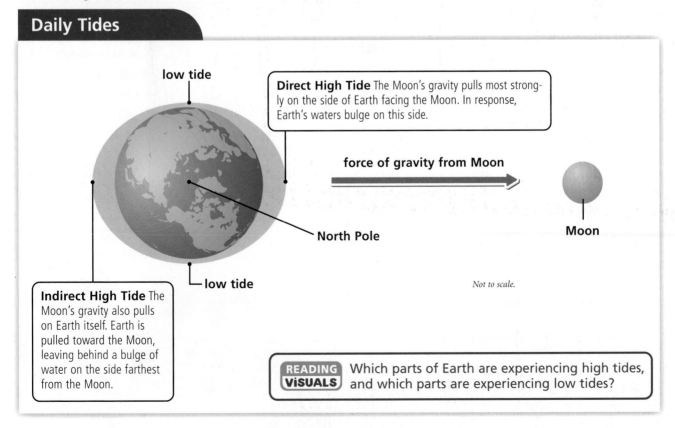

low tide

Direct High Tide The Moon's gravity pulls most strongly on the side of Earth facing the Moon. In response, Earth's waters bulge on this side.

force of gravity from Moon

North Pole

Moon

low tide

Indirect High Tide The Moon's gravity also pulls on Earth itself. Earth is pulled toward the Moon, leaving behind a bulge of water on the side farthest from the Moon.

Not to scale.

READING VISUALS Which parts of Earth are experiencing high tides, and which parts are experiencing low tides?

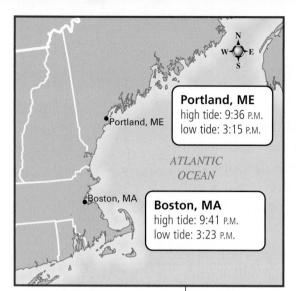

Portland, ME
high tide: 9:36 P.M.
low tide: 3:15 P.M.

ATLANTIC OCEAN

Boston, MA
high tide: 9:41 P.M.
low tide: 3:23 P.M.

A place farther east along a coastline experiences high and low tides earlier in the day, because it passes through the tidal bulge first. Times for high and low tides change daily.

The timing of high and low tides at one location on a coast may differ from the timing at other locations along that coast. As you can see on the map of the coastline of New England, the tides occur later as you move west along the coastline. As Earth rotates, the easternmost points on a coastline will pass through the tidal bulge before places farther west on the same coastline.

The timing of high and low tides is not the only way that tides can differ along a coastline. Some places experience higher high tides and lower low tides than other places. The shape of the land above and below the water affects tidal ranges. A **tidal range** is the difference in height between a high tide and the next low tide. The tidal range is greater in a narrow bay than on a wide-open shore. For example, the narrow harbor of Lympstone, England, shown in the photographs on page 96, has a very large tidal range. A coastline with a steeply sloped ocean floor has a larger tidal range than a coastline with a gradually dropping floor. For example, the coasts of Texas and western Florida have very small tidal ranges because of the gradual slope of the ocean floor there.

⬆ CHECK YOUR READING   In what two ways does the shape of the land affect the tidal range? What sentences tell you this?

INVESTIGATE Tides

How does the Moon make tides?

PROCEDURE

1. Cut the Tides datasheet in two, along the dotted line. Cut out the map of Earth on the bottom half of the sheet.

2. Use a paper fastener to connect the two pieces as shown in the photograph.

3. Now you are ready to model the tides. Rotate Earth one full turn in the direction of the arrow. One full turn is equal to one day.

WHAT DO YOU THINK?

- How does the model demonstrate the Moon's role in tides?

- How many times does each place in the ocean experience high tide and low tide each day?

CHALLENGE One full rotation of Earth takes place in a day, or 24 hours. About how much time passes between one high tide and the next high tide at any location on Earth?

SKILL FOCUS
Making models

MATERIALS

- Tides datasheet
- scissors
- brass paper fastener

TIME
15 minutes

Monthly Tides

The Moon is the main cause of tides, but the Sun affects tides as well. The Moon takes about a month to move around Earth. Twice during this month-long journey—at the new moon and the full moon—the Moon, the Sun, and Earth line up. The gravity of the Sun and the gravity of the Moon combine to pull Earth's waters in the same directions. The result is an extra-high tidal bulge and an extra-low tidal dip, called a **spring tide.**

During first- and third-quarter moons, the Sun and the Moon are not lined up with Earth. The gravity of each pulls from a different direction. The result is a smaller tidal bulge and tidal dip, called a **neap tide.** During a neap tide, high and low tides are less extreme.

Changes in the timing and the height of tides occur in a regular cycle. The timing of tides may be important to people who live near a coast or use coasts for fishing or boating. In many coastal communities, tide tables printed in newspapers give the exact times and heights of the tides.

RESOURCE CENTER
CLASSZONE.COM

Find out more about ocean tides.

READING TiP

Spring tides occur twice a month all year long, not just in spring. This use of the word *spring* is related to its meaning "to jump."

Monthly Tides

Spring Tide

Sun · Moon · Earth

Not to scale.

At new moon and full moon, Earth, the Moon, and the Sun are lined up. The gravity of the Sun and the gravity of the Moon pull Earth's waters in the same direction. As a result high tides are extra high and low tides are extra low.

Neap Tide

At first- and third-quarter moons, Earth, the Moon, and the Sun are not lined up. The gravity of the Sun pulls in a different direction from that of the Moon. As a result, high and low tides are less extreme.

READING VISUALS How are Earth, the Moon, and the Sun positioned during spring tides? How are they positioned during neap tides?

Tides can be used to generate electricity.

The energy of tides can be used to generate electricity. A tidal dam is built near a coast in the path of tidal waters. The water flows in during high tide and is trapped behind the gates of the dam. Then, when the tide is low, the gates open and the trapped water rushes out. As the water flows out, it spins turbines that power electric generators.

open ocean ← → shore

gate

turbine

1

The dam's gates are open as the tide rises. Notice that the water level is the same on both sides.

2

When the tide begins to lower, the gates close, trapping water behind the dam.

3

At low tide, the gates open and the water rushes out, spinning turbines that generate electricity.

Tidal dams cause much less pollution than many other methods of generating electricity. Also, tides are a renewable source of energy; the tides are not used up in the process. However, tidal dams have some drawbacks. Few places in the world are actually suitable for such dams. Another problem is that the times of day when tidal dams generate electricity might not be the times of day when people most need electricity. Tidal dams also sometimes block the paths of migrating fish and might hurt marine life by altering the regular flow of water.

CHECK YOUR READING What are the benefits and drawbacks of tidal power plants?

3.4 Review

KEY CONCEPTS

1. Describe the appearance of tidal changes at a coastline.

2. Explain the difference between the Sun's role and the Moon's role in creating tides.

3. How are tides used to generate electricity?

CRITICAL THINKING

4. **Synthesize** Contrast the daily and monthly patterns of tides. What role does the Moon's orbit around Earth play in both?

5. **Compare** Tidal range is the daily difference in high and low water levels. Compare the tidal ranges of neap and spring tides.

⬥ CHALLENGE

6. **Draw Conclusions** How would the tides be different if the Moon revolved around Earth twice a month instead of once a month?

Tidal Energy

Tidal power plants can work only in a few locations in the world. The best locations for tidal energy plants are ones with large differences between high and low tides. Why can't tides make electricity just anywhere?

The first and largest tidal energy plant in the world is in northern France, where the Rance River enters the English Channel. The plant opened in 1966.

Rance R.

Under Pressure

Each of these jugs contains the same amount of water. Water sprays out of the hole at the bottom of each—but why does it spray farther out of the narrow jug? The water pressure is greater in the tall, narrow jug because the water is deeper. The width of the jug does not matter—just the depth. The deeper the water, the greater the water pressure. The higher the water pressure, the faster the water comes out of the hole—and the farther the water sprays.

From Pressure to Power

Tidal dams use moving water to turn turbines that power generators. Turning turbines requires work. Work is the use of force to move an object. In this case, the force of the water is doing work on the turbines. The faster the water moves, the more work it can do.

Location, Location, Location

Think again about the two jugs. The water moves faster out of the hole in the tall, narrow jug—the one with the higher water pressure. Tidal power plants work best in places where high water pressure moves the water fast enough to turn the turbines. Remember that deeper water makes for higher water pressure. So tidal power plants work best in places with a large tidal range—the difference between high and low tide.

EXPLORE

1. **APPLY** When the water trapped behind a dam is released, it is channeled through openings in the dam and spins the turbines. From what you've learned about water pressure, where do you think the openings are, toward the top of the dam or toward the bottom? Explain your reasoning.

2. **CHALLENGE** Make a model of a tidal-energy plant. Use the side of a milk jug as a base, modeling clay to make the basin, and pieces of plastic for the dam and gates. Try different shapes for your basin and different sizes of gates to see how fast you can get the water to flow.

3

the BIG idea

The oceans are a connected system of water in motion.

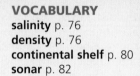

CONTENT REVIEW
CLASSZONE.COM

◀ **KEY CONCEPTS SUMMARY**

3.1 The oceans are a connected system.

- Much of Earth is covered by ocean water, which contains dissolved salts and gases.

- Ocean temperatures decrease with depth.

- The ocean floor has canyons, mountains, and many other features.

VOCABULARY
salinity p. 76
density p. 76
continental shelf p. 80
sonar p. 82

3.2 Ocean water moves in currents.

- Surface currents are set in motion by winds and carry heat around the globe.

- Deep currents are caused by differences in water density. Dense water sinks at the poles and very slowly flows toward the equator.

VOCABULARY
ocean current p. 84
upwelling p. 86
downwelling p. 86
El Niño p. 88

3.3 Waves move through oceans.

- Ocean waves transport energy, not water. When a wave passes, water particles end up in the same places they began.

- Longshore currents occur when waves hit shores at angles.

- Rip currents are narrow streams of water that break through sandbars.

VOCABULARY
longshore current p. 92
rip current p. 92

3.4 Waters rise and fall in tides.

The Moon's gravity pulls Earth's waters into bulges and dips. As Earth rotates, its movement through these bulges and dips causes tides.

direct high tide
indirect high tide
Earth
Moon

VOCABULARY
tide p. 96
tidal range p. 98
spring tide p. 99
neap tide p. 99

Reviewing Vocabulary

Make a description wheel like the one below for each of the following terms. Write the term in the circle. On the spokes, write words or phrases that describe the term.

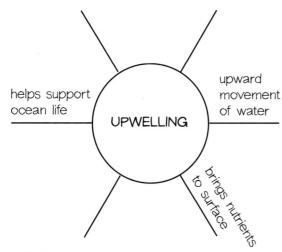

helps support ocean life

upward movement of water

UPWELLING

brings nutrients to surface

1. El Niño

2. longshore current

3. rip current

Reviewing Key Concepts

Multiple Choice *Choose the letter of the best answer.*

4. Warm water stays at the ocean surface because
  a. it is less dense than cold water
  b. it is more dense than cold water
  c. it is saltier than cold water
  d. it has more carbon dioxide than cold water

5. Sonar measures ocean depth by means of
  a. weighted lines   **c.** sound waves
  b. light waves   **d.** magnets

6. Surface currents are caused by
  a. waves   **c.** density
  b. winds   **d.** heat

7. El Niño is caused by changes in
  a. wave speed   **c.** salinity
  b. currents   **d.** tides

8. Deep currents are caused by differences in
  a. location   **c.** depth
  b. wind speed   **d.** density

9. Tides are caused by the gravitational pull of
  a. Earth and the Sun
  b. the Sun and the Moon
  c. Earth alone
  d. Earth and the Moon

10. What does wave action involve?
  a. the transfer of water molecules across the ocean surface
  b. the transfer of energy across the ocean surface
  c. oscillations generated by tides
  d. rip currents

Short Answer *Write a short answer to each question.*

11. What is the connection between salinity and density?

12. Explain why Earth's oceans are actually parts of one connected body of water.

13. Describe the relationship between ocean temperature and depth.

14. What are the characteristics of a wave? Copy the drawing below onto your paper, and label each part.

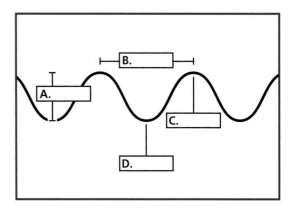

15. SYNTHESIZE One of these cups contains salt water, and the other contains fresh water. Without tasting the water, how could you figure out which sample is which? Describe two methods. You may specify tools or materials you would need to carry out the two methods. **Hint:** Think about the water cycle and density when considering the two methods.

16. INFER After the development of sonar, oceanographic researchers discovered much about the features of the ocean floor. How would the sonar readings of a research ship be affected as it passes above a mid-ocean ridge?

17. COMPARE AND CONTRAST How are space exploration and ocean exploration similar? How are they different?

18. PROVIDE EXAMPLES How could a change in the direction of a surface current in the ocean affect weather? Give examples of the weather in an area before and after the change.

19. INFER If global winds were to change, which ocean motions would be affected?

20. APPLY During a violent storm that causes huge waves to form on the ocean's surface, a submarine glides deep underwater, unaffected by the waves above. Explain why.

21. COMPARE AND CONTRAST Copy and fill in the Venn diagram below. In the overlapping section, list at least one characteristic that is shared by waves and tides. In the outer sections, list characteristics that are not shared. Then write a short summary of the information in the Venn diagram.

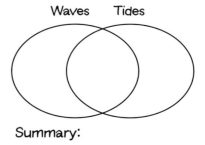

Summary:

22. APPLY Maria and her friends like to play soccer on a beach. Sometimes the water is very low at low tide, and there is plenty of room to play. At other times, the water does not get as low at low tide, and there is not enough room to play. What does Maria need to know about monthly tidal cycles so that she can plan to have the soccer games when there is plenty of room on the beach?

the BIG idea

23. IDENTIFY CAUSE AND EFFECT Look again at the photograph on pages 72–73. Now that you have finished the chapter, explain what is causing the waves in the photograph. Also explain what might cause the water level to rise and cover the area where the surfer is standing.

24. SYNTHESIZE One system can interact with another system. The oceans are a connected system of water in motion. The solar system is the Sun and its family of orbiting planets, moons, and other objects. Describe a connection between the solar system and the ocean system.

UNIT PROJECTS

Check your schedule for your unit project. How are you doing? Be sure that you have placed data or notes from your research in your project folder.

Standardized Test Practice

Analyzing a Table

The table below shows the times of high and low tides at a location on the Atlantic Ocean coast. Use the table to answer the questions below.

	Low Tide	High Tide	Low Tide	High Tide
Monday	12:01 A.M.	5:33 A.M.	11:58 A.M.	5:59 P.M.
Tuesday	12:57 A.M.	6:33 A.M.	12:51 P.M.	6:54 P.M.
Wednesday	1:51 A.M.	7:30 A.M.	1:45 P.M.	7:48 P.M.
Thursday	2:43 A.M.	8:25 A.M.	2:38 P.M.	8:40 P.M.

1. On which day was there a high tide at 7:48 P.M.?

   a. Monday   **c.** Wednesday

   b. Tuesday   **d.** Thursday

2. Low tide is a good time to find shells along the beach. What time would be best for finding shells on Wednesday?

   a. 8:00 A.M.   **c.** noon

   b. 10:00 A.M.   **d.** 2:00 P.M.

3. What was happening to the water level along the beach between 12:00 A.M. and 5:33 A.M. on Monday?

   a. The water level was getting higher.

   b. The water level was getting lower.

   c. The water level was at its lowest.

   d. The water level was at its highest.

4. Which of the following graphs best represents the tides during one day?

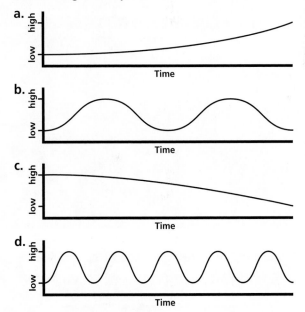

Extended Response

Answer the two questions below in detail.

5. How could you use a cork and a tank of water to demonstrate that waves transport energy, not water? You may include a diagram as part of your response if you wish.

6. The beaker contains both salt water and fresh water. Why do the two liquids form layers? Use the words *salinity* and *density* in your response.

TIMELINES in Science

EXPLORING THE OCEAN

People have been studying ocean waves and currents at least since Egyptians sailed in the Mediterranean Sea more than 5000 years ago. Almost 3000 years ago, Phoenicians in the Mediterranean and Polynesians in the South Pacific understood enough to sail the open sea with confidence. More than 2000 years ago, people developed special gear to provide divers with oxygen so that they could explore the undersea world.

The timeline shows some historical events in the study of the ocean. The boxes below the timeline show how technology has made this study possible and useful.

345 B.C.
Alexander Goes Undersea?
According to legend, Macedonia's powerful ruler Alexander the Great has himself lowered into the ocean in a glass ball so that he can explore what lies underwater.

EVENTS

360 B.C.   320 B.C.

APPLICATIONS AND TECHNOLOGY

APPLICATION

Measuring Ocean Depth

Around 85 B.C., the Greek philosopher Posidonius used a simple method to answer a simple question. He wanted to know the depth of the Mediterranean Sea. So he and a crew sailed out into the sea near Italy. There, they dropped a weight tied to a very long rope into the water. When the weight struck bottom, they measured how much rope they had let out. It was almost 2 kilometers (about 1 mi). This was the standard method for measuring depth for almost 2000 years. Today, instruments on ships emit sound waves that bounce off the sea floor. The instruments then calculate depth according to how long the sound waves take to return to the surface.

A sailor in 1916 prepares to lower a weight on a rope to measure the ocean's depth.

1775
Submarines Allow Undersea Travel

Connecticut inventor David Bushnell designs and builds a wooden submarine. It holds enough air for a person to stay underwater for 30 minutes. The *Turtle,* as his vessel is known, is among the first to allow people to travel underwater.

1876
Expedition Surveys the Oceans

The sailing ship *Challenger* completes one of the great scientific research efforts of the 1800s, and returns home to Great Britain. In 362 locations around the world, the crew recorded data on ocean depth, currents, temperature, and water chemistry. They identified more than 4000 previously unknown species of plants and animals.

1797
Explorer Designs First Diving Suit

German mechanic Karl Heinrich Klingert combines waterproof clothes and a helmet with two tubes, one for inhaling and one for exhaling. He calls his outfit a diving machine. It allows people to stay underwater for longer periods than ever before.

A.D. **1760**   **1800**   **1840**   **1880**

APPLICATION

Charting the Ocean Floor

In the 1800s, sailors began recording measurements of the deep Atlantic Ocean floor. The U.S. Navy lieutenant Matthew Maury collected 200 of these measurements and created the first chart showing water depths in such a large region. His chart, completed in 1855, provided the first evidence of mountains in the middle of the Atlantic. A decade later, Maury's studies of the ocean floor guided those who were laying the first telegraph cable connecting the United States and Europe.

1943

Explorer Breathes Underwater

In 1943, Jacques Cousteau, the most famous of 20th-century undersea explorers, helps develop scuba—a *s*elf-*c*ontained *u*nderwater *b*reathing *a*pparatus. The breathing gear allows divers to explore depths of 30 meters and beyond without having to wear heavy suits and metal helmets.

1938

Fish with Elbows Caught

Among the day's catch of the South African fisherman Hendrick Goosen is an odd five-foot-long fish with joints in its fins, like elbows and knees. Surprised scientists identify it as a coelacanth, a creature they thought had been extinct for 60 million years. The catch spurs people's imaginations about what else the ocean might contain.

1951

Exploration as Entertainment

Improvements in underwater breathing gear in the 1940s make recreational scuba diving possible. Then, a 1951 movie about scuba-wearing soldiers, *The Frogmen,* spurs popular interest in the activity. The movie inspires more people than ever before to start exploring the underwater world for themselves.

1953

Robotic Probe Searches Ocean

POODLE, the first remote operated vehicle (ROV), is invented. Since ROVs carry no people, they allow more research to be done in deep areas that are difficult for people to travel to.

| 1900 | 1920 | 1940 | 1960 | 1980 |

TECHNOLOGY

Sonar

In 1914, Reginald Fessenden developed the first practical instrument for using the echo of a sound to measure distances underwater. This technique, later named sonar, for "*so*und *na*vigation and *r*anging," allows scientists to study the undersea world without the expense and danger of going underwater. Sonar has been a valuable tool for measuring the depth of the ocean and the landforms along the bottom. Because temperature and salt concentration affect how sound travels, oceanographers can use sonar to measure these properties as well. One of sonar's most important early uses was to help sailors spot icebergs. Today, industry uses sonar to identify schools of fish, places likely to have oil, and other features.

This sonar image, recorded in October 1999, shows a shipwreck at the bottom of Delaware Bay.

1998

Aquarius *Keeps Researching*

After renovation, the 12-year-old *Aquarius* lab settles on the ocean floor in the Florida Keys. Its crew is investigating a nearby coral reef. They have studied the impact of sewage, the effects of ultraviolet radiation, and chemicals produced by organisms in the reef.

1994

Life Thrives Under Ocean

The discovery of microorganisms thriving in rock pulled up from 500 meters (1600 ft) below the ocean floor raises new questions for scientists. How did the bacteria get there? How do they survive? How many are there? Scientists call the region the deep biosphere.

RESOURCE CENTER
CLASSZONE.COM

Learn more about exploring the ocean.

2000

TECHNOLOGY

Ocean Buoys

Starting in 2000, scientists scattered in the ocean 3000 buoys equipped with the latest developments in floating technology. These Argo floats then started collecting information on water temperature and salinity. They transmitted data by satellite every 15 days. With this more detailed information about ocean water, scientists may be able to make weather predictions more accurate than ever before.

SPOTLIGHT on
SYLVIA EARLE

Many people call Dr. Sylvia Earle "Her Deepness." *Time* magazine named her its first "Hero of the Planet." Few people have spent more time underwater than Dr. Earle. No other woman has dived deeper than she has. Dr. Earle holds the women's record for solo diving at a depth of over a thousand meters (3,300 ft).

Currently, Dr. Earle is an Explorer-in-Residence at the National Geographic Society. Her passion is protecting the oceans. In cooperation with NOAA, she was project director for the Sustainable Seas Expeditions. The project's goal was to document the geology and creatures of the twelve U.S. marine sanctuaries. These are the underwater equivalents of national parks.

ACTIVITIES

Mapping the Sea Floor

Suppose you are in a boat that is traveling in a straight line. You take a sonar reading every one-half minute. Your readings, which show how long sound waves take to reach bottom and return to the surface, are as follows:

1. 2 seconds   **3.** 3 seconds
2. 0.5 second   **4.** 3 seconds

Sound travels at about 1500 meters per second (4900 ft/s) in seawater.

From this information, draw what the sea floor looks like under the path of your boat.

Writing About Science

Technology has been used for centuries to study the ocean. Trace the history of one piece of technology, such as a submarine, diving gear, sonar, or a depth gauge. Write a short history of that device.

Ocean Environments

the BIG idea

The ocean supports life and contains natural resources.

Key Concepts

SECTION 4.1
Ocean coasts support plant and animal life.
Learn about conditions in coastal environments and about the plants and animals that live there.

SECTION 4.2
Conditions differ away from shore.
Learn how conditions change as you move away from the shore and deeper into the ocean.

SECTION 4.3
The ocean contains natural resources.
Learn about the ocean's living and nonliving resources and how pollution affects the ocean.

Internet Preview

CLASSZONE.COM

Chapter 4 online resources: Content Review, Simulation, Visualization, three Resource Centers, Math Tutorial, Test Practice

How is the deep ocean different from the shore?

EXPLORE (the **BIG** idea)

It's Alive!

Carefully observe a fish in a fish tank. Pay attention to all of the fish's movements. Record what the fish does and what the fish's environment is like.

Observe and Think All animals, including fish, need oxygen to live. Where does the fish get its oxygen?

Beneath the Surface

What forms of life would you expect to see underwater in the ocean near shore? Draw a picture to show your ideas.

Observe and Think What do you need to know in order to make your picture more accurate? Write five questions you have about the ocean environment near shore.

Internet Activity: Ocean Environments

Go to **ClassZone.com** to learn more about organisms in the ocean. See which plants and animals live in different ocean environments.

Observe and Think What factors or conditions might affect the kinds of organisms that can live in each part of the ocean?

NSTA
scilinks.org
SCI**LINKS**

Ocean Resources **Code: MDL021**

Getting Ready to Learn

◄ CONCEPT REVIEW

- The ocean contains oxygen and other gases.
- Deep currents carry oxygen from the surface to the ocean floor.
- Upwelling carries nutrients from the bottom of the ocean to the surface.

◄ VOCABULARY REVIEW

point-source pollution p. 54

nonpoint-source pollution p. 54

continental shelf p. 80

ocean current p. 84

CONTENT REVIEW
CLASSZONE.COM
Review concepts and vocabulary.

▶ TAKING NOTES

MAIN IDEA WEB

Write each new blue heading—a main idea—in a box. Then put notes with important terms and details into boxes around the main idea.

SCIENCE NOTEBOOK

| Different parts of the ocean have different characteristics. | Almost 95 percent of the ocean is still unexplored. |

Ocean waters contain many environments.

| | Swimmers, floaters, and bottom dwellers are three groups of ocean life. |

CHOOSE YOUR OWN STRATEGY

Take notes about new vocabulary terms, using one or more of the strategies from earlier chapters—**four square, description wheel,** or **word triangle.** Feel free to mix and match the strategies, or use an entirely different vocabulary strategy.

See the Note-Taking Handbook on pages R45–R51.

Four Square

Description Wheel

Word Triangle

KEY CONCEPT

Ocean coasts support plant and animal life.

◀ BEFORE, you learned	▶ NOW, you will learn
• Ocean water contains gases such as oxygen • Salinity is a measure of the amount of salt in water • Coastal waters rise and fall each day because of tides	• What the intertidal zone is • What coastal environments exist where fresh water and salt water meet • How human activity affects shoreline environments

VOCABULARY

habitat p. 114
intertidal zone p. 114
estuary p. 116
wetland p. 116

THINK ABOUT

What are the characteristics of shoreline environments?

This map shows the migration route of the osprey, a type of bird. Each fall ospreys fly south to warmer weather. In the spring they fly north. Each dot on the map represents a place where ospreys stop along the way. What do you notice about where the birds stop? What resources might shoreline environments provide for birds?

Ocean waters contain many environments.

MAIN IDEA WEB
Remember to start a main idea web in your notebook for this blue heading.

Where on Earth can you find a living animal that is larger than the largest dinosaur that ever lived? Where can you find birds that use their wings to fly underwater, or animals that can eject their internal organs—and grow another set? Where can you find warm tropical zones thick with plants, or cold, empty plains where no plant can grow? The ocean contains all these and more.

Like the land, the ocean contains many different environments, each with its own special characteristics. Although scientists have learned a lot about the ocean and its environments, almost 95 percent of the ocean remains unexplored. It is possible that many millions more species of ocean life are yet to be discovered.

The many known ocean organisms are organized in three groups according to the way the organisms live. Bottom dwellers include plantlike organisms called algae (AL-jee) and other organisms that live on the ocean bottom—for example, seaweeds, crabs, corals, starfish, and shellfish. Swimmers are animals such as fish, dolphins, whales, and octopuses that swim in the ocean. Floaters are organisms that do not swim but float at or near the ocean surface. Some floaters, such as jellyfish, are large, but most are so small you need a microscope to see them. These tiny living things include plants, animals, bacteria, and single-celled organisms called protists (PROH-tihsts).

CHECK YOUR READING What are the three groups of ocean life?

The shoreline supports many plants and animals.

READING TiP

Word parts can help you remember the meaning of *intertidal zone.* The prefix *inter-* means "between." The root *tidal* means "relating to the tides." The *intertidal zone* is the area between high and low tides.

An environment that has all the necessary requirements for an organism to live is called a **habitat.** In this chapter you will explore some of the many different ocean habitats. Your journey begins on the coastline, where the ocean meets the land. The habitat at the edge of the ocean is the **intertidal zone** (IHN-tuhr-TYD-uhl)—the narrow ocean margin between the high tide mark and the low tide mark. The conditions constantly change in the intertidal zone. Organisms that live here must be able to survive both wet and dry periods. Plants and animals must also withstand the force of waves that constantly crash onto shore.

1 At **low tide,** the intertidal zone is dry and exposed to direct sunlight. Organisms must be able to live out of water. They must also be able to tolerate the air temperature, which may differ from the temperature of the water.

2 At **high tide,** the intertidal zone is covered with water, so it is not exposed to direct sunlight. Organisms must be able to live completely underwater and tolerate the temperature of the water.

Tidal pools are areas along the shore where water remains at low tide. Plants and animals that live in tidal pools must survive drastic changes in salinity, or salt content. When sunlight causes water to evaporate, the salinity increases. When rain falls, the salinity decreases.

Organisms have different ways of surviving the conditions of the intertidal zone. For example, crabs can move around and seek cover in the sand or in between rocks. Mussels attach themselves to rocks and close their shells to keep from drying out during low tide. Some seaweeds dry out at low tide but are able to regain moisture at high tide.

Intertidal Zone

The intertidal zone is the area along the coastline between the high tide mark and the low tide mark.

intertidal zone

① Low Tide

At low tide, the intertidal zone is exposed to the air.

Tidal pools are areas where water remains at low tide.

Some seaweeds can dry out during low tide and absorb water at high tide.

At low tide, mussels close their shells tightly to keep from drying out.

② High Tide

At high tide, the intertidal zone is covered with water.

Plants and animals must survive the constant crashing of waves against the shore.

At high tide, mussels open their shells to eat and take in oxygen.

READING VISUALS What organisms can you see in the photograph of low tide?

INVESTIGATE Coastal Environments

How do mussels survive?

Most intertidal zone organisms require water to survive, and they must endure long dry periods during low tides. Mussels close their shells tightly during low tide and open them during high tide.

DESIGN — YOUR OWN — EXPERIMENT

PROCEDURE

1. Using the materials listed, design an experiment to demonstrate why mussels close their shells during low tide.

2. Write up your procedure.

3. Test your experiment.

WHAT DO YOU THINK?

- How does your experiment demonstrate why mussels close their shells?

- What were the variables in your experiment?

CHALLENGE How could you redesign your experiment to better model what happens during low tide? What other variables would you include?

WATER

Fresh water and salt water meet on coasts.

This aerial photograph shows the Pawcatuck River estuary in the northeastern United States. Fresh water from the river mixes with salt water from the ocean.

You have read that rivers flow to the sea. What happens when they get there? The fresh water from rivers mixes with salt water from the ocean in shoreline areas called **estuaries** (EHS-choo-EHR-eez), which include bays, inlets, and harbors. The water in estuaries is not as salty as ocean water, nor as fresh as river water. The salinity changes as the tide flows in and out. Sometimes the water at the surface is fresh, while denser salt water remains below.

Estuaries are bursting with life. Plants and animals thrive on nutrients washed in by rivers. Worms and shellfish live along the bottom. Plants and animals too small to see without a microscope float in the water. Many different kinds of birds and sea animals breed in estuaries. Roots and grasses offer protection for young fish and other animals. These small fish and other animals are an important food source for larger fish and for birds.

Coastal wetlands form along the edges of estuaries. As the name suggests, **wetlands** are wet, swampy areas that are often flooded with water. There are two kinds of coastal wetlands. Away from the equator, in cooler regions, coastal wetlands are salt marshes. Closer to the equator, in tropical regions, coastal wetlands are mangrove forests.

CHECK YOUR READING How are coastal wetlands related to estuaries?

Salt Marshes

Away from the equator, in cooler regions, grassy salt marshes are found along the edges of estuaries. In the United States, salt marshes are found along the coasts of the Atlantic and Pacific oceans and the Gulf of Mexico. Salt marshes help keep the shoreline from washing away. They also provide an important habitat for fish, birds, and other wildlife.

The rivers that flow into estuaries carry nutrient-rich soil. When the rivers reach the sea, they drop the soil. This rich soil supports thick grasses. The grasses form a protective barrier against waves, tides, and storms. Thick root systems hold the muddy bottom together. Tiny organisms decompose, or break down, dead grasses and return the nutrients the grasses contained to the marsh.

Crabs, snails, and minnows thrive among the grasses. Ospreys and other fish-eating birds find food in salt marshes. Birds that migrate use salt marshes as rest stops when they fly back and forth each season.

In the past, people did not understand the importance of wetlands. Over the last 200 years, about half of all wetlands in the United States were destroyed. Many were drained or filled in with soil to provide solid ground to build on or to farm. In the 1970s, people started working to protect and restore coastal wetlands.

CHECK YOUR READING Why are grasses an important part of the salt marsh environment?

VIRGINIA

Marsh grasses have thick root systems that help hold the muddy soil together.

Many small fish and other animals live in the sheltered areas among the marsh grasses.

Fish-eating birds find plenty to eat in salt marshes.

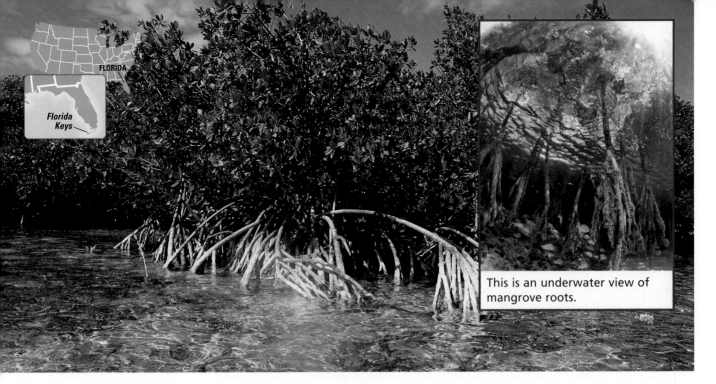

This is an underwater view of mangrove roots.

INFER This photograph shows mangrove plants along the coast of Florida. How do the roots brace the mangroves against waves and storms?

Mangrove Forests

In tropical regions, the main coastal wetland is the mangrove forest. In the United States, mangrove forests are found along the coast of southern Florida. A mangrove forest is a thick group of mangrove shrubs and trees. The mangrove plants' roots brace them against storms and waves. Without the protection of these plants, shorelines in tropical areas would be drastically changed by heavy storms.

The sheltered mangrove forest is home to many living things. Fiddler crabs may live in the shallow waters among the mangrove roots. You may find seaweeds, oysters, shrimp, and snails. You may even see tree-climbing fish! These fish, called mudskippers, climb mangrove roots to catch insects and crabs.

MAIN IDEA WEB
Remember to start a main idea web in your notebook for this blue heading.

Human activity affects shorelines.

Coastal environments are home not only to many plants and animals, but to many humans as well. About half of the world's population lives within 80 kilometers (50 mi) of a coastline. Big cities and important commercial ports are often located where rivers meet the sea. Many people use coastlines and estuaries for recreation, such as boating, swimming, and fishing.

Human activity can harm the estuary environment. For example, some coastal wetlands are cleared for shrimp farms and for raising crops. Other areas are filled in to make new land for houses and other development. Industry and shipping can disturb wildlife and alter the estuary habitat. In some places, human waste and other sewage drains directly into the water.

About half of the world's population lives near a coastline, such as this one in Mexico.

Even pollution that occurs far away from the shore can affect the coast. The rivers that empty into estuaries pass through farms and cities. Along the way, the rivers may pick up pollutants such as pesticides, fertilizers, oil, and other chemicals. Pollution that washes into the river—even kilometers away from the shore—will eventually end up in the estuary.

Governments, local organizations, and individuals work to protect and preserve shoreline environments in many states. Improved sewage treatment plants reduce the amount of human waste that ends up in shoreline environments. Laws that restrict dumping help reduce pollution along shorelines. Many states have shoreline sanctuaries where plants and animals are protected.

  What are three ways shorelines are protected?

4.1 Review

KEY CONCEPTS

1. Describe the characteristics of the intertidal zone.

2. Name and describe two coastal environments that border estuaries.

3. What human activities are harmful to shoreline environments?

CRITICAL THINKING

4. **Compare and Contrast** What similarities exist between salt marshes and mangrove forests? How are they different?

5. **Infer** Sometimes estuaries are called nursery areas. Why do you think estuaries may have been given that name?

⬤ CHALLENGE

6. **Identify Cause** A salinity meter placed in a tidal pool shows a dramatic decrease in salinity between 2 A.M. and 3 A.M. This decrease is followed by a gradual rise in salinity from 11 A.M. until 4 P.M. the next day. What might explain these changes?

MATH in SCIENCE

MATH TUTORIAL
CLASSZONE.COM
Click on Math Tutorial for more help with bar graphs.

Machines mounted on boats drill down into the ocean floor to collect sediment cores.

This tube contains a sediment core.

Tracking Contaminants

The layered sediments at the bottom of the ocean have formed over time. The particles in the deeper layers settled to the floor long ago, while those in the top layers settled out of the water more recently. By studying the amounts of pollutants in different layers of sediment, scientists can see how the water quality has changed over time. In 1991, scientists collected sediment cores north of Dash Point in Puget Sound. The table below shows levels of two pollutants, lead and arsenic, in the sediment layers for 1880, 1960, and 1990. The levels are measured in milligrams per kilogram dry weight (mg/kg d.w.).

Levels of Lead and Arsenic in Sediments		
Year	Lead (mg/kg d.w.)	Arsenic (mg/kg d.w.)
1880	10	6
1960	62	22
1990	45	17

You can use a double bar graph to analyze the data. A double bar graph shows two sets of data on the same graph. The first two bars of the graph are drawn for you below.

Example

(1) Copy the axes and labels.

(2) Draw bars for the lead data. Use the scale to determine the height of each bar, as shown.

(3) Draw the arsenic bars next to the lead bars.

(4) Shade the bars in different colors. Include a key.

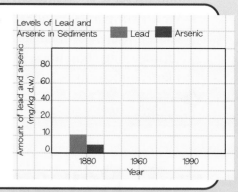

Make a double bar graph of the data by following the steps above. Use your graph to answer the following questions.

1. What happened to the levels of lead and arsenic between 1880 and 1960?

2. What happened to the levels of lead and arsenic between 1960 and 1990?

CHALLENGE Because lead can be harmful to humans, the use of leaded gasoline in new cars was banned in 1975 and the sale of lead-based paint was banned in 1978. How might these bans have affected the amount of lead in Puget Sound? Use evidence from your graph to support your answer.

Conditions differ away from shore.

◁ **BEFORE,** you learned	▷ **NOW,** you will learn
• Coasts support plants and animals • Estuaries and intertidal zones are coastal environments	• About ocean environments away from the coast • How ocean environments change with depth • How hydrothermal vents support life in the ocean

VOCABULARY

coral reef p. 122
kelp forest p. 124
phytoplankton p. 126
hydrothermal vent p. 128

EXPLORE Air Bladders

How can air make things float?

PROCEDURE

① Fill the container halfway with soda water.

② Add raisins to the container, one by one.

③ Observe for 5 minutes. Record your observations.

WHAT DO YOU THINK?

• How did the air bubbles control the movement of the raisins?

• Many ocean fish have an air-filled organ called an air bladder. The fish can control the amount of air in the bladder. How might the amount of air in the bladder change as a fish dives from the ocean surface to the bottom and then returns to the surface?

MATERIALS
• clear container
• soda water
• 5 raisins

Ocean environments change with depth and distance from shore.

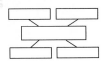

MAIN IDEA WEB
Remember to start a main idea web in your notebook for the blue heading.

Your journey through ocean environments continues as you leave the intertidal zone and move farther out into the ocean. First, you will visit the habitats found in the waters near shore. Next you will move out into the open ocean.

Near shore—in the waters over the continental shelf—sunlight reaches most of the way to the ocean bottom. Nutrients wash in from land. Temperature and salinity are nearly constant from the surface to the bottom. These conditions support many kinds of living things.

CHECK YOUR READING What are some characteristics of the environment near shore?

The waters near shore support diverse life forms.

More kinds of ocean life live in the waters near shore than in any other ocean environment. Microscopic organisms including bacteria, protists, plants, and animals live there. They share the waters near shore with plants as tall as ten-story buildings and animals larger than elephants. Each organism is part of a delicate and complex food web. You become part of this food web when you eat a fish from the waters near shore. In fact, most of the world's fish are caught in this ocean environment.

Two important habitats near shore are the kelp forest and the coral reef. Kelp forests are found in cooler waters, and coral reefs are found in tropical warm waters.

Coral Reefs

In warm, tropical regions of the globe, the waters near shore support coral reefs. **Coral reefs** are built-up limestone deposits formed by large colonies of ant-sized organisms called corals. Corals produce a hard limestone covering that remains after the corals die. New generations of corals grow on top of older limestone coverings. Although individual corals are small, coral reefs can be huge. Australia's Great Barrier Reef is about 2000 kilometers (1250 mi) long—as long as the distance from Chicago, Illinois, to San Antonio, Texas.

Corals rely on a special relationship with a kind of algae for almost all of their food needs. Tiny algae live inside individual corals. Like plants, the algae use sunlight to produce food through photosynthesis. The food algae produces provides the coral with most of its nutrition. In return, the coral provides some nutrients to the algae. Because the algae need sunlight to survive, coral reefs exist only in the ocean environment near shore, where sunlight reaches all the way to the ocean floor.

Coral reefs, which contain over 25 percent of all of the species of ocean life, help protect shorelines from wave and storm damage.

Coral Reefs

The nutrient-rich, sunlit waters near shore support a greater variety of life than any other part of the ocean.

near shore environment

The **anemone** can paralyze most fish with its stinging tentacles.

The **anemone fish** (also called the clown fish) is covered by mucus that protects it from the anemone. The anemone shelters the fish from predators. The anemone benefits by eating bits of food that the fish drops.

The **parrotfish** uses its hard teeth to chew on coral. It eats the algae that live in and on the coral. The hard coral skeletons get ground into sand as they pass through the parrotfish's digestive system.

The **moray eel** spends days hidden in cracks or holes in the reef. At night the eel comes out to hunt.

The **nudibranch** is related to snails but has no shell. It contains bad-tasting or poisonous chemicals that discourage fish from eating it.

The **giant clam** can grow to be over 1 meter (3 ft) long. It feeds by filtering tiny organisms from the water. Like corals, the giant clam gets some of its nutrients from algae that live within its own tissues.

READING VISUALS Which organisms in the diagram appear to be using nooks in the reef for shelter?

The huge amount and variety of life found at coral reefs compares with that found in rain forests. In fact, coral reefs contain over 25 percent of all the species of ocean life. Some reef inhabitants use nooks and crannies in the reef for shelter. Other inhabitants eat corals or feed on seaweed that grows on the corals. Clown fish, sea anemones, (uh-NEHM-uh-neez), sea urchins, starfish, giant clams, and parrotfish are some of the many colorful reef inhabitants.

Coral reefs are now endangered habitats. Pollution that drains off land or that is dumped directly into the water harms coral reefs. Some fishing practices also harm corals and other life at reefs.

 CHECK YOUR READING Why are coral reefs endangered?

Kelp Forests

In cold waters, a seaweed called kelp attaches itself to the ocean floor and grows as tall as 40 meters (130 ft)—about the length of an airline jet. Air-filled bulbs on the seaweed's stalks help it to float up toward the surface and remain upright underwater. Large communities of this seaweed form **kelp forests.** Like plants, kelps use sunlight to produce food. Because kelps need sunlight and grow in the ocean, kelp forests

Kelp forests, such as this one in California, provide food and shelter for many living things.

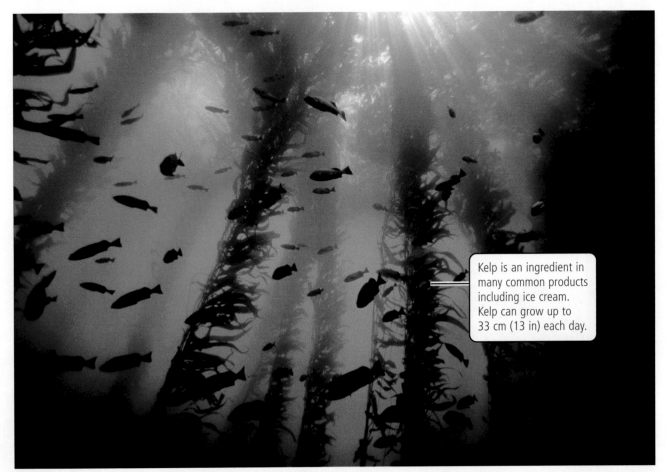

Kelp is an ingredient in many common products including ice cream. Kelp can grow up to 33 cm (13 in) each day.

A sea otter off the coast of California wraps itself in kelp.

are found only in the waters near shore, where sunlight reaches to the ocean floor. Thick kelp forests provide habitats for many organisms. Worms, starfish, lobsters, crabs, abalones, and octopuses are some of the animals that live among the crowded stands of kelp. Fish find shelter and food there. Sea otters dining on sea urchins anchor themselves to the thick mats that the kelps form on the surface.

 CHECK YOUR READING Why are kelp forests found only in waters near shore?

INVESTIGATE Floating

How do plankton float?

Plankton are microscopic organisms that drift in the ocean, where they are moved about by wind, waves, and currents. They must stay near the sunlit surface in order to live. Because plankton have no muscles, they cannot swim to stay afloat. In this lab, you will construct different-shaped clay models to determine how shape helps plankton stay near the ocean surface.

DESIGN —YOUR OWN—

PROCEDURE

(1) Fill the clear container with tap water.

(2) Use the clay to make several different shapes that you think will stay afloat.

(3) One by one, place your clay models on the surface of the water. Time how long each piece takes to reach the bottom. Record your observations.

WHAT DO YOU THINK?

• What were the characteristics of the clay shape that sank the slowest?

• What factors affected how fast your clay shape sunk?

CHALLENGE Some kinds of floating organisms release oil droplets or air bubbles to help them stay afloat. How could oil or air help them float?

SKILL FOCUS
Modeling

MATERIALS
• clear container
• water
• modeling clay
• watch with a second hand

TIME
30 minutes

Environments in the open ocean change with depth.

Out in the open ocean, conditions are different from these found in the waters near shore. Sunlight reaches through only the very top part of the open ocean. Nutrients sink down to the dark depths. There are no rocks, reefs, or big plants to provide shelter from predators. The open ocean covers a huge area but contains fewer living things than the waters near shore. Life is more spread out in the open ocean.

Surface Zone

The surface zone of the open ocean is the sunlit top 200 meters (650 ft). Microscopic floating organisms called **phytoplankton** (FY-toh-PLANGK-tuhn) live at or near the sunlit surface. Like plants, phytoplankton convert sunlight and carbon dioxide into food and oxygen. In fact, phytoplankton convert about as much carbon dioxide into oxygen as all land plants combined. Phytoplankton are an important source of the oxygen that you are breathing right now. Tiny floating animals called zooplankton eat phytoplankton. Zooplankton and phytoplankton then become food for fish, squids, and ocean mammals, such as whales.

Inhabitants of the surface zone must keep from sinking. To stay afloat, phytoplankton bodies have big surface areas and may use air bubbles or oil droplets to stay near the ocean surface. Many fish have an air-filled organ called an air bladder that helps the fish change depth. Changing the amount of air in the bladder allows these fish to move up and down in the water. When the bladder fills with air, the fish floats up toward the surface. Releasing air from the bladder allows the fish to dive down into deeper water.

READING TiP

Word parts can help you remember the meaning of *phytoplankton* and *zooplankton*. The prefix *phyto-* means "plant" and the prefix *zoo-* means "animal."

Deep Zone

The dark and cold deep zone of the open ocean lies under the surface zone. Because sunlight does not reach the deep zone, no plants can live there. Without plants for food, many deep-sea animals must either eat each other or rely on food drifting down from above.

The anglerfish in the photograph on page 127 has many of the common features of deep-sea animals. Its huge mouth and sharp teeth are typical of predators—animals that hunt and eat other animals. Many deep-sea animals glow in the dark, as fireflies do. A glowing extension sticks out from the head of the anglerfish and acts as bait to attract prey. Animals of the deepest waters often have small eyes—and some have no eyes at all. Among the animals found in the deep zone are lantern fish, squids, octopuses, and shrimp.

Life in the Open Ocean

The open ocean consists of a sunlit surface zone and a dark deep zone.

open ocean

dolphin

The **surface zone** is the top 200 meters of the ocean.

Many kinds of phytoplankton and zooplankton live in the surface zone.

zooplankton

jellyfish

The **deep zone** is the part of the ocean beneath the surface zone all the way to the ocean floor.

phytoplankton

No sunlight reaches below this line.

Sperm whales need to breathe air at the surface but may dive down hundreds of meters to hunt giant squid.

lantern fish

hatchet fish

mid-water shrimp

This extension glows in the dark and attracts prey.

The gulper eel's huge jaws can open wide enough to swallow animals as large as itself.

The anglerfish is a predator that lives in the deep zone.

Scientists estimate there are about 20 billion rattail fish in the ocean—over three times the number of people on Earth.

giant squid

The **deep zone** continues to the ocean floor.

Open ocean inhabitants shown here are not drawn to scale.

READING VISUALS Which are bigger, phytoplankton or zooplankton? How can you tell?

New discoveries about ocean life continue.

While investigating deep-sea sediments in 1977, scientists got quite a surprise. On the deep-ocean floor they found thriving communities of crabs, fish, mussels, shrimp, giant clams, and tubeworms. These animals live near openings in Earth's crust called **hydrothermal vents**. Cold ocean water that seeps into cracks in the ocean floor gets heated deep underground by hot magma. The heated water then rises up and gushes out into the ocean, forming hydrothermal vents.

Before the discovery of animal communities near vents, most scientists thought life was impossible on the dark ocean floor. On land, life depends on plants, which use sunlight to produce food. Without sunlight, how could these deep sea animals live?

Hydrothermal vents support many kinds of life, including clams, crabs, fish, tubeworms, and bacteria.

Scientists found that animals at hydrothermal vents depend on a special type of bacteria. Instead of making food from sunlight and carbon dioxide, like plants, these bacteria make food from chemicals released by the vents. The bacteria thus form the base of the food chain at the vents. Some of the animals living there eat the bacteria. Other animals, such as tubeworms, have the bacteria living within their bodies. Tubeworms do not eat and have no digestive system—they absorb all their food directly from the bacteria.

Because of its crushing pressure, darkness, and huge size, the deep ocean remains mostly unexplored. The discovery of animal communities at hydrothermal vents is a reminder that life may be possible even in seemingly impossible places. In fact, more recent explorations have even found life deep within the sediments of the ocean floor.

 CHECK YOUR READING Why were scientists surprised to find life at hydrothermal vents?

4.2 Review

KEY CONCEPTS

1. What are two environments in the waters near shore? Describe the characteristics of each.

2. How does the surface zone of the open ocean differ from the deep zone?

3. How do hydrothermal vents support life on the deep-ocean floor?

CRITICAL THINKING

4. **Predict** How might a change in the amount of phytoplankton in the ocean affect the world's atmosphere?

5. **Evaluate** Suppose you are seeking a site for a submarine station where scientists could live for months at a time. Which ocean environment would you choose, and why?

CHALLENGE

6. **Apply** Diatoms are tiny ocean organisms that convert carbon dioxide to oxygen. Describe the depth at which diatoms live and where they fit into the ocean food chain.

(magnified 200x)

Undersea Hot Spots

Deep within Earth, volcanic activity heats up water. When this water shoots out through a crack in the ocean floor, it forms a hydrothermal vent. These vents are among the world's strangest environments.

- The pressure of the ocean water is so high that the water emerging from the vents does not boil—even though it is as hot as 400°C (750°F).

- The water from the vents is so filled with minerals, particularly hydrogen sulfide, that it would poison most animals.

- Sunlight is so dim that the vents exist in near total darkness. However, they often glow slightly, perhaps due to heat radiation.

RESOURCE CENTER
CLASSZONE.COM

Learn more about hydrothermal vents.

When the hot water from the vent hits the nearly freezing ocean water, it cools rapidly. The minerals dissolved in the water settle out, sometimes creating a chimney around the vent. Some chimneys are as tall as 15-story buildings.

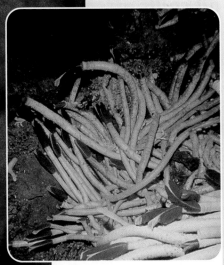

Tubeworms may grow up to 3 meters (10 ft) in length.

Home Sweet Home

Organisms that live anywhere else on Earth would not be able to survive the combination of pressure, heat, poisonous water, and darkness that exists near vents. Yet scientists have identified 500 species living near vents.

- Bacteria convert the sulfur in the water into energy. This is one of the few places on Earth where the living things at the base of a food chain get energy from chemicals rather than from sunlight.

- Tubeworms that grow up to 3 meters (10 ft) long and oversized clams thrive on the sulfur-eating bacteria.

- Crabs with gigantic legs that make them look like enormous spiders from a horror movie survive by eating the worms and other creatures.

Life Far Away

Organisms that live around the vents are like no others on Earth. However, could a different planet with a sulfur-rich environment support similar life forms? As scientists explore the possibility of life on other planets, they will look to hydrothermal vents for lessons on unusual life.

EXPLORE

1. **SEQUENCE** Create a diagram showing the relationship on the hydrothermal vent food chain between bacteria, crabs, and tubeworms.

2. **CHALLENGE** In 1997 scientists discovered features on Jupiter's moon Europa that look like icebergs floating on an ocean. Why did this discovery suggest that life might exist on Europa?

The ocean contains natural resources.

 BEFORE, you learned

- The waters near shore support diverse life forms
- The ocean environment changes with depth

▶ **NOW, you will learn**

- What living resources the ocean contains
- What mineral, energy, and other resources the ocean contains
- How pollution affects the ocean

VOCABULARY

overfishing p. 131
by-catch p. 132

EXPLORE Ocean Pollution

How do oil spills affect birds?

PROCEDURE

1. Fill the bowl with water.

2. Carefully place the feather on top of the water in the bowl.

3. Holding the end of the feather, blow on it to try to make the feather rise up out of the bowl. Record your observations.

4. Remove the feather and place three spoonfuls of oil into the bowl.

5. Repeat steps 2 and 3.

WHAT DO YOU THINK?

- How did the oil in the water affect the feather?
- Based on your findings, how do you think oil spills might affect birds?

MATERIALS
- bowl
- water
- feather
- spoon
- cooking oil

The ocean supports living resources.

MAIN IDEA WEB
Remember to start a main idea web in your notebook for the blue heading.

The ocean's many algae and animals are important food sources for people in many areas of the world, including the United States. In fact, the United States is the third largest consumer of seafood in the world. The ocean also supports living resources you do not eat for dinner. You have already read about phytoplankton, tiny ocean organisms. Phytoplankton are a very important resource because they produce much of the oxygen in Earth's air. Chemicals from other ocean organisms are used in medicines—including some that treat cancer. As research continues, scientists may find even more useful chemicals in ocean organisms.

Seafood and Algae

Across the United States, supermarkets sell ocean fish and shellfish. Most people, whether they realize it or not, eat seaweeds, too. These ocean algae are commonly used to thicken cheese, ice cream, and pudding. Seaweeds are also ingredients in nonfood products such as shaving cream and pesticides.

When you think of fishing, you might think of a person with a fishing pole catching one fish at a time. This method of fishing, however, is far too slow and inefficient for the commercial fishing industry to use. Instead, the fishing industry uses huge nets bigger than football fields or lines of fishing hooks kilometers long to catch large amounts of fish at a time. As you read this sentence, tens of thousands of nets and fishing lines trail in the ocean. The fishing industry uses sonar, satellites, airplanes, and other technology to find areas in the ocean that contain large numbers of fish.

Overfishing and By-Catch

Over the years, people have noticed that there are fewer and fewer fish than there once were. The main cause of the decrease in fish populations is **overfishing,** or catching fish at a faster rate than they can reproduce. Cod is one popular food fish that was nearly killed off by overfishing. Cod were once common in the North Atlantic, but now the cod population is very small. All of the world's fisheries, or main fishing areas of the ocean, are either overfished or very close to being overfished. Overfishing is a major threat to ocean environments.

VOCABULARY
You can use a description wheel to take notes about the term *overfishing.*

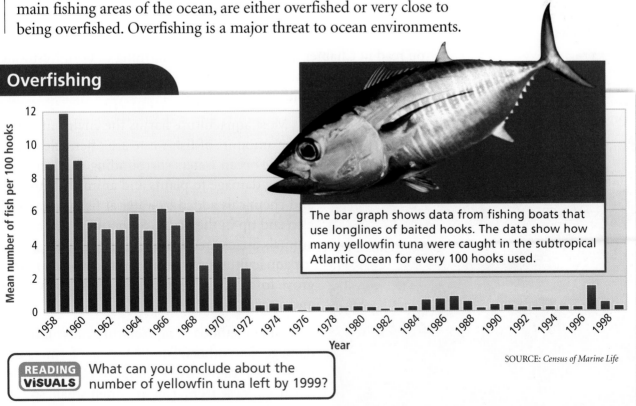

Overfishing

Mean number of fish per 100 hooks (vertical axis: 0, 2, 4, 6, 8, 10, 12)

Year (horizontal axis: 1958, 1960, 1962, 1964, 1966, 1968, 1970, 1972, 1974, 1976, 1978, 1980, 1982, 1984, 1986, 1988, 1990, 1992, 1994, 1996, 1998)

The bar graph shows data from fishing boats that use longlines of baited hooks. The data show how many yellowfin tuna were caught in the subtropical Atlantic Ocean for every 100 hooks used.

SOURCE: *Census of Marine Life*

READING VISUALS What can you conclude about the number of yellowfin tuna left by 1999?

Everything except the shrimp will be thrown away as by-catch from this boat in the Gulf of Mexico.

Fishing nets catch nearly everything in their path. A net that is being used to catch shrimp, for example, may also catch fish, turtles, sharks, dolphins, and other sea animals. The extra catch—everything besides the shrimp—gets tossed back into the ocean either dead or dying. **By-catch,** or by-kill, is the portion of animals that are caught in a net and then thrown away. Sometimes the by-catch is greater than the portion of fish or other animals the net is meant to catch.

To help reduce by-catch, fisheries started using nets designed to prevent animals such as turtles and dolphins from getting caught. Although these efforts have lessened the number of turtles and dolphins caught in fishing nets, fisheries worldwide still throw away about 30 percent of the fish they catch.

CHECK YOUR READING What harm does overfishing cause?

Saltwater Aquaculture

A shrimp farm extends out into the water off the island of Bora Bora in French Polynesia.

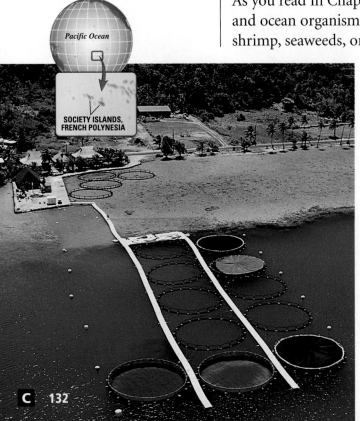

Pacific Ocean

SOCIETY ISLANDS, FRENCH POLYNESIA

As you read in Chapter 2, aquaculture is the farming of both freshwater and ocean organisms. Saltwater farmers may raise fish, oysters, mussels, shrimp, seaweeds, or other organisms.

Most aquaculture harms the environment. Huge amounts of fish waste are often released into the ocean waters surrounding fish farms, causing damage to plants and animals. Nutrients and chemicals added to water at fish farms may also end up in the ocean. Sometimes plants and animals are cleared from an area to make space for aquaculture. About half of the world's mangrove forests have been cleared for shrimp farms and similar uses.

Some methods of aquaculture cause more damage than others. For 4000 years, farmers in China have raised fish without causing much harm. Chinese fish farms are often small, so they release less waste than larger farms.

The ocean contains nonliving resources.

Ocean water itself is a valuable resource for people living in regions with little fresh water. As you read in Chapter 2, desalination is the process by which salt is removed from seawater. Desalinated seawater is a major portion of the fresh water used by many Middle Eastern countries, such as Saudi Arabia.

Many of the natural resources found on land are also found in the ocean. It is often less expensive to remove resources from the land than from the ocean, so many of the ocean's resources are not currently mined. However, as resources on land are used up and new technology makes ocean exploration and mining easier, ocean mining may increase.

Energy Resources

Oil and gas form from the remains of living organisms. In the ocean, organisms are concentrated in the waters over the continental shelf. Oil deposits, therefore, are found near shore. Oil and gas are pumped from the continental shelf of every continent but Antarctica. About 30 percent of the world's oil is pumped from deposits under the ocean floor.

Huge anchored platforms serve as artificial islands that house workers and the necessary equipment for drilling offshore oil wells. The platforms are built to withstand ocean currents, tides, and weather conditions such as storms. Underwater pipelines carry the oil to shore.

Oil is pumped from the ocean floor at huge anchored platforms such as this one in the North Sea.

Offshore Drilling

Oil and natural gas are pumped up to the platform, separated, and then pumped down to storage tanks on the sea floor.

Tankers load oil and gas at buoys.

Oil and gas are piped to shore.

storage tanks

natural gas reservoir

oil reservoir

Minerals and Rocks

When rivers empty into the sea, sediments carried by the rivers drop to the bottom. These sediments may contain phosphorite, iron, copper, lead, gold, tin, diamonds, and other minerals. Because these minerals wash into the ocean from land, most of them are found in areas near shore. It is currently too expensive to mine many of these minerals.

Some minerals are found away from shore. Nodules (NAHJ-oolz) are lumps of minerals that are scattered across the deep-ocean floor. The nodules are small at first, but they can build up over millions of years to a size of as much as a meter across. Nodules contain valuable manganese, iron, and cobalt, which are used to make metals such as steel. Nodules are not mined because it would be very expensive to remove them from the ocean floor. In the future, however, nodules may be removed—perhaps with giant vacuums.

Nodules are found away from the coast on the deep-ocean floor.

The Ocean's Energy and Mineral Resources

The ocean floor contains valuable energy and mineral resources.

Legend:
- Oil and gas
- Nodules
- Diamonds
- Gold
- Tin
- Phosphorite

READING VISUALS Which ocean environment contains most of the known energy and mineral resources?

When ocean water evaporates, salt is left behind.

Each of these mounds is a pile of salt harvested from ocean water in Thailand.

A mineral you eat is also removed from the ocean. About one-third of the world's table salt comes from the ocean. Ocean water is left to evaporate in flat, shallow areas. As the water evaporates, salts are left behind.

Sand and gravel might not be the first things you think of when you think of important resources. However, they are building materials used in concrete and cement. Sand and gravel are currently scraped off the sea floor in many locations near shore.

Pollution affects the ocean.

Every part of the ocean is polluted. Solid waste—such as plastic garbage, tar balls, and hypodermic needles—is a visible form of pollution along ocean shorelines. Trash washes up on beaches worldwide, even on the beaches of remote islands. Sea animals may mistake trash for food and eat plastic that can block their digestive systems. Animals also get tangled in and even strangled by plastic waste.

Although you may not see this much garbage on every beach, trash washes up on beaches all over the world—even on remote islands.

Most ocean pollution is harder to see than solid waste. Chemical pollutants, nuclear wastes, and heavy metals like mercury and lead are found in all parts of the ocean. These pollutants are known to harm and kill ocean life. They are also harmful to humans. Pregnant women are sometimes advised not to eat tuna and other fish because the fish may contain low levels of toxic mercury. Although the small amounts of mercury may not harm an adult, they could damage the developing child.

Human waste, sewage, and fertilizers have caused dead zones in the ocean—areas where no plants or animals can live. These pollutants contain nutrients and cause a huge increase in the amount of algae that live in an area. When the algae die, bacteria consume them. The large numbers of bacteria use up all the oxygen in an area of ocean. Without oxygen, the animals in the area cannot survive.

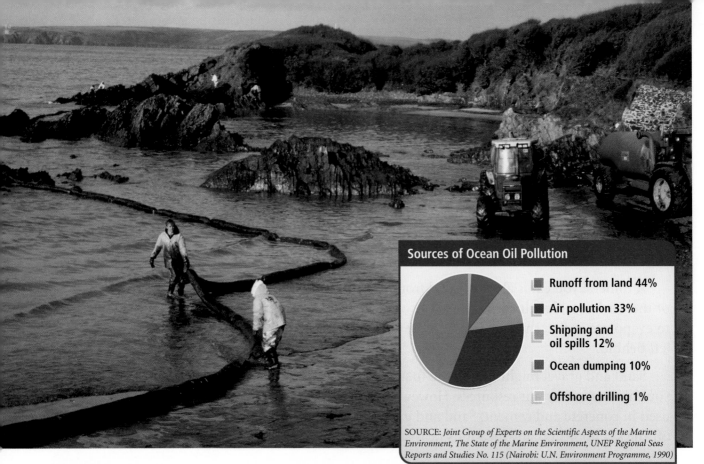

Sources of Ocean Oil Pollution

- ■ Runoff from land 44%
- ■ Air pollution 33%
- ■ Shipping and oil spills 12%
- ■ Ocean dumping 10%
- ■ Offshore drilling 1%

SOURCE: *Joint Group of Experts on the Scientific Aspects of the Marine Environment, The State of the Marine Environment, UNEP Regional Seas Reports and Studies No. 115 (Nairobi: U.N. Environment Programme, 1990)*

Oil spills are dramatic and disastrous events. However, most oil pollution in the ocean is washed in from land.

Some pollutants are dumped directly into the ocean. Many other pollutants wash from the land into the ocean or into rivers that flow into the ocean. Although oil spills are dramatic events that kill many animals, they account for only a small percentage of the oil pollution in the ocean. More oil enters the ocean by washing off the land than by being spilled. In addition to oil, pesticides, fertilizers, and many other pollutants wash into the ocean from land.

 CHECK YOUR READING What is the source of most of the ocean's oil pollution?

Preventing Ocean Pollution

 RESOURCE CENTER
CLASSZONE.COM

Find out more about ocean pollution and pollution prevention.

Ocean pollution can be prevented or reduced. In 1988, for example, the United States government restricted the use of a harmful chemical that had been used in ship paint. As a result, levels of the chemical dropped in certain areas of the ocean, and the health of some types of sea life, such as oysters, improved. Government organizations have also banned the dumping of some chemicals into the ocean. These bans have successfully reduced some kinds of pollution.

Individuals can help prevent or reduce ocean pollution. Many people may not realize that oil or other chemicals dumped in a drain or sewer or on the ground can end up in the ocean. The proper disposal of household chemicals and other toxic substances could reduce ocean pollution. The Environmental Protection Agency (EPA) has information about the proper disposal of many common chemicals.

Some oyster populations recovered after the use of a toxic chemical in ship paint was restricted. This photo shows an oyster farm in Washington State.

oyster

Global Pollution Problems

Remember that the ocean is a connected global body of water. Ocean currents circulate water around the globe and carry pollutants to all parts of the ocean. Pollution that occurs in any part of the world can affect the whole ocean.

The United Nations, through its 1994 Law of the Sea, attempts to manage ocean resources and to conserve ocean environments. The law calls on all countries to enforce pollution controls. It also sets pollution rules for ships operating in international waters, regulates fishing, and attempts to divide rights to undersea resources. This international law is an important step toward protecting the ocean and its resources for future generations.

 CHECK YOUR READING Why is ocean pollution a global problem?

Review

KEY CONCEPTS	CRITICAL THINKING	⬥ CHALLENGE
1. Describe one living resource contained in the ocean and how its use affects the ocean environment.	**4. Connect** How could ocean pollution affect your life?	**6. Evaluate** Most of the ocean does not belong to any country or government. Who do you think should be responsible for limiting pollution in areas outside country borders? Who should be able to claim ownership of resources in these areas?
2. Describe one nonliving resource contained in the ocean and how its use affects the ocean environment.	**5. Sequence** Describe how oil from a car many miles away from the shore could reach the ocean.	
3. How does pollution affect the ocean?		

CHAPTER INVESTIGATION

Population Sampling

OVERVIEW AND PURPOSE Scientists have found that overfishing is decreasing the population of many organisms. They have also found that the population of some other organisms are increasing. How do scientists know this? They count the number of individuals in a small measured area, called a quadrat, then estimate from their counts how many organisms live in a larger area. Repeated samplings over time allow them to determine whether populations are growing or decreasing. In this investigation you will

- count the number of items in a "population" using a quadrat technique
- use small and large quadrats to form two different estimates for the size of a "population"

MATERIALS
- calculator
- removable tape

▶ Procedure

1. As a class, brainstorm some objects that you might find in your classroom—for example: pencil, protractor, calculator, or ball cap. Choose one of those objects to count. You will estimate the population at your school of this object.

2. Remove all of the objects that your class decided to count from bags and drawers. For example, if your class is counting pencils, everyone should remove all of their pencils from their bags and place them on their desks.

3. Divide your classroom into four equal-sized pieces. Use removable tape to mark the boundaries of each quadrat. Label the quadrats A, B, C, and D.

4. Count the items in one of the quadrats—either A, B, C, or D. Record the number of objects in your **Science Notebook.**

5. Find the total classroom population of your object by combining your data with the data from groups who counted other quadrats. Record the total classroom population.

▶ Observe and Analyze

Write It Up

1. **RECORD** Make a data table like the one in the notebook.

2. **CALCULATE** Multiply the number of each item you counted in your quadrat by four. This will give you an estimate of the number of each item in your classroom. Record your answer.

3. **CALCULATE** For this investigation, assume that each classroom in your school is the same size as your classroom. Your teacher will provide you with the number of classrooms in your entire school. Multiply your answer from question 2 by the number of classrooms in your school. This will give you an estimate of the number of each item in your school. Record your answer.

4. **CALCULATE** Now estimate the population of the object in the whole school using the total count from the classroom. Multiply the total classroom population by the number of classrooms in your school. This will give you a second estimate for the population of each item in your school. Record your answer.

▶ Conclude

Write It Up

1. **COMPARE** How does your school population estimate based on your small quadrat count compare with your school population estimate based on your total classroom estimate?

2. **INFER** If there was a difference between your two total population estimates, what do you think could explain the difference?

3. **INFER** Do you think your total population estimate for your object in the school is accurate? Explain.

4. **COMPARE** How would your population estimate compare to one done the same way ten years ago? ten years from now? Explain your reasoning.

5. **IDENTIFY LIMITS** What possible limitations or sources of error could have affected your results?

6. **CONNECT** How would you need to change your procedure if you were sampling an ocean fish population? Give at least two examples.

▶ INVESTIGATE Further

CHALLENGE Suppose your quadrat size was one square meter. How would this have affected your accuracy? Imagine that you were given a wooden frame measuring one square meter in size. How would you change your procedure to best sample the school "population" using this smaller quadrat?

Population Sampling
Observe and Analyze
Table 1. Population Data

Quadrat	Number of Items	Classroom Population Estimate	School Population Estimate (No. in classroom × No. of classrooms in school)
A	7	$7 \times 4 = 28$	
B			
C			
D			
Total: classroom count			

the BIG idea

The ocean supports life and contains natural resources.

CONTENT REVIEW
CLASSZONE.COM

◀ **KEY CONCEPTS SUMMARY**

4.1 Ocean coasts support plant and animal life.

Organisms in the intertidal zone are covered by water during high tide and exposed to the air during low tide.

high tide mark

low tide mark

intertidal zone

- Fresh water and salt water mix in estuaries.
- Salt marshes and mangrove forests form along coasts.

VOCABULARY
habitat p. 114
intertidal zone p. 114
estuary p. 116
wetland p. 116

4.2 Conditions differ away from shore.

near shore environment
open ocean

Life in the open ocean is more spread out. The surface zone is lit by the Sun. The deep zone is dark.

The waters near shore support more life than any other part of the ocean.

VOCABULARY
coral reef p. 122
kelp forest p. 124
phytoplankton p. 126
hydrothermal vent p. 128

4.3 The ocean contains natural resources.

Living ocean resources include seafood and algae. Overfishing and pollution threaten ocean environments.

Nonliving ocean resources include oil, natural gas, and minerals.

VOCABULARY
overfishing p. 131
by-catch p. 132

Reviewing Vocabulary

Copy and complete the chart below. In the middle column, list characteristics of each environment. In the last column, list examples of organisms that live in each environment.

Vocabulary Term	Characteristics	Organisms
1. intertidal zone		
2. estuary		
3. coral reef		
4. kelp forest		
5. hydrothermal vent		

Reviewing Key Concepts

Multiple Choice *Choose the letter of the best answer.*

6. An environment that contains all the necessary requirements for an organism to live is called
   a. the surface zone   **c.** a habitat
   b. a nodule   **d.** an estuary

7. Where would you expect to find ocean organisms that are able to survive out of water and withstand drastic changes in salinity?
   a. the intertidal zone   **c.** the open ocean
   b. a coral reef   **d.** a hydrothermal vent

8. Two kinds of wetlands that border estuaries are
   a. coral reefs and mangrove forests
   b. salt marshes and mangrove forests
   c. tidal pools and salt marshes
   d. mangrove forests and tidal pools

9. Tiny plantlike organisms that float at the surface of the ocean are called
   a. phytoplankton   **c.** corals
   b. kelps   **d.** bottom dwellers

10. Where are hydrothermal vents located?
   a. in the intertidal zone
   b. on the deep-ocean floor
   c. on coral reefs
   d. in kelp forests

11. The bacteria that form the base of the food chain at hydrothermal vents convert
   a. dim sunlight that filters down into food
   b. heat from the vents into food
   c. phytoplankton that drift down into food
   d. chemicals released by the vents into food

12. Overfishing is best described as catching
   a. more fish than people can eat
   b. fish at a faster rate than they can reproduce
   c. other kinds of fish than the ones intended
   d. fish with huge nets and long lines of hooks

13. Why are 30 percent of the fish that are caught by commercial fishing boats thrown away?
   a. Fishing nets catch everything in their path.
   b. Smaller fish are thrown back into the ocean.
   c. Oil pollution has damaged many of the fish.
   d. Large phytoplankton interfere with nets and lines.

Short Answer *Write a short answer to each question.*

14. How does human activity affect shoreline environments?

15. Name the three categories of ocean life, and give an example of an organism for each category.

16. What resources does the ocean contain?

17. What kinds of pollution are found in the ocean?

18. Why is ocean pollution a global problem?

Thinking Critically

Use the maps shown below to answer the next three questions.

Catch per Hundred Hooks, 1958

Catch per Hundred Hooks, 1999

	<1
	1-2
	2-3
	3-4
	4-5
	5-6
	6-8
	8-10
	>10

SOURCE: *Census of Marine Life*

These maps show data from Japanese fishing boats of the total numbers of fish that were caught in 1958 and 1999. The color code shows the number of fish caught per 100 hooks on longlines.

19. INTERPRET What do these data show about how ocean fish populations have changed between 1958 and 1999?

20. INFER The data for 1999 were collected over a wider area than were the data for 1958. What might explain the wider area for the 1999 data?

21. PREDICT What would you expect a map with data for the current year to look like? Describe it in terms of color and the extent of the data.

22. COMPARE AND CONTRAST What similarities exist between kelp forests and coral reefs? How are they different?

23. INFER It is believed that life on Earth first appeared in the oceans. In which ocean zone might life have first appeared? Explain your reasoning.

24. APPLY The sargassum frogfish lives among sargassum algae, a type of algae that grows attached to the ocean floor. In which ocean zones could this species of frogfish possibly live? In which could it not live? Explain.

25. SYNTHESIZE A marine sanctuary is an area of the ocean that is protected from fishing and most human use. An environmental organization is trying to decide whether to establish a marine sanctuary. Based on what you have learned, write a short letter telling the organization whether you think a marine sanctuary is a good idea and in which ocean zone the sanctuary should be established.

the BIG idea

26. COMPARE AND CONTRAST Look again at the photograph on pages 110–111. Now that you have finished the chapter, make a Venn diagram to answer the question on the photograph in more detail. For information about Venn diagrams, see page R49.

27. PROVIDE EXAMPLES What types of habitats and resources does the ocean contain? To answer, copy the concept map below into your notebook and add to it. For information about concept maps, see page R49.

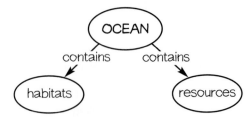

OCEAN
contains — habitats
contains — resources

UNIT PROJECTS

Check your schedule for your unit project. How are you doing? Be sure that you've placed data or notes from your research in your project folder.

Standardized Test Practice

For practice on your
state test, go to . . .
TEST PRACTICE
CLASSZONE.COM

Analyzing a Diagram

The diagram below shows a side view of part of the ocean. Use the diagram to answer the questions below.

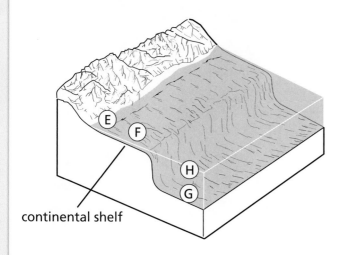

continental shelf

1. Which area is most affected by tides?
  a. E   **c.** G
  b. F   **d.** H

2. Kelps are plantlike algae that grow attached to the ocean bottom. At which points could kelps live?
  a. H and F   **c.** F and G
  b. F only   **d.** G only

3. Where is water the coldest?
  a. E   **c.** G
  b. F   **d.** H

4. Which statement best explains why plantlike algae do not live at G?
  a. The water is too salty at position G.
  b. The water is too cold at position G.
  c. There is not enough oxygen at position G.
  d. There is not enough sunlight at position G.

5. Which trait is most useful for fish in position H as they try to escape predators?
  a. the ability to hide in rocks
  b. the ability to blend in with plants
  c. the ability to swim very fast
  d. the ability to swim without sunlight

6. A limpet is an ocean snail whose flat shape allows it to remain attached to rocks even when waves are pounding against the rocks. Where does the limpet probably live?
  a. E   **c.** G
  b. F   **d.** H

Extended Response

The illustration on the right shows part of an ocean food web. Use the illustration to answer the next two questions in detail.

7. Describe how the killer whale, salmon, and zooplankton in the illustration are linked.

8. What would happen if overfishing caused herring to be removed from the food web? Describe how the other organisms would be affected.

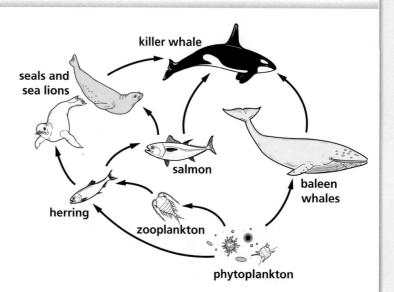

killer whale

seals and sea lions

salmon

baleen whales

herring

zooplankton

phytoplankton

Today's Scientist at Work

Name: Evan Forde	
Degree: MS, Marine Geology and, Geophysics, Columbia University	
Profession: Research Scientist, National Oceanic and Atmospheric Association (NOAA)	
Location: Miami, FL	

Photo courtesy of the National Oceanic and Atmospheric Administration (NOAA)

One day, Evan Forde heard that the National Oceanic and Atmospheric Administration (NOAA) was opening a lab near Miami, FL. He quickly applied for a job. When he went to interview, however, he was told there were no jobs. But one director had a technician position specifically created for him. That was back in 1973. Mr. Forde still works at NOAA. He has held several different jobs. Currently, he is a researcher in the AOML's Satellite Remote Sensing Group.

In his career, Mr. Forde has spent a lot of time at sea. He was the first African-American oceanographer to make dives in a submersible. A submersible is a submarine specially designed for scientific research. He studied how undersea canyons formed. His group also discovered some previously unknown sea creatures. His greatest accomplishment was discovering massive sediment slumping off the coast of New Jersey. Sediment slumping is similar to underwater landslides. The finding re-sulted in steps being taken to protect the area.

Today, Mr. Forde works with satellites. He looks at how ocean weather systems may affect the development of hurricanes. He also studies how ocean activity contributes to long term climate change. He uses comput-ers in his work, which allow him to do in minutes what it used to take him weeks to do when he first started.

This is a 3-D image of Norfolk Canyon. It is located off the coast of Virginia. Evan Forde has studied the geology of this canyon.

NORFOLK CANYON

In 2001 NOAA honored Mr. Forde as its Research Employee of the Year. He has spoken to more than 18,000 schoolchildren about science. He claims he loves his job so much that he would still do science even if he were a millionaire.

Captain Albert E. Theberge, NOAA Corps (ret.)

Student Resource Handbooks

Scientific Thinking Handbook

Making Observations

An **observation** is an act of noting and recording an event, characteristic, behavior, or anything else detected with an instrument or with the senses.

Observations allow you to make informed hypotheses and to gather data for experiments. Careful observations often lead to ideas for new experiments. There are two categories of observations:

- **Quantitative observations** can be expressed in numbers and include records of time, temperature, mass, distance, and volume.

- **Qualitative observations** include descriptions of sights, sounds, smells, and textures.

EXAMPLE

A student dissolved 30 grams of Epsom salts in water, poured the solution into a dish, and let the dish sit out uncovered overnight. The next day, she made the following observations of the Epsom salt crystals that grew in the dish.

Table 1. Observations of Epsom Salt Crystals

To determine the mass, the student found the mass of the dish before and after growing the crystals and then used subtraction to find the difference.

The student measured several crystals and calculated the mean length. (To learn how to calculate the mean of a data set, see page R36.)

Quantitative Observations	Qualitative Observations
• mass = 30 g • mean crystal length = 0.5 cm • longest crystal length = 2 cm	• Crystals are clear. • Crystals are long, thin, and rectangular. • White crust has formed around edge of dish.

Photographs or sketches are useful for recording qualitative observations.

Epsom salt crystals

MORE ABOUT OBSERVING

- Make quantitative observations whenever possible. That way, others will know exactly what you observed and be able to compare their results with yours.

- It is always a good idea to make qualitative observations too. You never know when you might observe something unexpected.

Predicting and Hypothesizing

A **prediction** is an expectation of what will be observed or what will happen. A **hypothesis** is a tentative explanation for an observation or scientific problem that can be tested by further investigation.

EXAMPLE

Suppose you have made two paper airplanes and you wonder why one of them tends to glide farther than the other one.

1. Start by asking a question.

2. Make an educated guess. After examination, you notice that the wings of the airplane that flies farther are slightly larger than the wings of the other airplane.

3. Write a prediction based upon your educated guess, in the form of an "If . . . , then . . ." statement. Write the independent variable after the word *if*, and the dependent variable after the word *then*.

4. To make a hypothesis, explain why you think what you predicted will occur. Write the explanation after the word *because*.

---

1. Why does one of the paper airplanes glide farther than the other?

2. The size of an airplane's wings may affect how far the airplane will glide.

3. Prediction: If I make a paper airplane with larger wings, then the airplane will glide farther.

To read about independent and dependent variables, see page R30.

4. Hypothesis: If I make a paper airplane with larger wings, then the airplane will glide farther, because the additional surface area of the wing will produce more lift.

Notice that the part of the hypothesis after *because* adds an explanation of why the airplane will glide farther.

MORE ABOUT HYPOTHESES

- The results of an experiment cannot prove that a hypothesis is correct. Rather, the results either support or do not support the hypothesis.

- Valuable information is gained even when your hypothesis is not supported by your results. For example, it would be an important discovery to find that wing size is not related to how far an airplane glides.

- In science, a hypothesis is supported only after many scientists have conducted many experiments and produced consistent results.

Inferring

An **inference** is a logical conclusion drawn from the available evidence and prior knowledge. Inferences are often made from observations.

EXAMPLE

A student observing a set of acorns noticed something unexpected about one of them. He noticed a white, soft-bodied insect eating its way out of the acorn.

> The student recorded these observations.

Observations
- There is a hole in the acorn, about 0.5 cm in diameter, where the insect crawled out.
- There is a second hole, which is about the size of a pinhole, on the other side of the acorn.
- The inside of the acorn is hollow.

> Here are some inferences that can be made on the basis of the observations.

Inferences
- The insect formed from the material inside the acorn, grew to its present size, and ate its way out of the acorn.
- The insect crawled through the smaller hole, ate the inside of the acorn, grew to its present size, and ate its way out of the acorn.
- An egg was laid in the acorn through the smaller hole. The egg hatched into a larva that ate the inside of the acorn, grew to its present size, and ate its way out of the acorn.

> When you make inferences, be sure to look at all of the evidence available and combine it with what you already know.

MORE ABOUT INFERENCES

Inferences depend both on observations and on the knowledge of the people making the inferences. Ancient people who did not know that organisms are produced only by similar organisms might have made an inference like the first one. A student today might look at the same observations and make the second inference. A third student might have knowledge about this particular insect and know that it is never small enough to fit through the smaller hole, leading her to the third inference.

Identifying Cause and Effect

In a **cause-and-effect relationship,** one event or characteristic is the result of another. Usually an effect follows its cause in time.

There are many examples of cause-and-effect relationships in everyday life.

Cause	Effect
Turn off a light.	Room gets dark.
Drop a glass.	Glass breaks.
Blow a whistle.	Sound is heard.

Scientists must be careful not to infer a cause-and-effect relationship just because one event happens after another event. When one event occurs after another, you cannot infer a cause-and-effect relationship on the basis of that information alone. You also cannot conclude that one event caused another if there are alternative ways to explain the second event. A scientist must demonstrate through experimentation or continued observation that an event was truly caused by another event.

EXAMPLE

Make an Observation

Suppose you have a few plants growing outside. When the weather starts getting colder, you bring one of the plants indoors. You notice that the plant you brought indoors is growing faster than the others are growing. You cannot conclude from your observation that the change in temperature was the cause of the increased plant growth, because there are alternative explanations for the observation. Some possible explanations are given below.

- The humidity indoors caused the plant to grow faster.

- The level of sunlight indoors caused the plant to grow faster.

- The indoor plant's being noticed more often and watered more often than the outdoor plants caused it to grow faster.

- The plant that was brought indoors was healthier than the other plants to begin with.

To determine which of these factors, if any, caused the indoor plant to grow faster than the outdoor plants, you would need to design and conduct an experiment.

See pages R28–R35 for information about designing experiments.

Recognizing Bias

Television, newspapers, and the Internet are full of experts claiming to have scientific evidence to back up their claims. How do you know whether the claims are really backed up by good science?

Bias is a slanted point of view, or personal prejudice. The goal of scientists is to be as objective as possible and to base their findings on facts instead of opinions. However, bias often affects the conclusions of researchers, and it is important to learn to recognize bias.

When scientific results are reported, you should consider the source of the information as well as the information itself. It is important to critically analyze the information that you see and read.

SOURCES OF BIAS

There are several ways in which a report of scientific information may be biased. Here are some questions that you can ask yourself:

1. Who is sponsoring the research?

   Sometimes, the results of an investigation are biased because an organization paying for the research is looking for a specific answer. This type of bias can affect how data are gathered and interpreted.

2. Is the research sample large enough?

   Sometimes research does not include enough data. The larger the sample size, the more likely that the results are accurate, assuming a truly random sample.

3. In a survey, who is answering the questions?

   The results of a survey or poll can be biased. The people taking part in the survey may have been specifically chosen because of how they would answer. They may have the same ideas or lifestyles. A survey or poll should make use of a random sample of people.

4. Are the people who take part in a survey biased?

   People who take part in surveys sometimes try to answer the questions the way they think the researcher wants them to answer. Also, in surveys or polls that ask for personal information, people may be unwilling to answer questions truthfully.

SCIENTIFIC BIAS

It is also important to realize that scientists have their own biases because of the types of research they do and because of their scientific viewpoints. Two scientists may look at the same set of data and come to completely different conclusions because of these biases. However, such disagreements are not necessarily bad. In fact, a critical analysis of disagreements is often responsible for moving science forward.

Identifying Faulty Reasoning

Faulty reasoning is wrong or incorrect thinking. It leads to mistakes and to wrong conclusions. Scientists are careful not to draw unreasonable conclusions from experimental data. Without such caution, the results of scientific investigations may be misleading.

EXAMPLE

Scientists try to make generalizations based on their data to explain as much about nature as possible. If only a small sample of data is looked at, however, a conclusion may be faulty. Suppose a scientist has studied the effects of the El Niño and La Niña weather patterns on flood damage in California from 1989 to 1995. The scientist organized the data in the bar graph below.

The scientist drew the following conclusions:

1. The La Niña weather pattern has no effect on flooding in California.

2. When neither weather pattern occurs, there is almost no flood damage.

3. A weak or moderate El Niño produces a small or moderate amount of flooding.

4. A strong El Niño produces a lot of flooding.

Flood and Storm Damage in California

Estimated damage (millions of dollars)

- Weak–moderate El Niño
- Strong El Niño

Starting year of season
(July 1–June 30)

SOURCE: *Governor's Office of Emergency Services, California*

For the six-year period of the scientist's investigation, these conclusions may seem to be reasonable. However, a six-year study of weather patterns may be too small of a sample for the conclusions to be supported. Consider the following graph, which shows information that was gathered from 1949 to 1997.

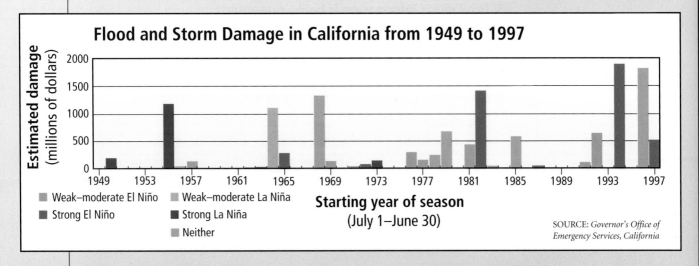

Flood and Storm Damage in California from 1949 to 1997

Estimated damage (millions of dollars)

- Weak–moderate El Niño
- Strong El Niño
- Weak–moderate La Niña
- Strong La Niña
- Neither

Starting year of season
(July 1–June 30)

SOURCE: *Governor's Office of Emergency Services, California*

The only one of the conclusions that all of this information supports is number 3: a weak or moderate El Niño produces a small or moderate amount of flooding. By collecting more data, scientists can be more certain of their conclusions and can avoid faulty reasoning.

Analyzing Statements

To **analyze** a statement is to examine its parts carefully. Scientific findings are often reported through media such as television or the Internet. A report that is made public often focuses on only a small part of research. As a result, it is important to question the sources of information.

Evaluate Media Claims

To **evaluate** a statement is to judge it on the basis of criteria you've established. Sometimes evaluating means deciding whether a statement is true.

Reports of scientific research and findings in the media may be misleading or incomplete. When you are exposed to this information, you should ask yourself some questions so that you can make informed judgments about the information.

1. **Does the information come from a credible source?**

   Suppose you learn about a new product and it is stated that scientific evidence proves that the product works. A report from a respected news source may be more believable than an advertisement paid for by the product's manufacturer.

2. **How much evidence supports the claim?**

   Often, it may seem that there is new evidence every day of something in the world that either causes or cures an illness. However, information that is the result of several years of work by several different scientists is more credible than an advertisement that does not even cite the subjects of the experiment.

3. **How much information is being presented?**

   Science cannot solve all questions, and scientific experiments often have flaws. A report that discusses problems in a scientific study may be more believable than a report that addresses only positive experimental findings.

4. **Is scientific evidence being presented by a specific source?**

   Sometimes scientific findings are reported by people who are called experts or leaders in a scientific field. But if their names are not given or their scientific credentials are not reported, their statements may be less credible than those of recognized experts.

Differentiate Between Fact and Opinion

Sometimes information is presented as a fact when it may be an opinion. When scientific conclusions are reported, it is important to recognize whether they are based on solid evidence. Again, you may find it helpful to ask yourself some questions.

1. **What is the difference between a fact and an opinion?**

   A **fact** is a piece of information that can be strictly defined and proved true. An **opinion** is a statement that expresses a belief, value, or feeling. An opinion cannot be proved true or false. For example, a person's age is a fact, but if someone is asked how old they feel, it is impossible to prove the person's answer to be true or false.

2. **Can opinions be measured?**

   Yes, opinions can be measured. In fact, surveys often ask for people's opinions on a topic. But there is no way to know whether or not an opinion is the truth.

HOW TO DIFFERENTIATE FACT FROM OPINION

Human Activities and the Environment

Unfortunately, human use of fossil fuels is one of the most significant developments of the past few centuries. Humans rely on fossil fuels, a non-renewable energy resource, for more than 90 percent of their energy needs.

This careless misuse of our planet's resources has resulted in pollution, global warming, and the destruction of fragile ecosystems. For example, oil pipelines carry more than one million barrels of oil each day across tundra regions. Transporting oil across such areas can only result in oil spills that poison the land for decades.

Opinions

Notice words or phrases that express beliefs or feelings. The words *unfortunately* and *careless* show that opinions are being expressed.

Opinion

Look for statements that speculate about events. These statements are opinions, because they cannot be proved.

Facts

Statements that contain statistics tend to be facts. Writers often use facts to support their opinions.

Lab Handbook

Safety Rules

Before you work in the laboratory, read these safety rules twice. Ask your teacher to explain any rules that you do not completely understand. Refer to these rules later on if you have questions about safety in the science classroom.

Directions

- Read all directions and make sure that you understand them before starting an investigation or lab activity. If you do not understand how to do a procedure or how to use a piece of equipment, ask your teacher.
- Do not begin any investigation or touch any equipment until your teacher has told you to start.
- Never experiment on your own. If you want to try a procedure that the directions do not call for, ask your teacher for permission first.
- If you are hurt or injured in any way, tell your teacher immediately.

Dress Code

goggles

apron

gloves

- Wear goggles when
  — using glassware, sharp objects, or chemicals
  — heating an object
  — working with anything that can easily fly up into the air and hurt someone's eye
- Tie back long hair or hair that hangs in front of your eyes.
- Remove any article of clothing—such as a loose sweater or a scarf—that hangs down and may touch a flame, chemical, or piece of equipment.
- Observe all safety icons calling for the wearing of eye protection, gloves, and aprons.

Heating and Fire Safety

fire safety

heating safety

- Keep your work area neat, clean, and free of extra materials.
- Never reach over a flame or heat source.
- Point objects being heated away from you and others.
- Never heat a substance or an object in a closed container.
- Never touch an object that has been heated. If you are unsure whether something is hot, treat it as though it is. Use oven mitts, clamps, tongs, or a test-tube holder.
- Know where the fire extinguisher and fire blanket are kept in your classroom.
- Do not throw hot substances into the trash. Wait for them to cool or use the container your teacher puts out for disposal.

Electrical Safety

electrical
safety

- Never use lamps or other electrical equipment with frayed cords.
- Make sure no cord is lying on the floor where someone can trip over it.
- Do not let a cord hang over the side of a counter or table so that the equipment can easily be pulled or knocked to the floor.
- Never let cords hang into sinks or other places where water can be found.
- Never try to fix electrical problems. Inform your teacher of any problems immediately.
- Unplug an electrical cord by pulling on the plug, not the cord.

Chemical Safety

chemical
safety

poison

fumes

- If you spill a chemical or get one on your skin or in your eyes, tell your teacher right away.
- Never touch, taste, or sniff any chemicals in the lab. If you need to determine odor, waft. Wafting consists of holding the chemical in its container 15 centimeters (6 in.) away from your nose, and using your fingers to bring fumes from the container to your nose.
- Keep lids on all chemicals you are not using.
- Never put unused chemicals back into the original containers. Throw away extra chemicals where your teacher tells you to.
- Pour chemicals over a sink or your work area, not over the floor.
- If you get a chemical in your eye, use the eyewash right away.
- Always wash your hands after handling chemicals, plants, or soil.

Wafting

Glassware and Sharp-Object Safety

sharp
objects

- If you break glassware, tell your teacher right away.
- Do not use broken or chipped glassware. Give these to your teacher.
- Use knives and other cutting instruments carefully. Always wear eye protection and cut away from you.

Animal Safety

- Never hurt an animal.
- Touch animals only when necessary. Follow your teacher's instructions for handling animals.
- Always wash your hands after working with animals.

Cleanup

disposal

- Follow your teacher's instructions for throwing away or putting away supplies.
- Clean your work area and pick up anything that has dropped to the floor.
- Wash your hands.

Using Lab Equipment

Different experiments require different types of equipment. But even though experiments differ, the ways in which the equipment is used are the same.

Beakers

- Use beakers for holding and pouring liquids.
- Do not use a beaker to measure the volume of a liquid. Use a graduated cylinder instead. (See page R16.)
- Use a beaker that holds about twice as much liquid as you need. For example, if you need 100 milliliters of water, you should use a 200- or 250-milliliter beaker.

Test Tubes

- Use test tubes to hold small amounts of substances.
- Do not use a test tube to measure the volume of a liquid.
- Use a test tube when heating a substance over a flame. Aim the mouth of the tube away from yourself and other people.
- Liquids easily spill or splash from test tubes, so it is important to use only small amounts of liquids.

Test-Tube Holder

- Use a test-tube holder when heating a substance in a test tube.
- Use a test-tube holder if the substance in a test tube is dangerous to touch.
- Make sure the test-tube holder tightly grips the test tube so that the test tube will not slide out of the holder.
- Make sure that the test-tube holder is above the surface of the substance in the test tube so that you can observe the substance.

Test-Tube Rack

- Use a test-tube rack to organize test tubes before, during, and after an experiment.

- Use a test-tube rack to keep test tubes upright so that they do not fall over and spill their contents.

- Use a test-tube rack that is the correct size for the test tubes that you are using. If the rack is too small, a test tube may become stuck. If the rack is too large, a test tube may lean over, and some of its contents may spill or splash.

Forceps

- Use forceps when you need to pick up or hold a very small object that should not be touched with your hands.

- Do not use forceps to hold anything over a flame, because forceps are not long enough to keep your hand safely away from the flame. Plastic forceps will melt, and metal forceps will conduct heat and burn your hand.

Hot Plate

- Use a hot plate when a substance needs to be kept warmer than room temperature for a long period of time.

- Use a hot plate instead of a Bunsen burner or a candle when you need to carefully control temperature.

- Do not use a hot plate when a substance needs to be burned in an experiment.

- Always use "hot hands" safety mitts or oven mitts when handling anything that has been heated on a hot plate.

Microscope

Scientists use microscopes to see very small objects that cannot easily be seen with the eye alone. A microscope magnifies the image of an object so that small details may be observed. A microscope that you may use can magnify an object 400 times—the object will appear 400 times larger than its actual size.

Body The body separates the lens in the eyepiece from the objective lenses below.

Nosepiece The nosepiece holds the objective lenses above the stage and rotates so that all lenses may be used.

High-Power Objective Lens This is the largest lens on the nosepiece. It magnifies an image approximately 40 times.

Stage The stage supports the object being viewed.

Diaphragm The diaphragm is used to adjust the amount of light passing through the slide and into an objective lens.

Mirror or Light Source Some microscopes use light that is reflected through the stage by a mirror. Other microscopes have their own light sources.

Eyepiece Objects are viewed through the eyepiece. The eyepiece contains a lens that commonly magnifies an image 10 times.

Coarse Adjustment This knob is used to focus the image of an object when it is viewed through the low-power lens.

Fine Adjustment This knob is used to focus the image of an object when it is viewed through the high-power lens.

Low-Power Objective Lens This is the smallest lens on the nosepiece. It magnifies an image approximately 10 times.

Arm The arm supports the body above the stage. Always carry a microscope by the arm and base.

Stage Clip The stage clip holds a slide in place on the stage.

Base The base supports the microscope.

VIEWING AN OBJECT

1. Use the coarse adjustment knob to raise the body tube.
2. Adjust the diaphragm so that you can see a bright circle of light through the eyepiece.
3. Place the object or slide on the stage. Be sure that it is centered over the hole in the stage.
4. Turn the nosepiece to click the low-power lens into place.
5. Using the coarse adjustment knob, slowly lower the lens and focus on the specimen being viewed. Be sure not to touch the slide or object with the lens.
6. When switching from the low-power lens to the high-power lens, first raise the body tube with the coarse adjustment knob so that the high-power lens will not hit the slide.
7. Turn the nosepiece to click the high-power lens into place.
8. Use the fine adjustment knob to focus on the specimen being viewed. Again, be sure not to touch the slide or object with the lens.

MAKING A SLIDE, OR WET MOUNT

1 Place the specimen in the center of a clean slide.

2 Place a drop of water on the specimen.

3 Place a cover slip on the slide. Put one edge of the cover slip into the drop of water and slowly lower it over the specimen.

4 Remove any air bubbles from under the cover slip by gently tapping the cover slip.

5 Dry any excess water before placing the slide on the microscope stage for viewing.

Spring Scale (Force Meter)

- Use a spring scale to measure a force pulling on the scale.

- Use a spring scale to measure the force of gravity exerted on an object by Earth.

- To measure a force accurately, a spring scale must be zeroed before it is used. The scale is zeroed when no weight is attached and the indicator is positioned at zero.

- Do not attach a weight that is either too heavy or too light to a spring scale. A weight that is too heavy could break the scale or exert too great a force for the scale to measure. A weight that is too light may not exert enough force to be measured accurately.

Graduated Cylinder

- Use a graduated cylinder to measure the volume of a liquid.

- Be sure that the graduated cylinder is on a flat surface so that your measurement will be accurate.

- When reading the scale on a graduated cylinder, be sure to have your eyes at the level of the surface of the liquid.

- The surface of the liquid will be curved in the graduated cylinder. Read the volume of the liquid at the bottom of the curve, or meniscus (muh-NIHS-kuhs).

- You can use a graduated cylinder to find the volume of a solid object by measuring the increase in a liquid's level after you add the object to the cylinder.

meniscus

Read the volume at the bottom of the meniscus. The volume is 96 mL.

LAB HANDBOOK

Metric Rulers

- Use metric rulers or meter sticks to measure objects' lengths.

- Do not measure an object from the end of a metric ruler or meter stick, because the end is often imperfect. Instead, measure from the 1-centimeter mark, but remember to subtract a centimeter from the apparent measurement.

- Estimate any lengths that extend between marked units. For example, if a meter stick shows centimeters but not millimeters, you can estimate the length that an object extends between centimeter marks to measure it to the nearest millimeter.

- **Controlling Variables** If you are taking repeated measurements, always measure from the same point each time. For example, if you're measuring how high two different balls bounce when dropped from the same height, measure both bounces at the same point on the balls—either the top or the bottom. Do not measure at the top of one ball and the bottom of the other.

EXAMPLE

How to Measure a Leaf

1. Lay a ruler flat on top of the leaf so that the 1-centimeter mark lines up with one end. Make sure the ruler and the leaf do not move between the time you line them up and the time you take the measurement.

2. Look straight down on the ruler so that you can see exactly how the marks line up with the other end of the leaf.

3. Estimate the length by which the leaf extends beyond a marking. For example, the leaf below extends about halfway between the 4.2-centimeter and 4.3-centimeter marks, so the apparent measurement is about 4.25 centimeters.

4. Remember to subtract 1 centimeter from your apparent measurement, since you started at the 1-centimeter mark on the ruler and not at the end. The leaf is about 3.25 centimeters long (4.25 cm – 1 cm = 3.25 cm).

Triple-Beam Balance

This balance has a pan and three beams with sliding masses, called riders. At one end of the beams is a pointer that indicates whether the mass on the pan is equal to the masses shown on the beams.

1. Make sure the balance is zeroed before measuring the mass of an object. The balance is zeroed if the pointer is at zero when nothing is on the pan and the riders are at their zero points. Use the adjustment knob at the base of the balance to zero it.

2. Place the object to be measured on the pan.

3. Move the riders one notch at a time away from the pan. Begin with the largest rider. If moving the largest rider one notch brings the pointer below zero, begin measuring the mass of the object with the next smaller rider.

4. Change the positions of the riders until they balance the mass on the pan and the pointer is at zero. Then add the readings from the three beams to determine the mass of the object.

300 g	position of largest rider
90 g	position of middle rider
+ 3 g	position of smallest rider
393 g	mass of beaker

Double-Pan Balance

This type of balance has two pans. Between the pans is a pointer that indicates whether the masses on the pans are equal.

1. Make sure the balance is zeroed before measuring the mass of an object. The balance is zeroed if the pointer is at zero when there is nothing on either of the pans. Many double-pan balances have sliding knobs that can be used to zero them.

2. Place the object to be measured on one of the pans.

3. Begin adding standard masses to the other pan. Begin with the largest standard mass. If this adds too much mass to the balance, begin measuring the mass of the object with the next smaller standard mass.

4. Add standard masses until the masses on both pans are balanced and the pointer is at zero. Then add the standard masses together to determine the mass of the object being measured.

```
            200 g        200 g
                100 g    100 g
                          50 g
                  50 g    20 g
  20 g                    20 g
      20 g                 2 g
          2 g       +      1 g
                         ───────────
 1 g                     393 g mass of beaker
```

Never place chemicals or liquids directly on a pan. Instead, use the following procedure:

1. Determine the mass of an empty container, such as a beaker.

2. Pour the substance into the container, and measure the total mass of the substance and the container.

3. Subtract the mass of the empty container from the total mass to find the mass of the substance.

The Metric System and SI Units

Scientists use International System (SI) units for measurements of distance, volume, mass, and temperature. The International System is based on multiples of ten and the metric system of measurement.

Basic SI Units		
Property	**Name**	**Symbol**
length	meter	m
volume	liter	L
mass	kilogram	kg
temperature	kelvin	K

SI Prefixes		
Prefix	**Symbol**	**Multiple of 10**
kilo-	k	1000
hecto-	h	100
deca-	da	10
deci-	d	$0.1 \left(\frac{1}{10}\right)$
centi-	c	$0.01 \left(\frac{1}{100}\right)$
milli-	m	$0.001 \left(\frac{1}{1000}\right)$

Changing Metric Units

You can change from one unit to another in the metric system by multiplying or dividing by a power of 10.

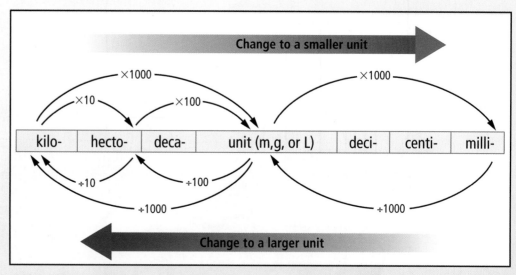

Example

Change 0.64 liters to milliliters.

(1) Decide whether to multiply or divide.

(2) Select the power of 10.

ANSWER 0.64 L = 640 mL

Change to a smaller unit by multiplying.

mL ◄——— × 1000 ——— L

0.64 × 1000 = 640.

Example

Change 23.6 grams to kilograms.

(1) Decide whether to multiply or divide.

(2) Select the power of 10.

ANSWER 23.6 g = 0.0236 kg

Change to a larger unit by dividing.

g ——— ÷ 1000 ——► kg

23.6 ÷ 1000 = 0.0236

Temperature Conversions

Even though the kelvin is the SI base unit of temperature, the degree Celsius will be the unit you use most often in your science studies. The formulas below show the relationships between temperatures in degrees Fahrenheit (°F), degrees Celsius (°C), and kelvins (K).

$$°C = \frac{5}{9}(°F - 32)$$

$$°F = \frac{9}{5}°C + 32$$

$$K = °C + 273$$

See page R42 for help with using formulas.

Examples of Temperature Conversions

Condition	Degrees Celsius	Degrees Fahrenheit
Freezing point of water	0	32
Cool day	10	50
Mild day	20	68
Warm day	30	86
Normal body temperature	37	98.6
Very hot day	40	104
Boiling point of water	100	212

Converting Between SI and U.S. Customary Units

Use the chart below when you need to convert between SI units and U.S. customary units.

SI Unit	From SI to U.S. Customary			From U.S. Customary to SI		
Length	When you know	multiply by	to find	When you know	multiply by	to find
kilometer (km) = 1000 m	kilometers	0.62	miles	miles	1.61	kilometers
meter (m) = 100 cm	meters	3.28	feet	feet	0.3048	meters
centimeter (cm) = 10 mm	centimeters	0.39	inches	inches	2.54	centimeters
millimeter (mm) = 0.1 cm	millimeters	0.04	inches	inches	25.4	millimeters
Area	When you know	multiply by	to find	When you know	multiply by	to find
square kilometer (km^2)	square kilometers	0.39	square miles	square miles	2.59	square kilometers
square meter (m^2)	square meters	1.2	square yards	square yards	0.84	square meters
square centimeter (cm^2)	square centimeters	0.155	square inches	square inches	6.45	square centimeters
Volume	When you know	multiply by	to find	When you know	multiply by	to find
liter (L) = 1000 mL	liters	1.06	quarts	quarts	0.95	liters
	liters	0.26	gallons	gallons	3.79	liters
	liters	4.23	cups	cups	0.24	liters
	liters	2.12	pints	pints	0.47	liters
milliliter (mL) = 0.001 L	milliliters	0.20	teaspoons	teaspoons	4.93	milliliters
	milliliters	0.07	tablespoons	tablespoons	14.79	milliliters
	milliliters	0.03	fluid ounces	fluid ounces	29.57	milliliters
Mass	When you know	multiply by	to find	When you know	multiply by	to find
kilogram (kg) = 1000 g	kilograms	2.2	pounds	pounds	0.45	kilograms
gram (g) = 1000 mg	grams	0.035	ounces	ounces	28.35	grams

Precision and Accuracy

When you do an experiment, it is important that your methods, observations, and data be both precise and accurate.

low precision

precision, but not accuracy

precision and accuracy

Precision

In science, **precision** is the exactness and consistency of measurements. For example, measurements made with a ruler that has both centimeter and millimeter markings would be more precise than measurements made with a ruler that has only centimeter markings. Another indicator of precision is the care taken to make sure that methods and observations are as exact and consistent as possible. Every time a particular experiment is done, the same procedure should be used. Precision is necessary because experiments are repeated several times and if the procedure changes, the results will change.

EXAMPLE

Suppose you are measuring temperatures over a two-week period. Your precision will be greater if you measure each temperature at the same place, at the same time of day, and with the same thermometer than if you change any of these factors from one day to the next.

Accuracy

In science, it is possible to be precise but not accurate. **Accuracy** depends on the difference between a measurement and an actual value. The smaller the difference, the more accurate the measurement.

EXAMPLE

Suppose you look at a stream and estimate that it is about 1 meter wide at a particular place. You decide to check your estimate by measuring the stream with a meter stick, and you determine that the stream is 1.32 meters wide. However, because it is hard to measure the width of a stream with a meter stick, it turns out that you didn't do a very good job. The stream is actually 1.14 meters wide. Therefore, even though your estimate was less precise than your measurement, your estimate was actually more accurate.

Making Data Tables and Graphs

Data tables and graphs are useful tools for both recording and communicating scientific data.

Making Data Tables

You can use a **data table** to organize and record the measurements that you make. Some examples of information that might be recorded in data tables are frequencies, times, and amounts.

EXAMPLE

Suppose you are investigating photosynthesis in two elodea plants. One sits in direct sunlight, and the other sits in a dimly lit room. You measure the rate of photosynthesis by counting the number of bubbles in the jar every ten minutes.

1. Title and number your data table.

2. Decide how you will organize the table into columns and rows.

3. Any units, such as seconds or degrees, should be included in column headings, not in the individual cells.

Table 1. Number of Bubbles from Elodea

> Always number and title data tables.

Time (min)	Sunlight	Dim Light
0	0	0
10	15	5
20	25	8
30	32	7
40	41	10
50	47	9
60	42	9

The data in the table above could also be organized in a different way.

Table 1. Number of Bubbles from Elodea

> Put units in column heading.

Light Condition	Time (min)						
	0	10	20	30	40	50	60
Sunlight	0	15	25	32	41	47	42
Dim light	0	5	8	7	10	9	9

Making Line Graphs

You can use a **line graph** to show a relationship between variables. Line graphs are particularly useful for showing changes in variables over time.

EXAMPLE

Suppose you are interested in graphing temperature data that you collected over the course of a day.

Table 1. Outside Temperature During the Day on March 7

	Time of Day						
	7:00 A.M.	9:00 A.M.	11:00 A.M.	1:00 P.M.	3:00 P.M.	5:00 P.M.	7:00 P.M.
Temp (°C)	8	9	11	14	12	10	6

1. Use the vertical axis of your line graph for the variable that you are measuring—temperature.

2. Choose scales for both the horizontal axis and the vertical axis of the graph. You should have two points more than you need on the vertical axis, and the horizontal axis should be long enough for all of the data points to fit.

3. Draw and label each axis.

4. Graph each value. First find the appropriate point on the scale of the horizontal axis. Imagine a line that rises vertically from that place on the scale. Then find the corresponding value on the vertical axis, and imagine a line that moves horizontally from that value. The point where these two imaginary lines intersect is where the value should be plotted.

5. Connect the points with straight lines.

Be sure to add a number and a title to your graph. ▶

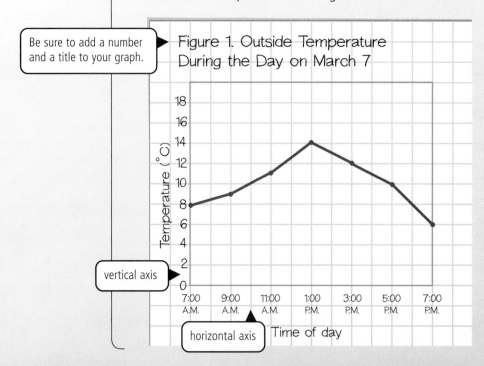

Figure 1. Outside Temperature During the Day on March 7

vertical axis

horizontal axis — Time of day

Making Circle Graphs

You can use a **circle graph,** sometimes called a pie chart, to represent data as parts of a circle. Circle graphs are used only when the data can be expressed as percentages of a whole. The entire circle shown in a circle graph is equal to 100 percent of the data.

EXAMPLE

Suppose you identified the species of each mature tree growing in a small wooded area. You organized your data in a table, but you also want to show the data in a circle graph.

1. To begin, find the total number of mature trees.

    $$56 + 34 + 22 + 10 + 28 = 150$$

2. To find the degree measure for each sector of the circle, write a fraction comparing the number of each tree species with the total number of trees. Then multiply the fraction by 360°.

    Oak: $\frac{56}{150} \times 360° = 134.4°$

3. Draw a circle. Use a protractor to draw the angle for each sector of the graph.

4. Color and label each sector of the graph.

5. Give the graph a number and title.

Table 1. Tree Species in Wooded Area

Species	Number of Specimens
Oak	56
Maple	34
Birch	22
Willow	10
Pine	28

Figure 1. Tree Species in Wooded Area

Willow 10
Birch 22
Pine 28
Oak 56
Maple 34

Instead of labeling each sector, you could make a color key.

- Oak 56
- Maple 34
- Pine 28
- Birch 22
- Willow 10

Bar Graph

A **bar graph** is a type of graph in which the lengths of the bars are used to represent and compare data. A numerical scale is used to determine the lengths of the bars.

EXAMPLE

To determine the effect of water on seed sprouting, three cups were filled with sand, and ten seeds were planted in each. Different amounts of water were added to each cup over a three-day period.

Table 1. Effect of Water on Seed Sprouting

Daily Amount of Water (mL)	Number of Seeds That Sprouted After 3 Days in Sand
0	1
10	4
20	8

1. Choose a numerical scale. The greatest value is 8, so the end of the scale should have a value greater than 8, such as 10. Use equal increments along the scale, such as increments of 2.

2. Draw and label the axes. Mark intervals on the vertical axis according to the scale you chose.

3. Draw a bar for each data value. Use the scale to decide how long to make each bar.

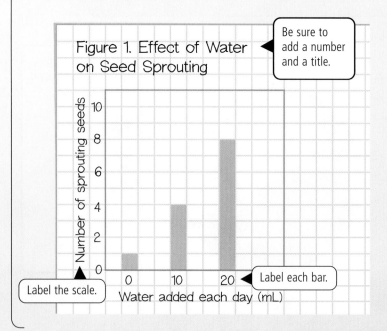

Figure 1. Effect of Water on Seed Sprouting

Be sure to add a number and a title.

Number of sprouting seeds

Water added each day (mL)

Label the scale.

Label each bar.

Double Bar Graph

A **double bar graph** is a bar graph that shows two sets of data. The two bars for each measurement are drawn next to each other.

EXAMPLE

The seed-sprouting experiment was done using both sand and potting soil. The data for sand and potting soil can be plotted on one graph.

1. Draw one set of bars, using the data for sand, as shown below.

2. Draw bars for the potting-soil data next to the bars for the sand data. Shade them a different color. Add a key.

Table 2. Effect of Water and Soil on Seed Sprouting

Daily Amount of Water (mL)	Number of Seeds That Sprouted After 3 Days in Sand	Number of Seeds That Sprouted After 3 Days in Potting Soil
0	1	2
10	4	5
20	8	9

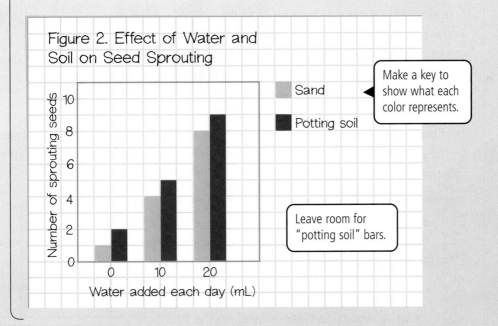

Figure 2. Effect of Water and Soil on Seed Sprouting

Make a key to show what each color represents.

Leave room for "potting soil" bars.

Designing an Experiment

Use this section when designing or conducting an experiment.

Determining a Purpose

You can find a purpose for an experiment by doing research, by examining the results of a previous experiment, or by observing the world around you. An **experiment** is an organized procedure to study something under controlled conditions.

1. Write the purpose of your experiment as a question or problem that you want to investigate.

2. Write down research questions and begin searching for information that will help you design an experiment. Consult the library, the Internet, and other people as you conduct your research.

> Don't forget to learn as much as possible about your topic before you begin.

EXAMPLE

Middle school students observed an odor near the lake by their school. They also noticed that the water on the side of the lake near the school was greener than the water on the other side of the lake. The students did some research to learn more about their observations. They discovered that the odor and green color in the lake came from algae. They also discovered that a new fertilizer was being used on a field nearby. The students inferred that the use of the fertilizer might be related to the presence of the algae and designed a controlled experiment to find out whether they were right.

Problem
How does fertilizer affect the presence of algae in a lake?

Research Questions
- Have other experiments been done on this problem? If so, what did those experiments show?
- What kind of fertilizer is used on the field? How much?
- How do algae grow?
- How do people measure algae?
- Can fertilizer and algae be used safely in a lab? How?

> **Research**
> As you research, you may find a topic that is more interesting to you than your original topic, or learn that a procedure you wanted to use is not practical or safe. It is OK to change your purpose as you research.

Writing a Hypothesis

A **hypothesis** is a tentative explanation for an observation or scientific problem that can be tested by further investigation. You can write your hypothesis in the form of an "If . . . , then . . . , because . . ." statement.

Hypothesis

If the amount of fertilizer in lake water is increased, then the amount of algae will also increase, because fertilizers provide nutrients that algae need to grow.

Hypotheses
For help with hypotheses, refer to page R3.

Determining Materials

Make a list of all the materials you will need to do your experiment. Be specific, especially if someone else is helping you obtain the materials. Try to think of everything you will need.

Materials
- 1 large jar or container
- 4 identical smaller containers
- rubber gloves that also cover the arms
- sample of fertilizer-and-water solution
- eyedropper
- clear plastic wrap
- scissors
- masking tape
- marker
- ruler

Determining Variables and Constants

EXPERIMENTAL GROUP AND CONTROL GROUP

An experiment to determine how two factors are related always has two groups—a control group and an experimental group.

1. Design an experimental group. Include as many trials as possible in the experimental group in order to obtain reliable results.

2. Design a control group that is the same as the experimental group in every way possible, except for the factor you wish to test.

Experimental Group: two containers of lake water with one drop of fertilizer solution added to each

Control Group: two containers of lake water with no fertilizer solution added

Go back to your materials list and make sure you have enough items listed to cover both your experimental group and your control group.

VARIABLES AND CONSTANTS

Identify the variables and constants in your experiment. In a controlled experiment, a **variable** is any factor that can change. **Constants** are all of the factors that are the same in both the experimental group and the control group.

1. Read your hypothesis. The **independent variable** is the factor that you wish to test and that is manipulated or changed so that it can be tested. The independent variable is expressed in your hypothesis after the word *if*. Identify the independent variable in your laboratory report.

2. The **dependent variable** is the factor that you measure to gather results. It is expressed in your hypothesis after the word *then*. Identify the dependent variable in your laboratory report.

Hypothesis
If the amount of fertilizer in lake water is increased, then the amount of algae will also increase, because fertilizers provide nutrients that algae need to grow.

Table 1. Variables and Constants in Algae Experiment

Independent Variable	Dependent Variable	Constants
Amount of fertilizer in lake water	Amount of algae that grow	• Where the lake water is obtained • Type of container used • Light and temperature conditions where water will be stored

Set up your experiment so that you will test only one variable.

MEASURING THE DEPENDENT VARIABLE

Before starting your experiment, you need to define how you will measure the dependent variable. An **operational definition** is a description of the one particular way in which you will measure the dependent variable.

Your operational definition is important for several reasons. First, in any experiment there are several ways in which a dependent variable can be measured. Second, the procedure of the experiment depends on how you decide to measure the dependent variable. Third, your operational definition makes it possible for other people to evaluate and build on your experiment.

EXAMPLE 1

An operational definition of a dependent variable can be qualitative. That is, your measurement of the dependent variable can simply be an observation of whether a change occurs as a result of a change in the independent variable. This type of operational definition can be thought of as a "yes or no" measurement.

Table 2. Qualitative Operational Definition of Algae Growth

Independent Variable	Dependent Variable	Operational Definition
Amount of fertilizer in lake water	Amount of algae that grow	Algae grow in lake water

A qualitative measurement of a dependent variable is often easy to make and record. However, this type of information does not provide a great deal of detail in your experimental results.

EXAMPLE 2

An operational definition of a dependent variable can be quantitative. That is, your measurement of the dependent variable can be a number that shows how much change occurs as a result of a change in the independent variable.

Table 3. Quantitative Operational Definition of Algae Growth

Independent Variable	Dependent Variable	Operational Definition
Amount of fertilizer in lake water	Amount of algae that grow	Diameter of largest algal growth (in mm)

A quantitative measurement of a dependent variable can be more difficult to make and analyze than a qualitative measurement. However, this type of data provides much more information about your experiment and is often more useful.

Writing a Procedure

Write each step of your procedure. Start each step with a verb, or action word, and keep the steps short. Your procedure should be clear enough for someone else to use as instructions for repeating your experiment.

If necessary, go back to your materials list and add any materials that you left out.

Procedure

1. Put on your gloves. Use the large container to obtain a sample of lake water.

2. Divide the sample of lake water equally among the four smaller containers.

3. Use the eyedropper to add one drop of fertilizer solution to two of the containers.

Controlling Variables
The same amount of fertilizer solution must be added to two of the four containers.

4. Use the masking tape and the marker to label the containers with your initials, the date, and the identifiers "Jar 1 with Fertilizer," "Jar 2 with Fertilizer," "Jar 1 without Fertilizer," and "Jar 2 without Fertilizer."

5. Cover the containers with clear plastic wrap. Use the scissors to punch ten holes in each of the covers.

6. Place all four containers on a window ledge. Make sure that they all receive the same amount of light.

Controlling Variables
All four containers must receive the same amount of light.

7. Observe the containers every day for one week.

8. Use the ruler to measure the diameter of the largest clump of algae in each container, and record your measurements daily.

Recording Observations

Once you have obtained all of your materials and your procedure has been approved, you can begin making experimental observations. Gather both quantitative and qualitative data. If something goes wrong during your procedure, make sure you record that too.

> **Observations**
> For help with making qualitative and quantitative observations, refer to page R2.

> For more examples of data tables, see page R23.

Table 4. Fertilizer and Algae Growth

Date and Time	Experimental Group		Control Group		Observations
	Jar 1 with Fertilizer (diameter of algae in mm)	Jar 2 with Fertilizer (diameter of algae in mm)	Jar 1 without Fertilizer (diameter of algae in mm)	Jar 2 without Fertilizer (diameter of algae in mm)	
5/3 4:00 P.M.	0	0	0	0	condensation in all containers
5/4 4:00 P.M.	0	3	0	0	tiny green blobs in jar 2 with fertilizer
5/5 4:15 P.M.	4	5	0	3	green blobs in jars 1 and 2 with fertilizer and jar 2 without fertilizer
5/6 4:00 P.M.	5	6	0	4	water light green in jar 2 with fertilizer
5/7 4:00 P.M.	8	10	0	6	water light green in jars 1 and 2 with fertilizer and in jar 2 without fertilizer
5/8 3:30 P.M.	10	18	0	6	cover off jar 2 with fertilizer
5/9 3:30 P.M.	14	23	0	8	drew sketches of each container

> Notice that on the sixth day, the observer found that the cover was off one of the containers. It is important to record observations of unintended factors because they might affect the results of the experiment.

Drawings of Samples Viewed Under Microscope on 5/9 at 100×

> Use technology, such as a microscope, to help you make observations when possible.

Jar 1 with Fertilizer

Jar 2 with Fertilizer

Jar 1 without Fertilizer

Jar 2 without Fertilizer

Summarizing Results

To summarize your data, look at all of your observations together. Look for meaningful ways to present your observations. For example, you might average your data or make a graph to look for patterns. When possible, use spreadsheet software to help you analyze and present your data. The two graphs below show the same data.

EXAMPLE 1

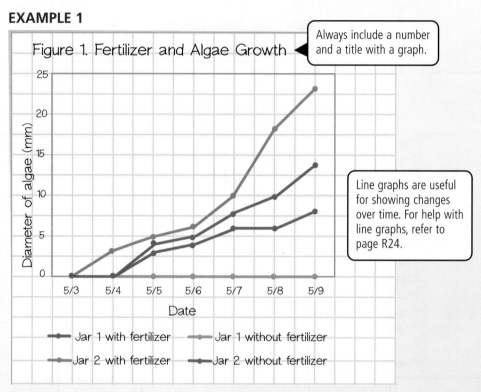

Always include a number and a title with a graph.

Line graphs are useful for showing changes over time. For help with line graphs, refer to page R24.

EXAMPLE 2

Bar graphs are useful for comparing different data sets. This bar graph has four bars for each day. Another way to present the data would be to calculate averages for the tests and the controls, and to show one test bar and one control bar for each day.

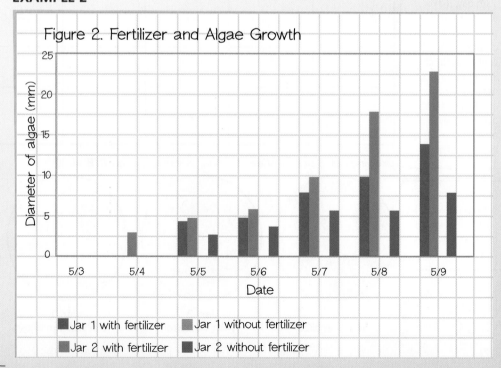

LAB HANDBOOK

Drawing Conclusions

RESULTS AND INFERENCES

To draw conclusions from your experiment, first write your results. Then compare your results with your hypothesis. Do your results support your hypothesis? Be careful not to make inferences about factors that you did not test.

For help with making inferences, see page R4.

Results and Inferences

The results of my experiment show that more algae grew in lake water to which fertilizer had been added than in lake water to which no fertilizer had been added. My hypothesis was supported. I infer that it is possible that the growth of algae in the lake was caused by the fertilizer used on the field.

Notice that you cannot conclude from this experiment that the presence of algae in the lake was due only to the fertilizer.

QUESTIONS FOR FURTHER RESEARCH

Write a list of questions for further research and investigation. Your ideas may lead you to new experiments and discoveries.

Questions for Further Research

• What is the connection between the amount of fertilizer and algae growth?
• How do different brands of fertilizer affect algae growth?
• How would algae growth in the lake be affected if no fertilizer were used on the field?
• How do algae affect the lake and the other life in and around it?
• How does fertilizer affect the lake and the life in and around it?
• If fertilizer is getting into the lake, how is it getting there?

Math Handbook

Describing a Set of Data

Means, medians, modes, and ranges are important math tools for describing data sets such as the following widths of fossilized clamshells.

13 mm   25 mm   14 mm   21 mm   16 mm   23 mm   14 mm

Mean

The **mean** of a data set is the sum of the values divided by the number of values.

Example

To find the mean of the clamshell data, add the values and then divide the sum by the number of values.

$$\frac{13 \text{ mm} + 25 \text{ mm} + 14 \text{ mm} + 21 \text{ mm} + 16 \text{ mm} + 23 \text{ mm} + 14 \text{ mm}}{7} = \frac{126 \text{ mm}}{7} = 18 \text{ mm}$$

ANSWER The mean is 18 mm.

Median

The **median** of a data set is the middle value when the values are written in numerical order. If a data set has an even number of values, the median is the mean of the two middle values.

Example

To find the median of the clamshell data, arrange the values in order from least to greatest. The median is the middle value.

13 mm   14 mm   14 mm   16 mm   21 mm   23 mm   25 mm

ANSWER The median is 16 mm.

Mode

The **mode** of a data set is the value that occurs most often.

> ### Example
>
> To find the mode of the clamshell data, arrange the values in order from least to greatest and determine the value that occurs most often.
>
> 13 mm   14 mm   14 mm   16 mm   21 mm   23 mm   25 mm
>
> **ANSWER** The mode is 14 mm.

A data set can have more than one mode or no mode. For example, the following data set has modes of 2 mm and 4 mm:

2 mm   2 mm   3 mm   4 mm   4 mm

The data set below has no mode, because no value occurs more often than any other.

2 mm   3 mm   4 mm   5 mm

Range

The **range** of a data set is the difference between the greatest value and the least value.

> ### Example
>
> To find the range of the clamshell data, arrange the values in order from least to greatest.
>
> 13 mm   14 mm   14 mm   16 mm   21 mm   23 mm   25 mm
>
> Subtract the least value from the greatest value.
>
> 13 mm is the least value.
> 25 mm is the greatest value.
>
> 25 mm − 13 mm = 12 mm
>
> **ANSWER** The range is 12 mm.

Using Ratios, Rates, and Proportions

You can use ratios and rates to compare values in data sets. You can use proportions to find unknown values.

Ratios

A **ratio** uses division to compare two values. The ratio of a value a to a nonzero value b can be written as $\frac{a}{b}$.

Example

The height of one plant is 8 centimeters. The height of another plant is 6 centimeters. To find the ratio of the height of the first plant to the height of the second plant, write a fraction and simplify it.

$$\frac{8 \text{ cm}}{6 \text{ cm}} = \frac{4 \times \overset{1}{\cancel{2}}}{3 \times \underset{1}{\cancel{2}}} = \frac{4}{3}$$

ANSWER The ratio of the plant heights is $\frac{4}{3}$.

You can also write the ratio $\frac{a}{b}$ as "a to b" or as $a:b$. For example, you can write the ratio of the plant heights as "4 to 3" or as $4:3$.

Rates

A **rate** is a ratio of two values expressed in different units. A unit rate is a rate with a denominator of 1 unit.

Example

A plant grew 6 centimeters in 2 days. The plant's rate of growth was $\frac{6 \text{ cm}}{2 \text{ days}}$. To describe the plant's growth in centimeters per day, write a unit rate.

Divide numerator and denominator by 2: $\quad \dfrac{6 \text{ cm}}{2 \text{ days}} = \dfrac{6 \text{ cm} \div 2}{2 \text{ days} \div 2}$

> You divide 2 days by 2 to get 1 day, so divide 6 cm by 2 also.

Simplify: $\quad = \dfrac{3 \text{ cm}}{1 \text{ day}}$

ANSWER The plant's rate of growth is 3 centimeters per day.

Proportions

A **proportion** is an equation stating that two ratios are equivalent. To solve for an unknown value in a proportion, you can use cross products.

Example

If a plant grew 6 centimeters in 2 days, how many centimeters would it grow in 3 days (if its rate of growth is constant)?

Write a proportion:	$\dfrac{6 \text{ cm}}{2 \text{ days}} = \dfrac{x}{3 \text{ days}}$
Set cross products:	$6 \text{ cm} \cdot 3 = 2x$
Multiply 6 and 3:	$18 \text{ cm} = 2x$
Divide each side by 2:	$\dfrac{18 \text{ cm}}{2} = \dfrac{2x}{2}$
Simplify:	$9 \text{ cm} = x$

ANSWER The plant would grow 9 centimeters in 3 days.

Using Decimals, Fractions, and Percents

Decimals, fractions, and percentages are all ways of recording and representing data.

Decimals

A **decimal** is a number that is written in the base-ten place value system, in which a decimal point separates the ones and tenths digits. The values of each place is ten times that of the place to its right.

Example

A caterpillar traveled from point *A* to point *C* along the path shown.

A   36.9 cm   **B**   52.4 cm   **C**

ADDING DECIMALS To find the total distance traveled by the caterpillar, add the distance from *A* to *B* and the distance from *B* to *C*. Begin by lining up the decimal points. Then add the figures as you would whole numbers and bring down the decimal point.

```
   36.9 cm
 + 52.4 cm
 ─────────
   89.3 cm
```

ANSWER The caterpillar traveled a total distance of 89.3 centimeters.

Example continued

SUBTRACTING DECIMALS To find how much farther the caterpillar traveled on the second leg of the journey, subtract the distance from *A* to *B* from the distance from *B* to *C*.

$$
\begin{array}{r}
52.4 \text{ cm} \\
- \ 36.9 \text{ cm} \\
\hline
15.5 \text{ cm}
\end{array}
$$

ANSWER The caterpillar traveled 15.5 centimeters farther on the second leg of the journey.

Example

A caterpillar is traveling from point *D* to point *F* along the path shown. The caterpillar travels at a speed of 9.6 centimeters per minute.

D   E   33.6 cm   F

MULTIPLYING DECIMALS You can multiply decimals as you would whole numbers. The number of decimal places in the product is equal to the sum of the number of decimal places in the factors.

For instance, suppose it takes the caterpillar 1.5 minutes to go from *D* to *E*. To find the distance from *D* to *E*, multiply the caterpillar's speed by the time it took.

> Align as shown.

$$
\begin{array}{rl}
9.6 & \quad 1 \quad \text{decimal place} \\
\times \ 1.5 & \quad + \ 1 \quad \text{decimal place} \\
\hline
480 & \\
96 \quad & \\
\hline
14.40 & \quad 2 \quad \text{decimal places}
\end{array}
$$

ANSWER The distance from *D* to *E* is 14.4 centimeters.

DIVIDING DECIMALS When you divide by a decimal, move the decimal points the same number of places in the divisor and the dividend to make the divisor a whole number.

For instance, to find the time it will take the caterpillar to travel from *E* to *F*, divide the distance from *E* to *F* by the caterpillar's speed.

$$
9.6 \overline{)33.6}
$$

> Move each decimal point one place to the right.

$$
\begin{array}{r}
3.5 \\
96 \overline{)336.} \\
\underline{288} \ \ \\
480 \\
\underline{480} \\
0
\end{array}
$$

> Line up decimal points.

ANSWER The caterpillar will travel from *E* to *F* in 3.5 minutes.

Fractions

A **fraction** is a number in the form $\frac{a}{b}$, where b is not equal to 0. A fraction is in **simplest form** if its numerator and denominator have a greatest common factor (GCF) of 1. To simplify a fraction, divide its numerator and denominator by their GCF.

Example

A caterpillar is 40 millimeters long. The head of the caterpillar is 6 millimeters long. To compare the length of the caterpillar's head with the caterpillar's total length, you can write and simplify a fraction that expresses the ratio of the two lengths.

Write the ratio of the two lengths: $\dfrac{\text{Length of head}}{\text{Total length}} = \dfrac{6 \text{ mm}}{40 \text{ mm}}$

Write numerator and denominator as products of numbers and the GCF: $= \dfrac{3 \times 2}{20 \times 2}$

Divide numerator and denominator by the GCF: $= \dfrac{3 \times \overset{1}{\cancel{2}}}{20 \times \underset{1}{\cancel{2}}}$

Simplify: $= \dfrac{3}{20}$

ANSWER In simplest form, the ratio of the lengths is $\frac{3}{20}$.

Percents

A **percent** is a ratio that compares a number to 100. The word *percent* means "per hundred" or "out of 100." The symbol for *percent* is %.

For instance, suppose 43 out of 100 caterpillars are female. You can represent this ratio as a percent, a decimal, or a fraction.

Percent	Decimal	Fraction
43%	0.43	$\frac{43}{100}$

Example

In the preceding example, the ratio of the length of the caterpillar's head to the caterpillar's total length is $\frac{3}{20}$. To write this ratio as a percent, write an equivalent fraction that has a denominator of 100.

Multiply numerator and denominator by 5: $\dfrac{3}{20} = \dfrac{3 \times 5}{20 \times 5}$

$= \dfrac{15}{100}$

Write as a percent: $= 15\%$

ANSWER The caterpillar's head represents 15 percent of its total length.

Using Formulas

A **formula** is an equation that shows the general relationship between two or more quantities.

The term *variable* is also used in science to refer to a factor that can change during an experiment.

In science, a formula often has a word form and a symbolic form. The formula below expresses Ohm's law.

Word Form

$$\text{Current} = \frac{\text{voltage}}{\text{resistance}}$$

Symbolic Form

$$I = \frac{V}{R}$$

In this formula, I, V, and R are variables. A mathematical **variable** is a symbol or letter that is used to represent one or more numbers.

Example

Suppose that you measure a voltage of 1.5 volts and a resistance of 15 ohms. You can use the formula for Ohm's law to find the current in amperes.

Write the formula for Ohm's law: $I = \dfrac{V}{R}$

Substitute 1.5 volts for V and 15 ohms for R: $I = \dfrac{1.5 \text{ volts}}{15 \text{ ohms}}$

Simplify: $I = 0.1 \text{ amp}$

ANSWER The current is 0.1 ampere.

If you know the values of all variables but one in a formula, you can solve for the value of the unknown variable. For instance, Ohm's law can be used to find a voltage if you know the current and the resistance.

Example

Suppose that you know that a current is 0.2 amperes and the resistance is 18 ohms. Use the formula for Ohm's law to find the voltage in volts.

Write the formula for Ohm's law: $I = \dfrac{V}{R}$

Substitute 0.2 amp for I and 18 ohms for R: $0.2 \text{ amp} = \dfrac{V}{18 \text{ ohms}}$

Multiply both sides by 18 ohms: $0.2 \text{ amp} \cdot 18 \text{ ohms} = V$

Simplify: $3.6 \text{ volts} = V$

ANSWER The voltage is 3.6 volts.

Finding Areas

The area of a figure is the amount of surface the figure covers.

Area is measured in square units, such as square meters (m²) or square centimeters (cm²). Formulas for the areas of three common geometric figures are shown below.

Area = (side length)²
$A = s^2$

Area = length × width
$A = lw$

Area = $\frac{1}{2}$ × base × height
$A = \frac{1}{2} bh$

Example

Each face of a halite crystal is a square like the one shown. You can find the area of the square by using the steps below.

3 mm

3 mm

Write the formula for the area of a square: $A = s^2$

Substitute 3 mm for s: $= (3 \text{ mm})^2$

Simplify: $= 9 \text{ mm}^2$

ANSWER The area of the square is 9 square millimeters.

Finding Volumes

The volume of a solid is the amount of space contained by the solid.

Volume is measured in cubic units, such as cubic meters (m³) or cubic centimeters (cm³). The volume of a rectangular prism is given by the formula shown below.

Volume = length × width × height
$V = lwh$

Example

A topaz crystal is a rectangular prism like the one shown. You can find the volume of the prism by using the steps below.

10 mm
12 mm
20 mm

Write the formula for the volume of a rectangular prism: $V = lwh$

Substitute dimensions: $= 20 \text{ mm} \times 12 \text{ mm} \times 10 \text{ mm}$

Simplify: $= 2400 \text{ mm}^3$

ANSWER The volume of the rectangular prism is 2400 cubic millimeters.

Using Significant Figures

The **significant figures** in a decimal are the digits that are warranted by the accuracy of a measuring device.

When you perform a calculation with measurements, the number of significant figures to include in the result depends in part on the number of significant figures in the measurements. When you multiply or divide measurements, your answer should have only as many significant figures as the measurement with the fewest significant figures.

Example

Using a balance and a graduated cylinder filled with water, you determined that a marble has a mass of 8.0 grams and a volume of 3.5 cubic centimeters. To calculate the density of the marble, divide the mass by the volume.

Write the formula for density: $\text{Density} = \dfrac{\text{mass}}{\text{Volume}}$

Substitute measurements: $= \dfrac{8.0 \text{ g}}{3.5 \text{ cm}^3}$

Use a calculator to divide: $\approx 2.285714286 \text{ g/cm}^3$

ANSWER Because the mass and the volume have two significant figures each, give the density to two significant figures. The marble has a density of 2.3 grams per cubic centimeter.

Using Scientific Notation

Scientific notation is a shorthand way to write very large or very small numbers. For example, 73,500,000,000,000,000,000,000 kg is the mass of the Moon. In scientific notation, it is 7.35×10^{22} kg.

Example

You can convert from standard form to scientific notation.

Standard Form	Scientific Notation
720,000	7.2×10^5
5 decimal places left	Exponent is 5.
0.000291	2.91×10^{-4}
4 decimal places right	Exponent is −4.

You can convert from scientific notation to standard form.

Scientific Notation	Standard Form
4.63×10^7	46,300,000
Exponent is 7.	7 decimal places right
1.08×10^{-6}	0.00000108
Exponent is −6.	6 decimal places left

Note-Taking Handbook

Note-Taking Strategies

Taking notes as you read helps you understand the information. The notes you take can also be used as a study guide for later review. This handbook presents several ways to organize your notes.

Content Frame

1. Make a chart in which each column represents a category.
2. Give each column a heading.
3. Write details under the headings.

NAME	GROUP	CHARACTERISTICS	DRAWING
snail	mollusks	mantle, shell	
ant	arthropods	six legs, exoskeleton	
earthworm	segmented worms	segmented body, circulatory and digestive systems	
heartworm	roundworms	digestive system	
sea star	echinoderms	spiny skin, tube feet	
jellyfish	cnidarians	stinging cells	

categories

details

Combination Notes

1. For each new idea or concept, write an informal outline of the information.
2. Make a sketch to illustrate the concept, and label it.

NOTES

Types of forces
- contact force
- gravity
- friction

informal outline

forces on a box being pushed

sketch with labels

contact force

gravity

friction

Make flash cards to help you study for a test. Write a concept on one side of each card and draw the sketch that goes with it on the other side. Use the cards to review concepts with a friend.

Main Idea and Detail Notes

1. In the left-hand column of a two-column chart, list main ideas. The blue headings express main ideas throughout this textbook.

2. In the right-hand column, write details that expand on each main idea.

You can shorten the headings in your chart. Be sure to use the most important words.

When studying for tests, cover up the detail notes column with a sheet of paper. Then use each main idea to form a question—such as "How does latitude affect climate?" Answer the question, and then uncover the detail notes column to check your answer.

MAIN IDEAS	DETAIL NOTES
1. Latitude affects climate. [main idea 1]	1. Places close to the equator are usually warmer than places close to the poles. [details about main idea 1]
	1. Latitude has the same effect in both hemispheres.
2. Altitude affects climate. [main idea 2]	2. Temperature decreases with altitude. [details about main idea 2]
	2. Altitude can overcome the effect of latitude on temperature.

Main Idea Web

1. Write a main idea in a box.
2. Add boxes around it with related vocabulary terms and important details.

You can find definitions near highlighted terms.

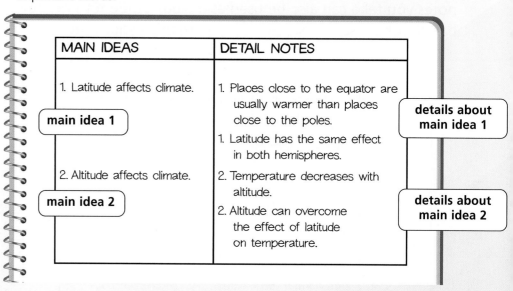

definition of *work*
Work is the use of force to move an object.

formula
Work = force · distance

main idea
Force is necessary to do work.

The joule is the unit used to measure work.
definition of *joule*

Work depends on the size of a force.
important detail

Mind Map

1. Write a main idea in the center.

2. Add details that relate to one another and to the main idea.

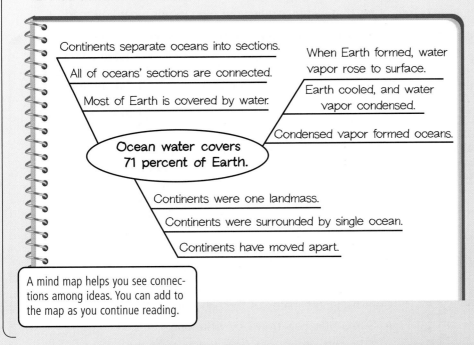

A mind map helps you see connections among ideas. You can add to the map as you continue reading.

Supporting Main Ideas

1. Write a main idea in a box.

2. Add boxes underneath with information—such as reasons, explanations, and examples—that supports the main idea.

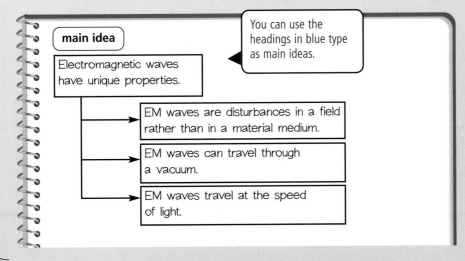

NOTE-TAKING HANDBOOK

Outline

1. Copy the chapter title and headings from the book in the form of an outline.

2. Add notes that summarize in your own words what you read.

Cell Processes

1st key idea

I. Cells capture and release energy.

1st subpoint of I

A. All cells need energy.

2nd subpoint of I

B. Some cells capture light energy.

1st detail about B

1. Process of photosynthesis

2nd detail about B

2. Chloroplasts (site of photosynthesis)
3. Carbon dioxide and water as raw materials
4. Glucose and oxygen as products

C. All cells release energy.
1. Process of cellular respiration
2. Fermentation of sugar to carbon dioxide
3. Bacteria that carry out fermentation

II. Cells transport materials through membranes.
A. Some materials move by diffusion.
1. Particle movement from higher to lower concentrations
2. Movement of water through membrane (osmosis)

B. Some transport requires energy.
1. Active transport
2. Examples of active transport

Correct Outline Form
Include a title.

Arrange key ideas, subpoints, and details as shown.

Indent the divisions of the outline as shown.

Use the same grammatical form for items of the same rank. For example, if A is a sentence, B must also be a sentence.

You must have at least two main ideas or subpoints. That is, every A must be followed by a B, and every 1 must be followed by a 2.

Concept Map

1. Write an important concept in a large oval.
2. Add details related to the concept in smaller ovals.
3. Write linking words on arrows that connect the ovals.

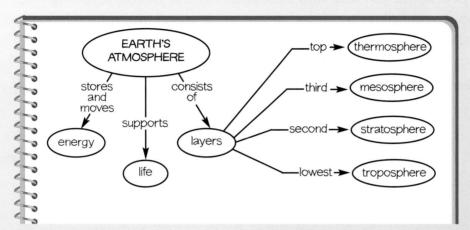

The main ideas or concepts can often be found in the blue headings. An example is "The atmosphere stores and moves energy." Use nouns from these concepts in the ovals, and use the verb or verbs on the lines.

Venn Diagram

1. Draw two overlapping circles, one for each item that you are comparing.
2. In the overlapping section, list the characteristics that are shared by both items.
3. In the outer sections, list the characteristics that are peculiar to each item.
4. Write a summary that describes the information in the Venn diagram.

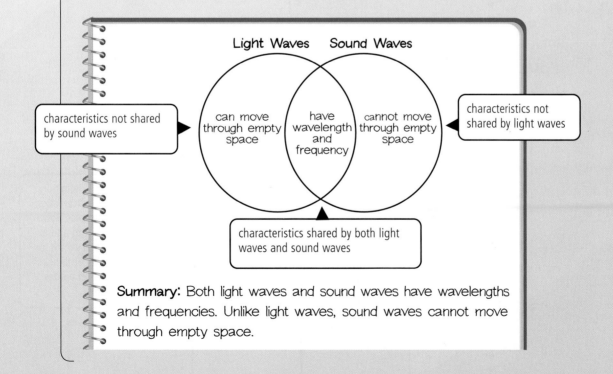

Summary: Both light waves and sound waves have wavelengths and frequencies. Unlike light waves, sound waves cannot move through empty space.

Vocabulary Strategies

Important terms are highlighted in this book. A definition of each term can be found in the sentence or paragraph where the term appears. You can also find definitions in the Glossary. Taking notes about vocabulary terms helps you understand and remember what you read.

Description Wheel

1. Write a term inside a circle.
2. Write words that describe the term on "spokes" attached to the circle.

When studying for a test with a friend, read the phrases on the spokes one at a time until your friend identifies the correct term.

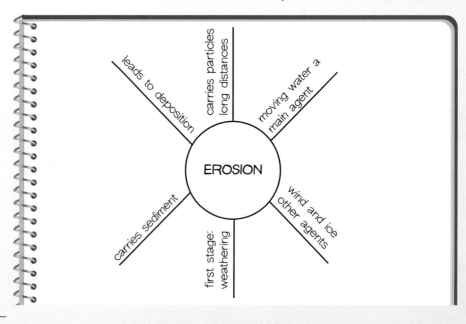

Four Square

1. Write a term in the center.
2. Write details in the four areas around the term.

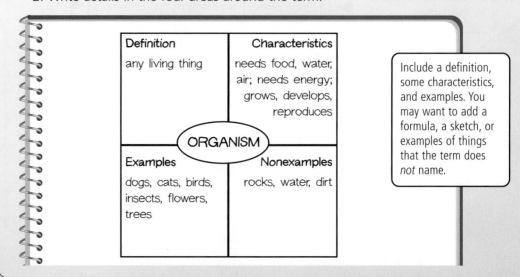

Include a definition, some characteristics, and examples. You may want to add a formula, a sketch, or examples of things that the term does *not* name.

NOTE-TAKING HANDBOOK

Frame Game

1. Write a term in the center.
2. Frame the term with details.

Include examples, descriptions, sketches, or sentences that use the term in context. Change the frame to fit each new term.

Magnet Word

1. Write a term on the magnet.
2. On the lines, add details related to the term.

You can also use phrases or sentences on the lines.

Word Triangle

1. Write a term and its definition in the bottom section.
2. In the middle section, write a sentence in which the term is used correctly.
3. In the top section, draw a small picture to illustrate the term.

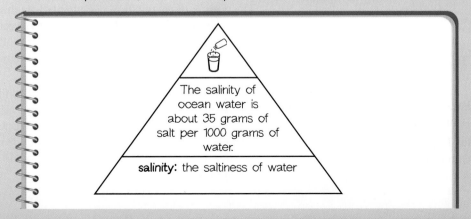

Glossary

A, B

aquaculture
The science and business of raising and harvesting fish in a controlled situation. (p. 45)

    acuacultura La ciencia y el negocio de criar y cosechar peces en una situación controlada.

aquifer
An underground layer of permeable rock that contains water. (p. 26)

    acuífero Una capa subterránea de roca permeable que contiene agua.

artesian well
A well in which pressurized water flows upward to the surface. (p. 28)

    pozo artesiano Un pozo en el cual el agua bajo presión fluye hacia arriba hasta la superficie.

atmosphere (AT-muh-SFEER)
The outer layer of gases of a large body in space, such as a planet or star; the mixture of gases that surrounds the solid Earth; one of the four parts of the Earth system. (p. xix)

    atmósfera La capa externa de gases de un gran cuerpo que se encuentra en el espacio, como un planeta o una estrella; la mezcla de gases que rodea la Tierra sólida; una de las cuatro partes del sistema terrestre.

atom
The smallest particle of an element that has the chemical properties of that element. (p. xvii)

    átomo La partícula más pequeña de un elemento que tiene las propiedades químicas de ese elemento.

biosphere (BY-uh-SFEER)
All living organisms on Earth in the air, on the land, and in the waters; one of the four parts of the Earth system. (p. xix)

    biosfera Todos los organismos vivos de la Tierra, en el aire, en la tierra y en las aguas; una de las cuatro partes del sistema de la Tierra.

by-catch
The portion of animals that are caught in a net and then thrown away as unwanted. (p. 132)

    captura incidental La porción de los animales que se capturan en una red y luego se desechan como no deseados.

C

climate
The characteristic weather conditions in an area over a long period of time. (p. xxi)

    clima Las condiciones meteorológicas características de un lugar durante un largo período de tiempo.

compound
A substance made up of two or more different types of atoms bonded together.

    compuesto Una sustancia formada por dos o más diferentes tipos de átomos enlazados.

concentration
The amount of a substance that is contained in another substance—such as dissolved sugar in water—often expressed as parts per million or parts per billion. (p. 51)

    concentración La cantidad de una sustancia contenida en otra sustancia, como el azúcar disuelto en agua; a menudo se expresa como partes por millón o partes por mil millones.

condensation
The process by which a gas changes into a liquid. (p. 13)

    condensación El proceso por el cual un gas se transforma en líquido.

continental shelf
The flat or gently sloping land that lies submerged around the edges of a continent and that extends from the shoreline out to the continental slope. (p. 80)

    plataforma continental La tierra plana o ligeramente inclinada que está sumergida alrededor de las orillas de un continente y que se extiende desde la costa hasta el talud continental.

convection
The transfer of energy from place to place by the motion of heated gas or liquid; in Earth's mantle, convection is thought to transfer energy by the motion of solid rock, which when under great heat and pressure can move like a liquid. (p. xv)

    convección La transferencia de energía de un lugar a otro por el movimiento de un líquido o gas calentado; se piensa que en el manto terrestre la convección transfiere energía mediante el movimiento de roca sólida, la cual puede moverse como un líquido cuando está muy caliente y bajo alta presión.

coral reef

A built-up limestone deposit formed by small ant-sized organisms called corals. (p. 122)

arrecife de coral Un depósito de piedra caliza formado por organismos pequeños del tamaño de una hormiga llamados corales.

cycle

n. A series of events or actions that repeat themselves regularly; a physical and/or chemical process in which one material continually changes locations and/or forms. Examples include the water cycle, the carbon cycle, and the rock cycle.

v. To move through a repeating series of events or actions.

ciclo *s.* Una serie de eventos o acciones que se repiten regularmente; un proceso físico y/o químico en el cual un material cambia continuamente de lugar y/o forma. Ejemplos: el ciclo del agua, el ciclo del carbono y el ciclo de las rocas.

D

dam

A structure that holds back and controls the flow of water in a river or other body of water. (p. 46)

presa Una estructura que retiene y controla el flujo de agua en un río u otro cuerpo de agua.

data

Information gathered by observation or experimentation that can be used in calculating or reasoning. *Data* is a plural word; the singular is *datum.*

datos Información reunida mediante observación o experimentación y que se puede usar para calcular o para razonar.

density

A property of matter representing the mass per unit volume.

densidad Una propiedad de la materia que representa la masa por unidad de volumen.

desalination (de-SAL-ih-NAY-shun)

The process of removing salt from ocean water. Desalination is used to obtain fresh water. (p. 66)

desalinización El proceso de eliminar la sal del agua de mar. La desalinización se usa para obtener agua dulce.

divide

A continuous high line of land—or ridge—from which water drains to one side or the other. (p. 17)

línea divisoria de aguas Una línea continua de tierra alta, o un cerro, desde donde el agua escurre hacia un lado o hacia el otro.

downwelling

The movement of water from the surface to greater depths. (p. 86)

sumergencia El movimiento de agua de la superficie hacia mayores profundidades.

drainage basin

An area of land in which water drains into a stream system. The borders of a drainage basin are called divides. (p. 17)

cuenca tributaria Un área de tierra en la cual el agua escurre a un sistema de corrientes. Los límites de una cuenca tributaria se denominan líneas divisorias de aguas.

drought (drowt)

A long period of abnormally low amounts of rainfall. (p. 61)

sequía Un período largo con cantidades inusualmente bajas de lluvia.

E

element

A substance that cannot be broken down into a simpler substance by ordinary chemical changes. An element consists of atoms of only one type.

elemento Una sustancia que no puede descomponerse en otra sustancia más simple por medio de cambios químicos normales. Un elemento consta de átomos de un solo tipo.

El Niño (el NEEN-yoh)

A disturbance of wind patterns and ocean currents in the Pacific Ocean that causes temporary climate changes in many parts of the world. (p. 88)

El Niño Un disturbio en los patrones de viento y las corrientes oceánicas del océano Pacifico que causa cambios climáticos temporales en muchas partes del mundo.

energy

The ability to do work or to cause a change. For example, the energy of a moving bowling ball knocks over pins; energy from food allows animals to move and to grow; and energy from the Sun heats Earth's surface and atmosphere, which causes air to move. (p. xv)

energía La capacidad para trabajar o causar un cambio. Por ejemplo, la energía de una bola de boliche en movimiento tumba los pinos; la energía proveniente de su alimento permite a los animales moverse y crecer; la energía del Sol calienta la superficie y la atmósfera de la Tierra, lo que ocasiona que el aire se mueva.

estuary (EHS-choo-EHR-ee)
A shoreline area where fresh water from a river mixes with salt water from the ocean. (p. 116)

estuario Un litoral donde se mezcla agua dulce de un río con agua salada del océano.

eutrophication (yoo-TRAF-ih-KAY-shun)
An increase in nutrients in a lake or pond. Eutrophication can occur naturally or as a result of pollution, and causes increased growth of algae and plants. (p. 20)

eutrofización Un aumento en los nutrientes de un lago o una laguna. La eutrofización puede ocurrir de manera natural o como resultado de la contaminación y ocasiona un aumento en el crecimiento de algas y plantas.

evaporation
The process by which liquid changes into gas. (p. 13)

evaporación El proceso por el cual un líquido se transforma en gas.

experiment
An organized procedure to study something under controlled conditions. (p. xxiv)

experimento Un procedimiento organizado para estudiar algo bajo condiciones controladas.

F

force
A push or a pull; something that changes the motion of an object. (p. xvii)

fuerza Un empuje o un jalón; algo que cambia el movimiento de un objeto.

fossil
A trace or the remains of a once-living thing from long ago. (p. xxi)

fósil Un rastro o los restos de un organismo que vivió hace mucho tiempo.

fresh water
Water that is not salty and has little or no taste, color, or smell. Most lakes and rivers are made up of fresh water. (p. 11)

agua dulce Agua que no es salada y que tiene muy poco o ningún sabor, color u olor. La mayoría de los lagos y los ríos están compuestos de agua dulce.

friction
A force that resists the motion between two surfaces in contact. (p. xxi)

fricción Una fuerza que resiste el movimiento entre dos superficies en contacto.

G

geosphere (JEE-uh-SFEER)
All the features on Earth's surface—continents, islands, and seafloor—and everything below the surface—the inner and outer core and the mantle; one of the four parts of the Earth system. (p. xix)

geosfera Todas las características de la superficie de la Tierra, es decir, continentes, islas y el fondo marino, y de todo bajo la superficie, es decir, el núcleo externo e interno y el manto; una de las cuatro partes del sistema de la Tierra.

glacier
A large mass of ice that exists year-round and moves over land.

glaciar Una gran masa de hielo que existe durante todo el año y se mueve sobre la tierra.

gravity
The force that objects exert on each other because of their mass. (p. xvii)

gravedad La fuerza que los objetos ejercen entre sí debido a su masa.

groundwater
Water that collects and is stored underground. (p. 24)

agua subterránea Agua que se acumula y almacena bajo tierra.

H

habitat
The natural environment in which a living thing gets all that it needs to live; examples include a desert, a coral reef, and a freshwater lake. (p. 114)

hábitat El medio ambiente natural en el cual un organismo vivo consigue todo lo que requiere para vivir; ejemplos incluyen un desierto, un arrecife coralino y un lago de agua dulce.

hydrothermal vent
An opening in the sea floor from which heated water rises and mixes with the ocean water above. (p. 128)

abertura hidrotermal Una salida en el fondo marino desde la cual asciende agua caliente que se mezcla con el agua del océano.

hydrosphere (HY-druh-SFEER)
All water on Earth—in the atmosphere and in the oceans, lakes, glaciers, rivers, streams, and underground reservoirs; one of the four parts of the Earth system. (p. xix)

    hidrosfera Toda el agua de la Tierra: en la atmósfera y en los océanos, lagos, glaciares, ríos, arroyos y depósitos subterráneos; una de las cuatro partes del sistema de la Tierra.

hypothesis
A tentative explanation for an observation or phenomenon. A hypothesis is used to make testable predictions. (p. xxiv)

    hipótesis Una explicación provisional de una observación o de un fenómeno. Una hipótesis se usa para hacer predicciones que se pueden probar.

I, J

iceberg
A mass of floating ice that broke away from a glacier. (p. 22)

    iceberg Una masa de hielo flotante que se separó de un glaciar.

impermeable
Resistant to the passage of water. (p. 25)

    impermeable Resistente al paso del agua.

intertidal zone
The narrow ocean margin between the high-tide mark and the low-tide mark. (p. 114)

    zona intermareal El estrecho margen oceánico entre el límite de la marea alta y el límite de la marea baja.

irrigation
The process of supplying water to land to grow crops. (p. 43)

    irrigación El proceso de suministrar agua a las tierras de cultivo.

K

kelp forest
A large community of kelp, a type of seaweed that can attach to the ocean floor. (p. 124)

    bosque de kelp Una comunidad grande de kelp, un tipo de alga marina que puede adherirse al fondo marino.

L

law
In science, a rule or principle describing a physical relationship that always works in the same way under the same conditions. The law of conservation of energy is an example.

    ley En las ciencias, una regla o un principio que describe una relación física que siempre funciona de la misma manera bajo las mismas condiciones. La ley de la conservación de la energía es un ejemplo.

lock
A section of a waterway, closed off by gates, in which the water level is rasied or lowered to move ships through. (p. 46)

    esclusa Una sección de un canal cerrado con compuertas, en la cual se eleva o se baja el nivel del agua para que pasen barcos.

longshore current
The overall direction and movement of the waves that strike the shore at an angle. (p. 92)

    corriente litoral La dirección y el movimiento general de las olas que golpean la costa en ángulo.

M, N

mass
A measure of how much matter an object is made of.

    masa Una medida de la cantidad de materia de la que está compuesto un objeto.

matter
Anything that has mass and volume. Matter exists ordinarily as a solid, a liquid, or a gas. (p. xvii)

    materia Todo lo que tiene masa y volumen. Generalmente la materia existe como sólido, líquido o gas.

molecule
A group of atoms that are held together by covalent bonds so that they move as a single unit.

    molécula Un grupo de átomos que están unidos mediante enlaces covalentes de tal manera que se mueven como una sola unidad.

neap tide
A tide of small range occurring during the first- and third-quarter phases of the Moon. (p. 99)

    marea muerta Una marea de poco rango que ocurre durante las fases cuarto menguante y cuarto creciente de la Luna.

nonpoint-source pollution
Pollution with a source that is hard to find or scattered. (p. 54)

    contaminación por fuentes difusas Contaminación de fuentes que son dispersas o difíciles de encontrar.

O, P, Q

ocean current
A mass of moving ocean water. (p. 84)

    corriente oceánica Una masa de agua oceánica en movimiento.

overfishing
The catching of fish at a faster rate than they can reproduce. (p. 131)

    sobrepesca La captura de peces a un ritmo mayor a la que pueden reproducirse.

permeable
Allowing the passage of water. (p. 24)

    permeable Que permite el paso del agua.

phytoplankton (fy-toh-PLANGK-tuhn)
Microscopic floating organisms that live in water and, like plants, convert sunlight and carbon dioxide into food. (p. 126)

    fitoplancton Organismos microscópicos que flotan y viven en el agua y, al igual que las plantas, convierten la luz del Sol y el dióxido de carbono en alimento.

point-source pollution
Pollution that enters water from a known source. (p. 54)

    contaminación por fuentes puntuales Contaminación que entra al agua proveniente de una fuente conocida.

precipitation
Any type of liquid or solid water that falls to Earth's surface, such as rain, snow, or hail. (p. 13)

    precipitación Cualquier tipo de agua líquida o sólida que cae a la superficie de la Tierra, como por ejemplo lluvia, nieve o granizo.

R

radiation (ray-dee-AY-shuhn)
Energy that travels across distances as certain types of waves. (p. xv)

    radiación Energía que viaja a través de las distancias en forma de ciertos tipos de ondas.

rip current
A narrow stream of water that breaks through sandbars and drains rapidly back into deeper water. (p. 92)

    corriente de retorno Una estrecha corriente de agua que atraviesa barras de arena y drena rápidamente hacia aguas más profundas.

S

salinity (suh-LIHN-ih-tee)
The measure of the amount of dissolved salt contained in water. (p. 76)

    salinidad La medida de la cantidad de sal disuelta en el agua.

salt water
Water that contains dissolved salts and other minerals. Oceans consist of salt water. (p. 11)

    agua salada Agua que contiene sales disueltas y otros minerales. Los océanos están compuestos de agua salada.

septic system
A small sewage system, often for one home or business, that uses an underground tank to treat wastewater. (p. 54)

    sistema séptico Un pequeño sistema de aguas residuales, a menudo para un hogar o un negocio, que usa un tanque subterráneo para tratar las aguas de desecho.

sewage system
A system that collects and treats wastewater from a city or a town. (p. 53)

    sistema de aguas residuales Un sistema que recolecta y trata las aguas de desecho de una ciudad o población.

sonar (SO-NAHR)
A system that uses underwater sound waves to measure distance and locate objects. (p. 82)

    sonar Un sistema que usa ondas sonoras subacuáticas para medir distancias y ubicar objetos.

spring
A flow of water from the ground at a place where the surface of the land dips below the water table. (p. 28)

    manantial Un flujo de agua proveniente del suelo en un punto donde la superficie de la tierra desciende por debajo del nivel freático.

spring tide

A tide of large range occurring during the new and full moons, resulting in an extra-high tidal bulge and an extra-low tidal dip. (p. 99)

marea viva Una marea de amplio rango que ocurre durante la luna nueva y la luna llena y que resulta en una protuberancia mareal más alta de lo normal y un descenso de la marea más bajo de lo normal.

system

A group of objects or phenomena that interact. A system can be as simple as a rope, a pulley, and a mass. It also can be as complex as the interaction of energy and matter in the four spheres of the Earth system.

sistema Un grupo de objetos o fenómenos que interactúan. Un sistema puede ser algo tan sencillo como una cuerda, una polea y una masa. También puede ser algo tan complejo como la interacción de la energía y la materia en las cuatro esferas del sistema de la Tierra.

T

technology

The use of scientific knowledge to solve problems or engineer new products, tools, or processes.

tecnología El uso de conocimientos científicos para resolver problemas o para diseñar nuevos productos, herramientas o procesos.

theory

In science, a set of widely accepted explanations of observations and phenomena. A theory is a well-tested explanation that is consistent with all available evidence.

teoría En las ciencias, un conjunto de explicaciones de observaciones y fenómenos que es ampliamente aceptado. Una teoría es una explicación bien probada que es consecuente con la evidencia disponible.

tidal range

The difference in height between high tide and low tide. (p. 98)

rango de marea La diferencia en altura entre la marea alta y la marea baja.

tide

The periodic rising and falling of the water level of the ocean due to the gravitational pulls of the Moon and the Sun. (p. 96)

marea La subida y caída periódica del nivel del agua del océano debido a las atracciones gravitacionales de la Luna y del Sol.

turnover

The yearly rising and sinking of cold and warm water layers in a lake. (p. 19)

renovación La ascensión y el hundimiento anual de las capas de agua fría y agua cálida en un lago.

U, V

upwelling

The vertical movement of deep water up to the surface. (p. 86)

surgencia El movimiento vertical del agua profunda a la superficie.

variable

Any factor that can change in a controlled experiment, observation, or model. (p. R30)

variable Cualquier factor que puede cambiar en un experimento controlado, en una observación o en un modelo.

volume

An amount of three-dimensional space, often used to describe the space that an object takes up.

volumen Una cantidad de espacio tridimensional; a menudo se usa este término para describir el espacio que ocupa un objeto.

W, X, Y, Z

water cycle

The continuous movement of water on Earth, through its atmosphere, and in the living things on Earth. (p. 12)

ciclo del agua El movimiento continuo de agua sobre la Tierra, por su atmósfera y dentro de los organismos vivos de la Tierra.

water table

The highest part in the ground that is saturated, or completely filled with water. (p. 25)

nivel freático La parte más alta del suelo que está saturada, o completamente llena de agua.

wetland

A wet, swampy area that is often flooded with water. (p. 116)

humedal Un área húmeda y pantanosa que a menudo está inundada de agua.

Index

Page numbers for definitions are printed in **boldface** type.
Page numbers for illustrations, maps, and charts are printed in *italics*.

F, G

H, I, J

INDEX

P, Q, R

Acknowledgments

Photography

Cover © Denis Scott/Corbis; **i** © Denis Scott/Corbis; **iii** *left (top to bottom)* Photograph of James Trefil by Evan Cantwell; Photograph of Rita Ann Calvo by Joseph Calvo; Photograph of Linda Carnine by Amilcar Cifuentes; Photograph of Sam Miller by Samuel Miller; *right (top to bottom)* Photograph of Kenneth Cutler by Kenneth A. Cutler; Photograph of Donald Steely by Marni Stamm; Photograph of Vicky Vachon by Redfern Photographics; **vi** © Photographer's Choice/Getty Images; **vii** © Darrell Jones/Getty Images; **ix** Photographs by Sharon Hoogstraten; **xiv–xv** Doug Scott/age fotostock; **xvi–xvii** © Aflo Foto Agency; **xviii–ix** © Tim Fitzharris/Masterfile; **xx–xxi** AP/Wide World Photos; **xxii** © Vince Streano/Corbis; **xxiii** © Roger Ressmeyer/Corbis; **xxiv** *left* University of Florida Lightning Research Laboratory; *center* © Roger Ressmeyer/Corbis; **xxv** *center* © Mauro Fermariello/Science Researchers; *bottom* © Alfred Pasieka/Photo Researchers; **xxvi–xxvii** © Stocktrek/Corbis; *center* NOAA; **xxvii** *top* © Alan Schein Photography/Corbis; *right* Vaisala Oyj, Finland; **xxxii** © The Chedd-Angier Production Company; **2–3** © Ralph White/Corbis; **3** *center* © Roger Steene/imagequestmarine.com; *bottom* Wolcott Henry/National Geographic Image Collection; **4** *top* NOAA/Pacific Marine Environmental Laboratory; *bottom* © The Chedd-Angier Production Company; **5** © Orbital Imaging Corporation and processing by NASA Goddard Space Flight Center. Image provided by ORBIMAGE; **6–7** © John Lawrence/Getty Images; **7** *top* © Anderson Ross/Getty Images; *bottom* Photograph by Sharon Hoogstraten; **9, 12** Photograph by Sharon Hoogstraten; **14** © Jagdish Agarwal/Alamy Images; **15** *left, inset* AP/WideWorld Photos/NASA Jet Propulsion Laboratories; **16** Photograph by Sharon Hoogstraten; **18** *center inset* © NASA/Getty Images; *bottom* © Claver Carroll/photolibrary/PictureQuest; **20** © Bruce Heinemann/Photodisc/PictureQuest; **21** Photograph by Sharon Hoogstraten; **22** © The Image Bank/Getty Images; **23** © Ron Erwin Photography; **24, 27** Photograph by Sharon Hoogstraten; **28** Peter Essick/Aurora; **30** © Michael S. Lewis/Corbis; **31** *left, right* © Jon Arnold/Jon Arnold Images/Alamy Images; **32** *top* Peter Essick/Aurora ; *bottom* Photograph by Sharon Hoogstraten; **36** Photograph by Sharon Hoogstraten; **38–39** © Photographer's Choice/Getty Images; **39** *top, bottom* Photograph by Sharon Hoogstraten; **41** AP/Wide World Photos; **42** © Charles E. Rotkin/Corbis; **43** *top* Photograph by Sharon Hoogstraten; *bottom* © Michael Andrews/Animals Animals/Earth Scenes; **44** *top* © Geoff Tompkinson/Photo Researchers; *bottom* AP/Wide World Photos; **45** © Macduff Everton/Corbis; **46** © Shubroto Chattopadhyay/Index Stock Imagery/PictureQuest; **47** © 1987 Tom Bean; **48** AP/Wide World Photos; **49** © J.C. Carton/Bruce Coleman, Inc./PictureQuest; **50** Photograph by Sharon Hoogstraten; **51** AP/Wide World Photos; **56** *left* © Brand X Pictures; *right* © Photodisc/Getty Images; **57** AP/Wide World Photos; **58** *top* © William Taufic/Corbis; *bottom left, right* Photograph by Sharon Hoogstraten; **60** © Dieter Melhorn/Alamy Images; **61** AP/Wide World Photos; **62** *top left* © Digital Vision; *top right* © Bob Melnychuk/Getty Images; *center left* © Photodisc/Getty Images; *center right* © Digital Vision; *bottom* AP/Wide World Photos; **63** Photograph by Sharon Hoogstraten; **65** NASA Goddard Space Flight Center Scientific Visualization Studio; **67** *left* © Denny Eilers/Grant Heilman Photography; *left inset* © Bob Rowan/Progressive Image/Corbis; *right* AP/WideWorld Photos; **68** *top* AP/Wide World Photos; *bottom* NASA Goddard Space Flight Center Scientific Visualization Studio; **72–73** © Darrell Jones/Getty Images; **73** *top, center* Photograph by Sharon Hoogstraten; **75** Photograph by Sharon Hoogstraten; **77** © Roger Antrobus/Corbis; **78** *top* Photograph by Sharon Hoogstraten; *bottom* © Jane Burton/Bruce Coleman, Inc.; **79** *bottom* NASA/Photo Researchers; **81** Emory Kristof/National Geographic Image Collection; **83** Walter H. F. Smith/NOAA; **84** Photograph by Sharon Hoogstraten; **85** © AFP/Corbis/NASA; **86** © Dan Gair Photographic/Index Stock Imagery/PictureQuest; **87** Photograph by Sharon Hoogstraten; **88** *left* Ron Erwin Photography; *right* © Bettmann/Corbis; **89** Photograph by Sharon Hoogstraten; **92** © C.C. Lockwood/Bruce Coleman, Inc.; **93** © Buddy Mays/Corbis; **94** *top* AP/Wide World Photos; *bottom left, right* Photograph by Sharon Hoogstraten; **96** *top, bottom* © M. H. Black/Bruce Coleman, Inc.; **98** Photograph by Sharon Hoogstraten; **101** *left* © Attar Maher/Corbis; **104** Photograph by Sharon Hoogstraten; **106** *top* NOAA/OAR/National Undersea Research Program; *bottom* NOAA; **107** *top left* NOAA/OAR/National Undersea Research Program; *top right* The Granger Collection, New York; *bottom* NOAA Central Library; **108** *top* AP Wide World Photos; *center* © Silva Joao/Corbis Sygma; *bottom* Alan Schietzch/ARSTI/NOAA; **109** *top left* OAR/National Undersea Research Program/Fairleigh Dickinson University; *top right* © Macduff Everton/Corbis *left bottom* Photograph by Ben Allsup/Webb Research Corporation; **110–111** © Brandon Cole; *top right* © Maximilian Weinzierl/Alamy Images; *center right* Photograph by Sharon Hoogstraten; **113** © Eric and David Hosking/Corbis; **115** *top, bottom* © Brandon Cole; **116** *top* Photograph by Sharon Hoogstraten; *bottom* © Robert Perron; **117** © W.K. Almond/Stock Boston/PictureQuest ; **118** *top* © Lee Foster/Bruce Coleman, Inc.; *right inset* © Masa Ushioda/V&W/Bruce Coleman, Inc.; **119** AP/Wide World Photos; **120** *left, inset* © Lowell Georgia/Corbis; **121** Photograph by Sharon Hoogstraten; **122, 124** © Stone/Getty Images; **125** *top* © Mark A. Johnson/Alamy; *bottom* Photograph by Sharon Hoogstraten; **127** © Norbert Wu; **128** *top* © Dr. Ken Mac Donald/Photo Researchers; *center left* © The Natural History Museum, London; *bottom* © John Burbidge/Photo Researchers; **129** *left* © B. Murton/Southampton Oceanography Centre/Photo Researchers; *inset* © NSF Oasis Project/Norbert Wu Productions; **130** Photograph by Sharon Hoogstraten; **131** © Stephen Frink Collection/Alamy Images; **132** *top* © Norbert Wu; *bottom* © Dani/Jeske/Animals Animals/Earth Scenes; **133** *bottom* Jan Stromme/Strom/Bruce Coleman, Inc.; **134** © Institute of Oceanographic Sciences/NERC/Photo Researchers; **135** *top* © James Marshall/Corbis; *bottom* © Dr. Morley Read/Photo Researchers; **136** © Simon Fraser/Photo Researchers; **137** *top left* © Richard A. Cooke/Corbis; *top right* © Dorling Kindersley; **138** *top* © Gary Bell/Alamy Images; *bottom* Photograph by Sharon Hoogstraten;**140** *bottom left* © Norbert Wu; *bottom right* Jan Stromme/Strom/Bruce Coleman, Inc.; **142** © Lawson Wood/Corbis; **R28** © Photodisc/Getty Images.

Illustrations and Maps

Accurate Art Inc. **143**
Ampersand Design Group **93**
Richard Bronson/Wildlife Art Ltd. **13, 19, 25, 26, 29, 34**
Peter Bull/Wildlife Art Ltd. **52, 53, 55, 68**
Steve Cowden **91**
Stephen Durke **11, 31, 47, 54, 66, 133**
Chris Forsey **17, 20, 34**

Gary Hincks **80–81**
Ian Jackson **115, 123, 127, 140**
Mapquest.com, Inc. **10, 30, 42, 44, 45, 47, 56, 61, 64, 65, 76, 77, 85, 88, 98, 101, 113, 117, 118, 122, 132, 134**
Morgan, Cain & Assoc. **77, 82, 85, 100, 133**
Dan Stuckenschneider **R11–R19, R22, R32, 101**
Raymond Turvey **86, 90–92**